英汉
思维模式
转换研究

YINGHAN SIWEI MOSHI ZHUANHUAN YANJIU

（下）

张 辉 / 著

电子科技大学出版社
University of Electronic Science and Technology of China Press
·成都·

图书在版编目（CIP）数据

英汉思维模式转换研究. 下 / 张辉著. 一成都：电子科技大学出版社，2018. 4

ISBN 978-7-5647-6133-2

Ⅰ. ①英… Ⅱ. ①张… Ⅲ. ①英语－教学研究 Ⅳ. ①H319.3

中国版本图书馆 CIP 数据核字（2018）第 084951 号

本书系亳州学院教学质量工程项目“亳州中药文化翻译与传播教学团队（2016jxtd01）”；
安徽省级教学质量工程：亳州中医药文化翻译教学团队（2017jxtd053）；
安徽高校人文社会科学研究项目：“一带一路”下的亳州中医药文化外宣翻译研究（SK2018A0859）研究成果

英汉思维模式转换研究（下）

张　辉　著

策划编辑　郭蜀燕
责任编辑　郭蜀燕　马　瑶

出版发行　电子科技大学出版社
　　　　　成都市一环路东一段 159 号电子信息产业大厦九楼　邮编　610051
主　　页　www.uestcp.com.cn
服务电话　028-83203399
邮购电话　028-83201495

印　　刷　四川煤田地质制图印刷厂
成品尺寸　185 mm×260 mm
印　　张　11
字　　数　303 千字
版　　次　2018 年 4 月第一版
印　　次　2018 年 4 月第一次印刷
书　　号　ISBN 978-7-5647-6133-2
定　　价　36.00 元

前　言

我从事英语教学多年，在中学教过初、高中英语，在高校主要从事“基础英语”教学，可以说对英语教学有深刻的认识和体会。以前教“精读”时，主要讲解英语单词、短语及一些语法知识，并对课文中重点句型进行分析及翻译。备一篇课文需要几个小时，自己感觉备课辛苦，但学生感觉课堂枯燥。上完一轮课之后，再教新生时，以前备的课基本上都忘了，不得不重新备课。曾因此厌倦过“基础英语”教学，后改教“英语阅读”及“英语翻译”，最后发现自己的作用只是一个组织者，并没有带给学生有启发或震撼的东西，这样的教学与学生自学没有什么大的区别。如果没有强制性措施，学生难免会逃课，即使被迫到了教室，也一心二用，敷衍了事。好多英语专业学生学了四年，专八也考过了，但又感觉什么都没学到。主要原因是，学到的知识是零散的，没有系统性，同时翻译能力没有得到很好的培养。

这样的经历让我痛下决心，寻找新的教学之路，思考老师的作用。老师的作用不应只是一个课堂组织者，更重要的是一个启迪者，引导学生关注语言规律，帮助学生找到适合他本人的学习方法。同时对英语学习也有了新的认识：基于英语是法治语言，有严谨的特点，对于把英语作为外语的学习者来说，过了“语言定式学习”阶段以后，若想在“写、译”方面获得实质性突破，可以像学习数学一样学习英语。

众所周知，学习数学时，先学习“数学定理及公式”，然后再通过做题目来消化和巩固，等到一学期结束之后，做过的题目可能会忘记，当然也不需要记住，最后在学生脑海中留下的是那些公式和定理，同时学生的逻辑思维及运算能力得到了发展。同样英语教学时，老师可以引导学生通过英汉对比发现英语中的语言规律，并通过大量阅读寻找能够反映这些规律的类似句型。然后把这些句型进行分类整理，像语法书一样，条分缕析，最终弄清楚英汉思维模式的差异，并用这些规律指导自己的翻译与写作实践。通过反复实践，最后把这些规律内化，形成能力。

基于以上认识，泛读、精读、翻译与写作不一定分开上，当然教师之间也可以协作，不是各讲各的。如果大家都围绕英语思维模式教学，就像学习数学把公理和定式掌握一样，学生放下书本，脑海中仍有一个清晰的图像。

由于水平有限，错误在所难免，欢迎专家批评指正。

另外，本书部分内容已在本人新浪微博“中高级英语学习平台”上发表。

编　者

2018 年 3 月 1 日

前言

目 录

第一章　英汉思维模式差异形成的原因及表现形式

由于英汉语思维模式之间存在相同之处，加上现代汉语欧化的原因，部分汉语句子词序与对应的英语词序是一致的，如“I have a book.”与“我有一本书。”碰到这种情况，只要知道英语单词就会翻译。英语学习的难点在于英汉思维模式差异上，如“我想到一个主意。”与“An idea came to me.”学习者需要在学习过程中发现这样的英汉思维模式差异，并不断积累、总结，最后内化。本章简单讨论一下英汉思维模式差异形成的原因。

第一节　语言与思维

列维·布留尔认为“事实上人类的思维方式在历史上有一个共同的起源，那就是原始思维。原始民族的语言永远是精确地按照事物和行动呈现在眼睛里和耳朵里的那种形式来表现关于它们的观念。”霍尔·荣格认为：“一个民族在历史发展的长河中，也在不断构筑其内在的心理模式，形成有别于其他民族的心理特征。这种心理模式和心理特征，对其他民族来讲，可能是陌生的、迥异的、相斥的，从而引起理解困难，交际障碍。人的心理不仅同自己的往昔联接在一起，更重要的是与种族的往昔相联接，甚至在那以前，还与有机界进化的漫长过程联接在一起。”他相信所有的人不仅都有着个人无意识而且同时也都具有一种集体无意识。集体无意识是指人类自原始社会以来世世代代的普遍性的心理经验的长期积累。每一种语言铸就了一种独特的文化传统，铸就了一种独特的认知方式和思维习惯。一种语言训练出一套思维方式。语言给一个民族思维习惯定位，给一个民族思维习惯安家。

萨丕尔有一个极端的表述，人很大程度上受他们所操语言的摆布，在很大程度上思想是由语言决定的。林语堂在 *My Country and My People* 一书中提到，汉语讲得很好的欧洲人会养成与中国人相同的思维习惯，从而被自己的同胞视为“怪物”。英语讲得很好的中国人则已养成了西方人的思维习惯，被“异族化”了。钱冠连认为这些人在习得语言的同时习得对方国的思维习惯。“有些生在美国的中国人，在另一环境中长大，绝无一般中国人的特质。他们可以用粗鲁的重鼻音和直率有力、不事雕琢的演讲搅乱一个教职员会议，他们缺乏炎黄子孙那种压倒一切、独一无二的老成温厚。”值得注意的是“生在美国”这个前提。这些中国人，一生下来就在习得语言的同时，形成了思维习惯，也习得了美国文化。语言不仅创造了文化，而且制约着人之为人的感觉。因此语言符号从根本上制约着人们对客体世界的概念和印象。

语言与思维的先后关系，应该是先有个体思维，后有交际需要，催生了语言，在语言发展完善的过程中，集体的无意识也慢慢形成，构成民族文化的一部分，这种集体无意识作为文化的一部分具有传承性，最后语言又反过来制约个体的思维过程，决定着一代又一代人的思维方式。

第二节　地理环境与民族思维过程

在古代中国，黄河流域与长江流域优越的地理条件和气候条件，使得中国古人能够从事大规模的农业合作，较少受到来自大自然的压力。对于绝大多数从业者来说，经济生存要求他们既要关注负责的人，又要关注一同耕作的人。人们做事讲究天时、地利、人和。这种宽松融洽的氛围塑造了中国古代哲学"天人合一"观，没有人与自然的明显对立，习惯于从总体方面认识事物，把世界看成本质上是一个不可分割的有机体，并用这种观点去解释一切事物和现象。因此对于中国人来说首先想到的是人，其次是自然，经常是"天人合一"。与此形成对照的是，古代希腊社会——西方社会的原型——主要特征是个体行为，如狩猎、捕鱼和小规模农业耕作。

不同的实践活动，导致不同的思维过程。关注整体的人慢慢形成看事物从认识主体到到客体，从大到小，从整体到个体的思维过程。思维过程最终通过语言以口语和书面语的形式体现出来，在语言形式上，汉语句型之主语几乎千篇一律以人称作主语，或省略主语。关注个体的人则形成从认识客体到主体，从小到大，从个体到整体的思维过程。因此英语中的"非人称主语"用得要比汉语多些，即认识的客体在前（相对于"我"以外的任何事物都是客体），主体在后，这就给句子的衔接与连贯带来麻烦，不同的客体要建立联系，句型之间必须通过关联词来实现衔接与连贯。而汉语中，由于人的无处不在，不同的客体之间由于人的参与而建立了联系，这就是汉语句子没有过多的关联词，更多的是"流水句"，却同样能够实现语篇的衔接与连贯的原因。

不同民族的地理环境也存在相同的部分，因此部分思维过程也是一致的。尽管思维过程存在差异，由于不同的民族面对的客观事物基本上是相同的，所以思考的结果基本上是一致的，这就使得不同的语言能够进行语码转换。不同民族思维过程的差异必然会表现出语言思维顺序的差异，思维顺序的差异就成了外语学习的难点和重点。

第三节　语言形式差异

语言的许多形式问题实则都是基于其内在的机制（intrinsic mechanism）而发之于外在的表现现象（刘宓庆，1994）。内在机制即民族思维过程，由民族思维过程导致的英汉语言形式差异主要体现在以下四个方面。

一、客体与主体的顺序

比较现代汉语文章和现代英语文章，就会发现英语动词使用的频率远比汉语动词低。英语民族的祖先生活在气候相对恶劣的海洋环境中，西方人早早地选择了一种"天人相分"的认知态度，认为人与自然、主体与客体不是有机和谐地融合在一起，而是分离与对立的。体现在语言形式上，就是英语中的及物动词一定要有宾语，表明主体对客体的认识、改造。同时由于当时认识能力及手段的局限，部分客观世界对人们来说是不可知的，因此英语中及物动词与不及物动词的区分比较明显。中国哲学中"天人合一"的思想以及人的无处不在，主体与客体是统一的，表现在语言形式上，汉语的动词几乎都可以用作及物动词，而且宾语可以省略。英汉主体与客体的位置差异体现在以下两个方面。

1. 被动与主动

付鸿军在《英汉被动句及其民族性》一文中把劳伦斯的 *Lady Chatterley's Lover*《情人》和钱钟书的《围城》两书的前 70 页作比较。发现《情人》和《围城》的主动形式之比是 50 句和 170 句（而被动句之比则是 160 句和 10 句）。可见，英语中客体是第一位的，主体次之。（1）It was proposed to build a hotel in the following spring. 本句中的客体是"建一个宾馆的提议”，而主体是“大家”给省略了，此处需要指出的是“思想”相对于人来说也是客体，它是主体认识的结果。(2) She was conducted out of the gardens, and passed along the pavement till she disappeared from view. 本句中“she”是客体，而认识主体则省略了。而汉语中，主体是第一位的，客体次之，只有主体面对客体遭遇失败时，才使用被动句。汉语的被动句绝大多数局限在表示不好的、不幸的、不如意的意思上。如用“被”“让”“受”“给”“遭”“挨”“叫”“教”的句子。如（1）旅馆被大火烧了。（2）发电厂遭到敌人的破坏。而英语中被动句一方面是为了行文需要，更多的是为了凸显客体。

2. 非人称主语句（Impersonal Subject Sentence）

由于英语强调主客体的对立，人可以认识改造世界，反过来客观世界也会影响人，因此人称及非人称的一切事物，无论具体的、抽象的、意念的、心理的，都可用来作主语。外界事物包括思想是客观存在的，你发现了这个事物，或想到了这个主意，别人也会发现或想到，因为那是对客观世界的反映，客观事物的存在或消失并不取决于哪个人，这样我们就能理解为什么英语会多用非人称主语，或认识客体在前。（1）A splash of bright orange caught my eye. 我看到一片鲜艳的橘色。（2）Not a sound reached our ears. 我们没听到任何声音。

下面两句英语的主语都是客观事物，而对应的汉语，如果不加上人称主语则不符合汉语表达习惯。(1)The first question went to him.(有人向他提了第一个问题。)(2)Her question received no answer.（没有人回答她的问题。）在汉语中，“人是万物之主体”，天经地义，不可动摇。因此无论作文，无论言语，均不能违反此金科玉律，皆得以人（或人称）作主语。国人对人称主语句的使用和接受发展到“心有灵犀一点通”的地步，“人称主语”的有无，已无关紧要。

二、动词名物化

英语文章中大量抽象名词的使用与民族文化和思维习惯也有一定关系。名词的使用不仅仅是减少了动词，而更重要的是使英语句子简洁紧凑，同时也避免了因使用动词而不得不把人牵扯进来。动词名物化的使用也是为了突出认识的客体，淡化认识主体的角色。如：

The denial of these principles and the placement of man at the core of the universe results in a paralyzing mass selfishness, and the sights of it are already frighteningly evident.（如果我们否认这些基本原理，把个人置于宇宙的中心，其结果是大家就会变得自私自利。这使一切都处于瘫痪。这方面表现出来的迹象已经十分明显。）上面英语句中的“主语”与汉语句中的“谓语”相对应，而汉语句中的主语“我们”则在英语中省略了。

三、现在分词与过去分词

英语中用分词来强调主客体的关系。如：Nokia released high-end phones aimed at both the consumer and business user and is showing strength in emerging and mature markets alike.（诺基亚推出了面向普通消费者和商务用户两种人群的高端手机，在新兴的和成熟的市场上都展现出强劲的实力。）在这一句中，汉语中的主谓结构“诺基亚推出”则变成了英语中的定语“Nokia released”“phones”是过去分词“released”施动的客体。

四、时空顺序

中国学生最不习惯的是英语中时空顺序从小到大，而且通常把时间地点放在句子最后。英语把主谓先摆出，然后把各种标志一条条补述，一步步交代，形成头短尾长的线性链。如：I saw Mr. Smith at the gate of the college at 2 o'clock yesterday afternoon, whom I have not seen three years. 汉语头大尾小，先交代环境与附带标志，最后是信息中心，谓之雄狮型序列。如：昨天下午两点钟，在学院大门口，我看见了三年未曾谋面的的史密斯先生。

汉语中“万物皆备于我”的思想体现在语言中，就是判断周围物体的方位时，首先想到的是以自我为中心，从宏观到微观这样一个顺序。而英语中正相反，首先先到的是具体方位。如：

（1）inner left thigh（左大腿内侧）

（2）north London house（伦敦北部的一座房子）

通过以上几部分，我们可以看到英语中“天人相分”与汉语中“天人合一”的思想，在语言形式上得到了充分体现。

第二章 非人称主语句

毛荣贵给“非人称主语句”的定义是：非人称主语句指非人称主语后续一般为人称主语所使用的表示感觉、意识、情感或动作之类的动词谓语构成的句式。因为，通常折射一定生命内涵的动词被“挪用”于不具生命的主语（Inanimate Subject），这样的句式新颖独特，结构严谨，言洁意丰，并染上了拟人化（Personification）的修辞色彩。为了与被动结构对比学习，这里把非人称主语句范围又做了扩展，把主语不是人称的句型，都称作“非人称主语句”。

第一节 描述自然现象

描述自然现象时，通常使用“非人称主语句”，但也可以使用“人称主语句”。

1. Monday dawned warm and rainless. 星期一清晨，温暖无雨。

2. The next morning opened calmly. 第二天早上平静地开始了新的一天。

3. The night was windy and flew on black wings. 夜晚风很大，就像鼓着漆黑的翅膀。

4. Wind sent a puff of red mayflowers through the air.
空气中弥漫着随风飘来的五月花花香。

5. A cloud passed across the sun. 一片云飘过太阳。

6. Large, black clouds announced a coming storm. 大堆的乌云预示着暴风雨即将来临。

7. The Rose in the garden slipped her bud. 园中玫瑰绽开了蓓蕾。

8. Water stood in pools on the gravel paths. 石子路上有一潭潭的积水。

9. Lovina offers beautiful sea views at dawn.
露薇娜的黎明时分可以看到美丽的海景。

10. The sun burst through the clouds. 太阳从云层钻出来了。

11. Suddenly, the curve of a brilliant sun burst through the dark forest. The world begins to awaken. 突然间，一轮灿烂的太阳冲出阴暗的丛林。万物开始复苏。

12. And it was so still. The silence of the fields seemed to enter and move familiarly through the house. The wind used the open hall.
房间里是如此安静，似乎是田野中的寂静进入了房间，并且在房内无拘无束地随意走动。风儿在敞开的大厅内飘荡。

13. The great night duly（及时地）arrived, moonlit and cloudless.
值得纪念的那一夜终于来到了，月光清澈，万里无云。

14. A storm broke. Lightning writhed above his head, rain poured into the hollow cylinder of the tree. 暴风雨也来了，闪电在他的头顶上发威，大量的雨水涌入这圆筒状的树洞里。

15. A few hours later Mr. Warburton watched the coast of England recede into the mist, and he left behind everything which to him made life worth living.
几小时以后，沃伯顿注视着渐渐消失在雾中的英国海岸，这也意味着他丢下一切对他来说弥足珍贵的东西。

16. The river flowed ominously silent. It was like a great serpent gliding with sluggish movement towards the sea. And the trees of the jungle over the water were heavy with a breathless menace. No bird sang. No breeze ruffled the leaves of the cassias. The river seemed to come from nowhere and flow nowhere.

这条河水流平缓，却又让人有不详之感。它就像一条巨大的毒蛇行动迟缓地滑向大海。河岸上丛林中的树充满了危险，让人感到窒息。不仅听不到鸟叫声，也没有微风轻抚肉桂树叶的声音。这条河似乎没有源头，也不知流向哪里。

17. Water in vast quantities tumbles through here each spring on its way to the river two miles west. I hope with my pond to make it pause awhile. Over two days of heavy rainfall in November, the pond filled completely.

每年春天都有大量的水从这里滚滚流过，流向西南两英里外的那条河。我希望用我的池塘挽留它一刻。11 月份下了两天大雨后，池塘积满了水。

18. On the surrounding hills, in sunlight that seemed almost blinding after days of gray mist, the forests of larch and fir glowed a rich green.

周围山上的落叶松和冷杉树林沐浴在阳光里，闪耀着浓浓的绿色。

19. Spring is shining upon these lanes and meadows; I feel as if I must follow every winding track that opens by my way. Spring has restored to me something of the long-forgotten vigour of youth. I walk without weariness; I sing to myself like a boy, and the song is one I knew in boyhood.

春色照亮了小径和原野，同时也点燃了我心中那股遗忘许久的青春活力。我开始有一股冲动，想走遍眼前所看见的每一条小道。我一边走着一边哼着童年时代的歌曲，丝毫不感到疲累。

第二节　去主观化

与汉语形成鲜明对比的是，英语喜欢去主观化，在表达中使用“非人称主语”，或把人当作动作的承受者，从而使表述更加客观。

2.1 “非人称主语句”表达有人类参与的活动

在下面这些句子里面，虽然活动有人的参与，但主语都是非人称主语。

1. Part of the pleasure and genius of language may well arise out of this slight “misuse” of words. 对一些词汇稍加“误用”，不仅是语言天分的体现，而且能够增加趣味。
2. The Supreme Court’s decision to deny bail to Awami League leader, Sheikh Hasina, came days before she is due back in the country. 就在执政党人民联盟领袖谢赫·哈西娜原定回国日期的前几天，最高法院做出裁决——拒绝对她的保释。
3. “All over the world,” came the reply. 回应是“全世界”。
4. Couldn’t the letter have waited until the morning? 这封信不能等到上午寄么？
5. My garden, a world in miniature, needed a pond.
我的花园，一个微型的世界，需要一个池塘。
6. When sorrow ceases to be speculative sleep sees her opportunity.

一个人在悲伤停止的时候，睡眠就会乘虚而入。

拓展学习：I was on the verge of sleep. 我快睡着了。

7. After dinner, my sleepiness returned. 饭后，困意再次袭来。

8. When at last the opportunity came, Mr.Warburton laughed aloud.
当机会最后来临时，沃伯顿先生大笑起来。

9. The conversation stopped, and it refused to start again. 谈话终止以后，没有人再愿意开口。

10. Their conversation touched upon a multitude of topics. Lord M. would criticize books, throw out a remark or two on the British Constitution, make some passing reflections on human life.
他们的谈话涉及很多话题，有时墨尔本勋爵会对一些书做出批评，有时对英国宪法做一番评论，有时会附带表达对人生的看法。

11. The tears came into her eyes. 她的眼中涌出泪水。

12. Silence fell upon the room where the boy and woman sat together.
房间里，那个男孩和一个女人安静地坐在一起。

13. It was Feb. 14, and Valentine's fever had taken over the whole shopping center.
那天是2月14日，情人节的狂热浪潮席卷了整个购物中心。

14. The reply came that he was to remain and await developments.
得到的回复是他要留下来关注事态发展。（同位语后置）

15. But the life of Paris had not seemed beautiful to her.
但是巴黎的生活对她来说似乎一直不是那么美好。

16. Even a butcher's shop in Paris was a pleasure to the eye.
甚至巴黎的一家肉铺都让人赏心悦目。

17. The inner decoration favored the First Empire and William Morris.
内部装潢以拿破仑时代和威廉·莫里斯风格为主。

18. Death approaches, and the shadow which foreruns him has thrown a softening influence over my spirit.
死亡临近，带给他的阴影已经影响到我的情绪，虽然不像对他影响那么强烈。

19. Imagination would fail in describing to itself the appearance of such a procession, and of the anxiety of the events which a few hours or a few minutes might produce.
你无法想象会出现这样一个游行以及这些事情在几小时或几分钟内可能造成的焦虑。

20. In the kitchen the carefully timed preparations had fulfilled their promise. The main course awaited only the consumption of the soup.
厨房里所有的菜已精心备好，只等汤喝完就上菜。

21. A feast was also provided for our reception, at which we sat cheerfully down; and what the conversation wanted in wit was made up in laughter. 为了欢迎我们的到来，他们请我们吃饭，席间大家都很开心，言谈间虽无甚妙语，却不乏笑声。

22. By lunch time, however, decorum had reasserted itself with enhanced rigour as a natural rebound from its recent overthrow.
然而到了午餐的时候，刚被破坏的礼仪，又自然而然地重新恢复了原来的状态，而且执行得更为严格。

23. Although I felt a little lonely, my exaltation of the morning had not worn off.
尽管我感到有点孤独，但我上午一直很开心。

24. Each city is writing a new chapter. 每座城市都在谱写着各自的新篇章。

25. Back in the early 1970s, an interest in Chinese clothing from the era of the imperial dynasties, and a strong desire to explore a China closed to foreign eyes, led Valery Garrett to embark on a 30-year journey of cultural discovery.
那是在20世纪70年代初，怀着对帝国王朝时代流传下来的中国服装的兴趣和对当时关闭了国门的中国进行探索的强烈愿望，瓦莱丽·加雷特便开始了她30年的文化发现之旅。

26. See which funny, sad, or inspired flicks made our list of the best sports movies.
看看我们列出的最佳体育电影榜单中都收入了哪些逗趣、悲伤或催人奋进的影片。

27. When a door opened we all got on. 车门开了，我们都上了车。

28. Electricity arrives in that village. 那个村庄通电了。

29. The power goes out. 停电。与汉语中的“通电”“坠机”对比。

30. The day we had been waiting for finally arrived. 我们期待已久的这一天终于到了。

31. The days of his youth appeared like dreams before him.
青春的岁月如梦一般浮现在他的眼前。

32. It all began with the howl of chain saws, the screech of a chipper big enough to devour trees, and the gut-tightening roar of earth-moving machinery.
一切都是在电锯的鸣啸声、大得足以吞噬大树的切削机的尖叫声和掘土机那令人胆战心惊的轰鸣声中开始。

33. Opposing to him grew in the Senate. 参议院里反对他的人增多。

34. He wanted to say “handwriting”, but the word still refused to come.
他想说“书法”，但就是说不出口。

2.2 主客体对调

人往往是认知的主体，做主语；客观事物一般是认知客体，做宾语。但实际语言运用中，主体与客体可以对调，人成为被认知的对象。这种现象在英语比较常见，汉语中也有这种情况，可以对比学习。

2.2.1 施动者是物，受动者是人

在这种结构里，把“物”作为施动者，人作为受动者。这种用法在汉语中较少见。

1. That’s how today’s robots will look to people in the year 2035.
生活在2035年的人也会以同样的眼光来看待今天的机器人。

2. Smiles decked the face of Mrs. Bennet. 贝内特夫人满脸堆笑。

3. The logic of this eluded most people. 大部分人不能理解它的逻辑。

4. Both left and right are focused on climate change with an intensity that eluded their elders.
左派和右派的年轻政治家们密切关注气候变化问题的程度都为他们的前辈所不及。

5. In that single moment, desperation wells up inside me. 就在那个瞬间，绝望涌上了心头。

6. It has come to my attention/ notice that some money is missing. 我发现一些钱弄丢了。

7. The whole unorthodox procedure appealed to him. 他对整个非同寻常的过程很感兴趣。

8. But what is wrong is that these things often come in at a high price to their health and the welfare of their families.
让人不能接受的是他们的健康及家人的幸福都会因为这些事情而付出代价。
9. A five-foot sausage gazes at you from a wall-painting.
壁画上一个五英尺高的香肠在凝视着你。
10. No complaints passed her lips. 她从不抱怨。
11. Later the realization struck me. 我后来意识到了。
12. As this realization sank into me I stopped running and began to cry.
当我有了这种意识时，我不再奔跑，开始大哭。
13. A strange peace came over her when she was alone. 她独处时便感到一种特殊的安宁。
14. Alarm began to take entire possession of him. 他开始变得惊恐万状。
15. Darkness engulfs me as I hear the sound of nails being hammered into the coffin.
我四周一片漆黑，我听到钉子敲进棺材的声音。
16. I remember you well, but your name has slipped my mind.
我确实记得你，只是一时想不起你的名字。
17. Reason had forsaken him. 他失去了理性。
18. Beauty and wonder had departed from him. 他已经感受不到美与神奇。
19. As he did so an exclamation of concern escaped him.
当他要离开时，他发出一声关切的惊叫。
20. Even my voice did not escape him. 甚至我的声音都被他听到了。
21. You may find it difficult to understand the thought of Hume，and if you have no philosophical training its implications will doubtless escape you.
你会发现很难理解休姆的思想，而且如果你没有受到过哲学训练，毫无疑问，你将无法理解它的含义。
22. So that that habit of obedience should not desert him at this perilous moment.
以致于他那服从的习惯在这危险的时刻就派上了用场。
23. The dread word shook me to my foundations. 可怕的字眼使我浑身颤抖。
24. A chance meeting took you by surprise in a supermarket. 超市的偶遇让你感到惊讶。
25. From the moment we stepped into the People's Republic of China, care and kindness surrounded us on every side.（H. and N. Johnson: *To China at Ninety*）
自从踏上中华人民共和国国土那一刻，我们随时随地受到关怀与照顾。
26. A splash of bright orange caught my eye. 一片闪烁明亮的橘黄跃入我的眼帘
27. A snap-shot（快照）near the beginning of the musty-smelling album caught Peter's eye.
在那个散发着霉味的相册首页，有一张快照吸引了皮特的注意。
28. Just at this moment a plashy tramp by the side of the bridge caught the sensitive ear of Ichabod. 就在这时，伊卡博德敏感的耳朵听到了桥边的湿地有人行走的响声。
29. Gradually the sound penetrated to him. 渐渐地他听到这个声音。
30. Not a sound reached our ears. 我们没听到任何声音。
31. It was already growing dark when at last he opened the door, and stood listening. Not a sound! A milky twilight crept about the landing below. He had turned back when a sound

caught his ear. 当他最后打开门时，天已经变黑了，站那儿，听了一会。没有任何声音！乳白色的光照射在下面的楼梯平台上，这时他听到一个声音，便转过身去。

32. Something felt very small and tight inside the girl. 小女孩感到心里憋得慌。

33. A lump formed in my throat. 我的喉咙被一团东西塞住（说不出话来）。

34. Her voice was strangled in his throat. 他的喉咙发不出声音。

35. Offering Squeak a balanced diet became my main concern.
如今为吱吱提供营养均衡的饮食成了我最关心的问题。

36. No other great city can provide these glimpses.
只有在这个城市你才会不经意间看到这些情景。

37. But their turns came at last, and they found themselves in Greatorex's presence.
最后终于轮到他们了，但发现在他们面前的是格雷特雷克斯。

38. When the money comes to me, I must be able to pay all my debts.
当我有钱了，我一定能偿还所有的债务。

39. All the time the creeping fear that he would never come back to her grew strong within her.
她的心一直被那越来越强烈的恐惧感揪着，她感到他是永远不能回到她身边来了。

40. After more than a week of neglect the rubbish-heap had suddenly regained its fascination for me.
一周多没倒垃圾，我突然发现垃圾已经成堆。

41. The solution lies in a return to "traditional family values".
出路在于恢复"传统家庭价值观"。

42. The ultimate responsibility for the violence lies with the country's president.
暴乱的最终责任归咎于该国总统。

43. a habit that grows on you　在你身上日益根深蒂固的习惯

44. a book that grows on you　你喜爱的一本书

45. Some financial element was entering their talk.
他们的谈话中开始涉及一些金钱问题。

46. The absolute magnitude of my misfortune only loomed upon me by degrees.
我的许多灾难逐步隐现。

47. The doctor lost four hours' sleep. These pains returned at intervals of few days, and naturally the child's convalescence was retarded.
医生为此少睡了四个小时，在随后的几天这些疼痛间或发作，孩子的康复自然而然地被延缓了。

48. A sense of my whereabouts returned to me: I noticed for the first time where I was—on the causeway（堤道）leading to the sluice.
我意识到了我所在的位置，而且是第一次注意到我处在——通往水闸的堤道上。

49. Not that the lust to kill had suddenly descended on her, or that she felt that she would leave India safer and more wholesome（有益健康的）than she had found it, with one fraction less of wild beast per million of inhabitants.（每一百万居民中减少一部分野兽）
这并不是因为她突然感到有一种非杀害点什么东西不可的欲望，也不是因为她觉得在印度，猛兽与人口的比率偏高了一点，想要略加削减，使印度成为一个比她初来时更为安全舒适的地方。

50. The noise of the water drumming in the kettle deadened her pain.
水壶口的水发出咕咕的声音减弱了她的疼痛。

51. Bosinney's phrase came back to him: "women are the evils!"
他想起波辛尼的话："女人是魔鬼！"

52. His strength left. 他浑身无力。

53. A mix of excitement and fear **registers** on Jamie-Lynn Sigler's face as she contemplates the end of television's ground-breaking drama *The Sopranos*.
杰米-林恩·西格勒反复琢磨着具有开创性意义的电视连续剧《黑道家族》的结局，脸上流露出一种兴奋与担心相混杂的神色。

54. The tea received a great deal of praise from Sophia, but neither of them ate much.
索菲亚对茶大加赞赏，但她们俩吃的都不多。

55. She wanted to cry out with joy because of the words that had **come from** the lips of her son, but the expression of joy had become impossible to her.
由于这话从她儿子嘴里出来，她高兴地想大喊，但她却无法表达她的快乐。

56. Sometimes as they sat thus a picture of village life **presented** itself to them.
有时候，他们俩这样坐着，一幅乡村生活的画面呈现在他们的眼前。

57. As the events of the day **formulated**（明确表达）themselves in his mind, Davies wrote and turned over page after page.
当这一天的事情在戴维斯的脑海里逐步清晰以后，他一边写一边不停地翻页。

58. Scarcely any predicament, moral or psychological has **escaped** its study, and it has so refined and perfected its methods that antiseptic surgery itself has already made a more beneficent advance.
无论是道德困境还是心理困境都在它的研究范围，它还对研究方法进行了完善和优化，以致于抗菌研究本身也取得了有益的进步。

59. The decision to build had been **weighing on** his mind all the week, and he had not made up his mind to tell her.
关于在罗宾山建造别墅的想法，他已经思考了一周，还没想好是否告诉她。

60. "Does any one know where this negro lived?" he asked heavily, a growing sense of his duty **weighing upon** him.
他缓慢地问道："有人知道这个黑人住哪么？"同时感到责任越来越重。

61. The problem /responsibility **weighs on** him/his mind.
那个难题（责任）沉重地压在他的身上（心上）。

62. The criticism that has hitherto（迄今）**met** Mr. Washington has not always been of this broad character. 迄今为止，华盛顿受到的批评从未如此广泛过。

63. He had been away for months and a sense of emptiness was **creeping into** my life.
他离开已经有几个月了，我感到生活空虚。

64. When he spoke these last words, a thrill of amazement **went through** every one.
当他说出这最后几个字时，大家都感到一阵惊讶。

65. Almost imperceptibly a change **came over** the settlement.

几乎是不知不觉间殖民地发生了变化。

66. And again the scornful smile curled her lips. 她的嘴唇再次露出轻蔑的微笑。

67. A smile lit（up）her face. 微笑使她容光焕发。light up（with）使容光焕发

68. A smile lit the eyes of the expiring Kentuck. 弥留之际的肯塔克眼里闪现着笑容。

69. I staggered forward at once, and a few steps brought me to the vestibule of the building.
我立刻踉踉跄跄往前走，不消几步，就到了屋子的门厅。

70. Every step takes me nearer home. 每一步都让我离家更近。

71. She frowned at a piece of toast and ate it very slowly, as though she wished to convey the impression that the process hurt her more than it hurt the toast, but no extension of hospitality on Clovis's behalf **rose to her lips**.

似乎（吃面包）这个动作使她遭受到的损害比面包遭受到的损害更大。（形容她无心吃面包，而在盘算如何回答。）但她没有说要延长对克洛维斯的款待。（意即她没有说愿意再留克洛维斯住下去。）

2.2.2　想出一个主意或形成一个观点

这种用法在英语中较常见，但汉语中并不多见，值得注意。

1. It never entered anyone's head that she could have had a motive for killing her husband.
没有人会想到她有杀死她丈夫的动机。

2. It never entered my head to be a poet. 我从没想过成为一名诗人。

3. His best ideas came to him in dreams. 他最好的主意是在梦中想到的。

4. An idea came to me. 我想到了一个主意。

5. At last the idea came to him of sending the dog for help. 最后他想到了让狗去求助。

6. A thought had come into her mind. 她想到一个主意。

7. An idea has occurred to me. 我已经想到了一个主意。

8. The bright idea occurred to her that she could casually broach the subject while moving round among the spectators.
她想到一个好主意，当她在观众中间走动时，她可以不经意间提出这个话题。

9. It somehow never occurred to one to think of the flesh-and-blood side of it.
似乎人们从未想到他们是血肉之躯这一面。

10. There were several things they never guessed, and one of them was that for a striking scene in the novel, in which a footman briefly figured, it occurred to me to make use of Major Monarch as the menial. 有几件事是他们从未想到的，其中之一就是一个仆人短暂出现过，我想到把梅杰·默纳克用作仆人。

11. Suddenly Alastair MacIntyre looked as if an unpleasant thought had just struck him. He quickly recovered himself and began to whistle casually.
艾乐斯泰尔.麦克恩泰尔好像忽然想起了什么不快乐的事情，他迅速恢复了常态并开始漫不经心地吹起口哨来。

12. It crossed my mind that the store would be closed at five o'clock.
我想到商店将会在五点关门。

13. Then it dawned upon him that there was no further need to escape the bacteriologist.

那时他忽然醒悟，他再也不必逃避细菌学家。

14. It dawned on him what he had done. 他突然想到他曾经做过的事。

15. A sense of strangeness seemed to dawn on the lady.
这位太太突然有一种奇怪的感觉。

16. Then, immediately arose the idea of a non-reasoning creature capable of speech.
那时，立刻意识到没有理性的生物能够说话。

17. A disturbing thought struck him. 他感到心烦意乱。

18. For a time no thoughts would come to me, I was so blasted by her anger.
我被她的愤怒吓住了，一时没了主意。

19. An idea suddenly struck me. 我突然想到一个主意。

20. A thousand ideas raced through her head. 她思绪万千。

21. To make her his queen never entered his mind. 他从来没有想到要把她娶为皇后。

22. The idea flashed into/through/ across his mind. 他的脑海中闪现一个主意。

23. A definite determination had come into the mind of the defeated wife of the Winsburg hotel keeper. 遭受失败的温斯堡饭店管理员的妻子想到要坚决果断。

24. Everywhere bright red flags strike the eye. 到处是鲜艳夺目的红旗。

25. His mind was occupied with a desire not to appear green. 他满脑子想的是要表现成熟。

26. The idea stuck in Mama's head. 这个主意牢牢盘踞在老伴的心头。

27. When I saw this the conviction flew across my mind like a flash of lighting that the preparation had been made under other eyes than those of the servants.
当我看到靴子这样放法，我瞬间意识到这样的安排是别人而不是佣人想出来的。

28. Such frightful thoughts ran endlessly through Constance's mind as she bent over the fire endeavoring to keep alive a silly conversation with Maria Crithlow.
当康斯坦斯俯身向炉火时，她的脑海中充斥着这种可怕的想法，尽力维持她与玛利亚·克里斯露之间愚蠢的谈话。

29. There came into his mind a flood of unaccustomed thoughts. 他想到一系列奇怪的想法。

30. As these thoughts came, his anger against the mulatto died away, and in its place there sprang up a great pity. 想到这些，他不再生这个白黑混血儿的气，取而代之的是怜悯。

31. Then it came over me that she had made a great effort for me—made it with a kind of nobleness—and that I owed her a compensation.
那时想到他已为我做了很多，而且是一种高尚的行为，我应该补偿他。

32. When it came over me, the latent eloquence of what they were doing.
他们虽默默无言，但所作所为却具有说服力。

33. An idea slowly took shape in his mind. 一个想法在他脑海中慢慢形成了。

34. Tom had a remarkably smooth, soft voice, and a habitually respectful manner, that had given Legree an idea that he would be cowardly, and easily subdued.
汤姆的声音非常平缓、温柔，并且习惯性地毕恭毕敬，这在莱格里看来，是懦弱的表现，容易驯服。

35 My thoughts immediately swung back to the first time I wore this outfit in performance.
我立刻回想到我第一次穿这套服装表演的情形。

36. Instead, my thoughts drift back to the Nile valley and to two young sisters who call Egypt home. 而是任思绪飘回了尼罗河河谷，飘回了将埃及称作故乡的两个年轻姐妹身上。

37. "Good God!" Things were coming back to me. 天哪！我想起来了。

38. This reflection, which had been occupying him for most of the day at the Public Library.
在公共图书馆的大半天时间他都在想这个问题。

39. Nagging thoughts began to stir in Mary's mind. 玛丽开始有了抱怨的冲动。

40. Many thoughts besieged my mind but only one found lodging, and it was overwhelming.
我想到了许多主意，但最后只剩下一个，并且是无法抗拒的。

41. A $ 3 trillion figure for the total cost strikes us as judicious, and probably errs on the low side.
我们觉得 3 万亿美元的总开销是比较谨慎的估计，而且这个数字很可能是估计得偏低了。

42. The idea struck her as odd. 那个想法让她感到很奇怪。

43. What adjectives arrive in your mind? 你想到什么形容词？

44. What adjectives arrive when I ask you: what are the qualities of this person?
当我问及这个人的品质时，你会想到什么形容词？

45. Mrs. Packletide had already **arranged in her mind** the lunch she would give at her house in Curzon Street, ostensibly in Loona Bimberton's honor.
帕克尔泰德夫人心里早就筹划好了，她准备在柯纵街的住宅里设午宴专请鲁娜・宾波敦。

46. She had also already **designed in her mind** the tiger-claw brooch that she was going to give Loona Bimberton on her next birthday.
她也已经想好在她的下一次生日聚会上送给她一个虎爪胸针。

47. Nanjing remained only on the periphery of her thought. 南京未引起她的关注。

48. You may be asking what brought on this morbid of thought.
你可能会问，为什么会产生这种病态想法？

第三节 描述客观事物

这种用法与汉语思维模式基本一致。

1. The story unfolds as the film goes on. 随着影片的放映，故事情节展开了。

2. My portmanteau had of course come open. 我的旅行箱当然已经开了。

3. The rifle flashed out with a loud report. 一声很响的枪声。

4. The prepared tea-table in front of the fire made a glittering array.
火堆前准备好的茶桌闪闪发光。

5. To the right the road continued up the main valley; to the left it went over the big bridge.
往右，这条路继续往这个主山谷的上方延伸；往左，经过一座大桥。

6. Just where she had paused, the brook chanced to form a pool, so smooth and quiet that it reflected a perfect image of her little figure. 就在她停下的地方，水流汇成一个小水坑，水面光滑而又平静，完美地映出她那娇小的身材。

7. Irony makes the world go around. 讽刺无处不在。

第四节 身体的局部做主语

这种用法与汉语思维模式一致。

1. "I walk, but now my back is giving me a hard time, so the nurses say I should not walk that distance," she said. And she pointed to the lily-lawn with the hand that didn't hold the bread-and-butter. 她说："我走了走，结果我的背部现在很难受，因此护士们说我不该走那么远，"然后她用那只没拿黄油面包的手指向长着百合花的草坪。

2. Her eyes filled as she regarded her position further.
她进一步想到了自己的情形，眼睛里充满了泪水。

3. And the tears are running down their faces. 他们泪流满面。

4. He suddenly stretched himself up, and, looking earnestly to heaven, while the tears and blood flowed down his face mingled,
他突然站直了身子，热切地望向天空，此时鲜血混合着泪水留下他的面庞。

5. Tom put up his hand to wipe the blood that trickled down his face.
汤姆抬起手擦掉脸上一滴一滴留下的鲜血。

6. Tess stood there staring at him with eyes that did not weep.
苔丝站在那里用那双没有泪水的眼睛呆呆地看着他。

7. My brain, that precision instrument, slipped into high gear.
我的大脑像精确的仪器一样，开始高速运转

8. His heart thumping hard, and the sweat breaking out all over his forehead.
他的心脏跳得厉害，并且整个额头都渗出了汗。

9. The cold sweat ran from forehead. 额头直冒冷汗。

10. Aziz wiped his head, and sweat began to stream inside his clothes.
阿齐兹擦着他的头，而衣内已汗流成河。

11. Sweat pearled his forehead. 他额上满是汗珠。

12. A cold perspiration had gathered on his forehead, and his teeth were chattering with affright. 他的前额冒出冷汗，甚至他的牙齿也因为害怕打战。

13. Perspiration ran down his forehead. 汗水从他的前额流下来。

14. As he approached the stream his heart began to thump. 当他靠近小溪时，心里砰砰跳。

15. His heart began to sink within him. 他的心情开始变得沉重。

16. The prisoner's arm was bleeding from a fresh wound. 犯人胳膊上的新伤口在流血。

17. His cheek-bones showed painfully. 他的颧骨露出痛苦的样子。

18. The fists and the abdominal muscles did their work, for the door of the house suddenly burst open and Ruth came running down the steps, carrying Baby on her arm.
拳头和腹部肌肉此时大显身手，因为房门突然砰地一声开了，露丝怀中抱着婴儿跑下楼梯。

19 At that her eyes blazed. 看到这，她的眼睛一亮。

20. His ears picked up a familiar braying noise, and a broad back that had been turned towards him was abruptly reversed, becoming a broad chest. 他听到一个熟悉的大嗓门声音，接着一个刚才转过去背对着他的宽大躯体又突然转过来，面对着他。

21. Three years ago, a spinal cord injury left 25-year-old Mathew Nagle unable to do much more than speak and shrug his shoulders. 三年前，脊髓损伤使25岁的马修·内格尔除了说话和耸肩以外几乎不能做其他更多的动作。

第五节 无须提到施动者

下面这些句子的动作是人发出的，但施动者信息在句中并不重要，可以省去。汉语中有时也会这样表达。

1. The first question went to him. 第一个问题是问他的。
2. Her question received no answer. 没人回答她的问题。
3. A telegram came from Moscow. 一份来自莫斯科的电报。
4. Reports are coming in of a major earthquake in Mexico.
传来的消息说墨西哥发生一场大地震。
5. My TV came in yesterday. 我的电视是昨天送来的。
6. Your TV is ready. 你的电视修好了。
7. No card or note came with it. 上面既没有卡片也没有便条。
8. Calls to the florist are in vain, it was a cash purchase.
多次打电话询问花店，均无所获，用现金支付。
9. All of those calls have to go to a personal phone. 这些电话都会打到个人电话上。
10. Cars are stopping to look. 好多车都停下来观看。
11. It discusses why human beings are interested in the outer space.
这一章讨论了人类为什么对外空感兴趣。
12. The second chapter discusses different approaches to the treatment of cancer.
第二章讨论了治疗癌症的不同方法。
13. A list gives prices. 一张价格列表。
14. The job pays a decent wage. 这份工作报酬不错。
15. And recreation centres couldn't find enough indoor space for playing; consequently, it was moved outdoors, as early as 1908.
由于娱乐中心不能提供足够的空间开展这项运动，使得它早在1908年成了户外运动。
16. The letter failed to arrive. 这封信未能送达。
17. Shortly after midnight, the truck arrived at our hotel. 刚过午夜，卡车到了我们的宾馆。
18. A conversation leading to mutual mystification followed.
就这样，两个人在互不明白的情况下继续他们的谈话。
19. In a country which increasingly improves the material aspect of life, the question will linger " What is the future all about?"
在一个物质生活水平不断提高的国家，“未来会怎样？”这个问题仍悬而未决。
20. The dishes we had laboured over disappear in less than a half hour.
不到半小时，我们辛辛苦苦做的菜都被吃了个精光。
21. Credit goes to CEO Mark Hurd. 这要归功于惠普公司首席执行官马克·赫德。
22. The door stood open onto a scene of boyish pandemonium.

教室的门敞开着，但见男孩们把教室弄得一片混乱。

23. In the past few days, a debate has arisen in the Kenyan government over the fate of prominent rights activist Al Amin Kimathi and several suspects facing charges of terrorism in Uganda. 在过去的几天内，肯尼亚政府内部掀起一场辩论，事关著名的人权活动家Al Amin Kimathi及其他几个嫌犯的命运，他们面临着乌干达政府的涉嫌恐怖指控。

24. Thirty-three pairs of eyes were trained on me. 三十三双眼睛注视着我。

25. The hall soon filled. 会堂很快坐满了。

26. The cinema was filling fast. 电影院很快就坐满了。

27. Back home, more newspapers began printing his articles.
国内更多的报纸开始刊登他的文章。

28. It（*Bull Durham* 《百万金臂》）took an ex-ballplayer to craft the ultimate ode to America's pastime. 影片请来了一位前棒球运动员来为美国的娱乐生活编织最美妙的颂歌。

29. New York is a judging town, and often invokes standards that the rest of the country deplores or ignores. 纽约是一个裁判城市，经常炮制出一些全国其他地方的人不是为之感到遗憾就是完全不予理睬的规范标准。

30. The shops and markets well provided. 有商店和市场，百货齐全。

31. At length notice arrived that executors were prepared to settle with Mr. Rymer.
最后传来通知，执法者准备与雷默先生和解。

32. But the unlucky suggestion met with fierce and unanimous opposition.
然而这个倒霉的建议遭到了激烈而一致的反对。

33. School learning must have been a deadening experience for children, for lapses in knowledge were often met with brutal punishment.
学校学习对孩子来说一定是一个热情消退的过程，因为知识上的错误经常会招致残酷的惩罚。

34. A polite skepticism would have greeted the slightest hint at a prospective reformation.
哪怕是极微弱的认为克洛维斯今后会改过自新的暗示，别人都将会有礼貌地表示怀疑。

35. The school was now thudding with activity and I could see boys out of the assembly hall and into the classrooms. 校内响起了孩子们活动的乒乒乓乓的声音，我看见男生从大礼堂蜂拥而出，继而进入了教室。

36. The arrow thudded into the target. 箭噗的一声射中靶子。

37. A great silence seemed to lie heavily over the station and press on their lips.
车站无比安静，以致于他们不敢说话。

38. Before the end of a week smiles and cheerful remarks ruled in the family.
在一周结束之前，家中不乏欢声笑语。

39. Chaos reigned in the classroom. 教室里大乱。

40. A kind of buzzing stillness reigned throughout the schoolroom.
学生轻声背诵课文的嗡嗡声。

41. The house was alive with soft, quick steps and running voices.
整个房子充满了轻快的脚步声和急促的交谈声。

42. The green baizer door that led to the kitchen regions swung open and shut with a muffled thud. 那扇通往厨房方向的绿色毛毡们，“吱”的打开，然后又“砰”的关上，发出

一声沉闷的响声。

43. Every Friday five crates of oranges and lemons arrived from a fruiterer in New York—every Monday these same oranges and lemons left his back door in a pyramid of pulpless halves. 每星期五，五箱橙子和柠檬从纽约一家水果行送到。每星期一，这些橙子和柠檬变成一座半拉半拉的果皮堆成的小金字塔从他的后门运出去。

44. The whole village was up and about,(起床活动)its one street alive and running with people. Heads appeared at doors and windows.

整个村庄都开始起床了，它的一条街道上满是流动的人群。一些门窗里探出了人头。

45. It began at the time when war memories and ideals were rapidly passing; a day of astonishing commercial development was dawning; a sense of doubt and hesitation overtook the freedom's sons, —then it was leading began.

对战争的记忆及理想一闪而过，令人惊讶的商业发展来临，这位自由之子开始怀疑和犹豫，他的领导地位就是在那时开始确立的。

46. A new period of self-assertion and self-development dawned.

出现了一个新的自信与自我发展的阶段。

47. With the prosperity of the camp came a desire for further improvement.

随着咆哮营的繁荣，人们盼望着更好的发展。

48. A silence followed Stumpy's speech. 斯达姆讲完之后，接着是一片安静。

49. For a moment the conversation hung upon that declaration.

有一会儿，会谈围绕这句话继续下去。

50. In that instance business had simply moved a few yards to the east.

在那种情况下，商业无非向东移了几码远。

51. A hushed and anonymous voice broke in. 传来一个陌生人的平静的声音。

第六节 与人有关的活动做主语

英语中与人有关的的心理活动、身体动作、人的外表都可以用作主语。

1. The memory she'd been resisting came back to her. 她又想起一直不愿想的事情。

2. Reminiscences, the most trifling and immaterial, passages of infancy and school-days, sports, childish quarrels, and the little domestic traits of her maiden years, came swarming back upon her, intermingled with recollections of whatever was gravest in her subsequent life; one picture precisely as vivid as another; as if all were of similar importance, or all alike a play.

她回忆起那些最琐碎零散最无关紧要的事情，孩提时期和学校生活，儿时的游戏和争吵，以及婚前在娘家的种种琐事蜂拥回到她的脑海，其中还混杂着她后来生活中最重大的事件的种种片断，一切全都历历在目似乎全都同等重要，或者全都像一出戏。

3. But the urge to play it for the most part deserted her. 只是弹琴的冲动已多半离她远去。

4. And even the memory of the deed is now dying. 甚至都快忘了这件事。

5. The matter of the rent must have altogether escaped his mind.

他一定把房租这件事一起给忘了。

6. His name escapes me/my memory. 我记不得他的名字了。

7. Her memory lingered for a moment over visions of the past. 他想了一会儿过去的情景。

8. Toward ten in the evening, his coat collar turned up against the fine drizzle that pervaded the air, his hands in his pockets, his elbows gripping his sides. 快到晚上十点时，为了躲避天空中细密的毛毛细雨，他把外套的领子卷起，手插到口袋里，两个肘夹住身体两侧。

9. The thought hurt him, then lost edge, as if it had come in contact with a breastplate.
这种想法曾让他心痛，慢慢地他也习以为常了，就像尖刀遇到了胸铠一样。

10. His gaze flattered Sophia. 他的注视让索菲亚很开心。

11. But the idea of leaving Constance, having once rejoined her, did not please Sophia.
她曾经再三考虑离开康丝坦斯，但索菲亚对此不悦。

12. His retreating figure vanished slowly into the shadows.
老人离去的身影渐渐消失在夜幕之中。（Saki *Dusk*）

13. Mrs. Sheridan's voice floated down the stairs. 谢里丹夫人的声音传到楼下。

14. An awkward little silence fell. 出现了令人尴尬的沉默。

15. A deep silence spread over the whole school. 整个学校开始沉寂下来。

16. A quick whisper ran through the class. 班里很快地私语起来。

17. But his breathing came with difficulty, and he had to stop to rest.
但他呼吸困难，不得不停下来休息。

18. The hope faded away in 1919. 1919 年，希望越来越渺茫。

19. His voice choked at the thought of it. 一想到它，他的声音哽咽。

20. His voice was strangled in his throat. 他的喉头哽住。

21. The beating was cruel and bloody as that of grown-ups, no mercy was shown. I have had three holes in my head, and many black eyes and puffed lips from our street wars.
这种殴打就像成人打架一样残酷而血腥，没有同情可言。因为街头打架，我的头已经烂过三个洞，有过多次熊猫眼和泡芙的嘴唇。

22. "Oh, my God!" he whispered, his voice losing power. 他有气无力地说"喔，我的天哪！"

23. A noticeable movement on the part of the crowd ceased.
这伙人停止了他们引人注意的行动。

24. Footsteps walked the floor above his head. 他听到楼上有走动的声音。

25. A quick glance told her that one of the men was bald, and the other had a crew cut.
他匆匆一瞥，看到其中一个男人秃头，另一个留着小平头。

26. This album is a collection of some of my favorite classic music songs. My greatest thanks go to the amazing songwriters who were responsible for these wonderful works of art and to the original artists who provided their everlasting stamp. 这张专辑收录的都是我最喜爱的一些经典歌曲。我最要感谢的是那些了不起的歌曲作者，是他们创作出了这些美妙的艺术作品，还有那些原唱艺术家，他们在这些作品上刻下他们永恒的记忆。

27. Your note will explain. 你的笔记可以说明问题。

28. Quite unexpectedly, the strange emotion which had overwhelmed me at the station returned.
出人意料的是，刚到广岛车站时袭扰我的那种异样的忧伤情绪竟在这时重新袭上心头。

29. My feelings towards Martin had suffered a sea-change.
我对马丁的印象来了一个一百八十度的转弯。

30. Peter's complain came to an end. 皮特不再抱怨。
31. Deep, loving pride in her stirred in me. 一种为她而产生的深切疼爱的自豪感。
32. And then a sudden hope filled my heart. 那时我内心突然充满了希望。
33. All the old bitterness began to well up inside her again.过去的苦难又一次在她心中涌起。
34. She comes into the room. A sound between sob and a sniff escapes her.
她进了房间，既不是哭也不是吸气的声音也随之消失。
35. Her pride rose at the bare thought of return.
只要想到回去，他内心自豪感油然而生。
36. The strangeness of the hazards of life overwhelmed her.
她一直沉浸在生命充满危险的怪感中。
37. A thrill passed over all of us. 我们大家都感到十分惊异
38. An awed hush fell upon the bystanders. 旁观者都惊愕得说不出话来。
39. All his anger seemed to have drifted away from him.
他所有的愤怒似乎都慢慢消失了。
40. And soon the first shock of meeting had worn off.
很快见面时最初的惊讶消失了。
41. The pain is wearing off. 痛苦在慢慢消失。
42. Although I felt a little lonely, my exaltation of the morning had not worn off.
尽管我感到有点孤单，但上午的快乐还没有消退。
43. And this feeling of personal dependence on her Minister steadily increased.
她本人对首相的情感依赖与日俱增。
44. The Major enquired with the comfortable candour that now prevailed between us.
上校询问时的坦率让人感觉舒适，而且现在这种坦率是我们之间常有的。
45. A leisured friendly atmosphere prevailed among the crowds.
人群中流行着闲适友好的气氛。
46. These somber recollections gave way at length to more cheerful feelings as he began to approach his home coolly.
当他开始沉着地走近家时，那些忧伤的回忆也随之消失，取而代之的是更为欢快的心情。
47. And a frown gathered on her brow. 她皱起了眉头。
48. Then her happiness reached its height, her eye sparkled.
随之，她的幸福达到巅峰，眼睛闪烁着光芒。
49. His nervousness about this disclosure irritated him profoundly.
他对这件事败露后的忧虑感到极度不快。
50. Because her curiosity did not extend beyond Bursley. 因为她的好奇仅限于伯斯利。
51. A smile softened her lips and she opened her blue eyes very wide.
她的嘴唇露出了微笑，一双蓝色的眼睛睁得大大的。
52. Marian's brow darkened. 玛丽安表情铁青。
53. A cold shudder ran through me. 我浑身一阵寒颤。
54. Languor and uneasiness would seize on everyone, even the denizens of the forest, betraying it by their motions. 大家都是无精打采、焦躁不安，连树林里的动物也烦躁起来。

55. A look of disappointment went around the crowd. 人群中流露出失望的表情。

56. An impulse came to her. 她有一种冲动。

57. And their ambition takes a different form—not a better form, but one produced by the preference of enjoyment to power.

他们欲望的表现形式不同，但并非比我们的好，只是因为他们好享受胜于好权力。

第七节　拟人化的句子

这类非人称主语句使用了“拟人”修辞，让无生命的事物具有人的感情。

But the complexion even of external things seemed to suffer transmutation as her announcement progressed. The fire in the grate looked impish - demoniacally funny, as if it did not care in the least about her strait. The fender grinned idly, as if it too did not care. The light from the water-bottle was merely engaged in a chromatic problem. All material objects around announced their irresponsibility with terrible iteration. And yet nothing had changed since the moments when he had been kissing her; or rather, nothing in the substance of things. But the essence of things had changed.

但是随着她的讲述，甚至连外界事物的面貌也似乎发生了变化。炉桥里的火苗露出恶作剧的样子，变得凶恶可怖，仿佛一点儿也不关心苔丝的不幸。壁炉的栅栏懒洋洋的，也似乎对一切视而不见。从水瓶里发出来的亮光，只是一心在研究颜色的问题。周围一切物质的东西，都在可怕地反复申明，它们不负责任。但是自从他吻她的时候以来，什么也没有发生变化；或者不如说，一切事物在本质上都没有发生变化。但是一切事物在本质上又发生了变化。

第八节　英汉思维模式对比

中国人受传统哲学思想的影响，在他们的意识里，人的主体意识、人的重要性是相当强的。而英语重视客体意识，思维的目标往往指向外界，探求外部客观世界对人的影响。这种思维差异反映到语言表达上，就是汉语习惯用表示人的词作句子的主语（或潜在的主语），而英语则有用非生物主语的倾向。钱歌川在《英语疑难详解》中指出，“我们说中文时，惯常都要用人或生物作主语，而英文则爱用无生命物作主语。下面这些例句中，“a.”可以说是汉语思维模式，或英汉思维模式有相通之处，而“b.”则完全是英语思维模式。

1. 不同的人对退休有不同的态度。

a. Different people have different attitudes towards retirement.

b. Attitudes towards retirement vary from person to person.

2. 我永远不会忘记这个教训。

a. I will never forget the lesson.

b. The lesson will be rooted in my memory forever.

3. 由于计划不够完善，我不仅浪费了金钱，也浪费了时间。

a. Because of poor planning, I wasted all my money as well as my time.

b. Poor planning wasted all my money as well as my time.

4. 当我因工作繁忙而必须搬家时，玛丽不得不转学。

Mary had to change schools when my busy work schedule made it necessary for me to move house.（Mitch Miller *Popularity That Counts*）

汉语是两个短句，而英语用了一个主从复合句。

5. 跑了有一百码，想说些幽默和鼓励的话，但我气喘吁吁，说不出话来。

After a hundred yards or so I tried to speak to, to offer some great words of wisdom and motivation, but my words and my breath failed.（Charles A. Coonradt *Her Newly-discovered Self*）

汉语“气喘吁吁”的主语是“我”，英语用“my words and my breath”作主语。

6. 整个晚上和他在一起就是听他一个人讲。任何人只要稍微有点和他不同的看法，哪怕是琐事，也足以使他几个小时不停地驳斥。

An evening with him was an evening spent in listening to a monologue. The slightest hint of disagreement, from anyone, on the most trivial point, was enough to set him off on a harangue that might last for hours.

上面汉语中，用人作主语；而英语中，全部用物作主语，凸显了英语的非人称主语特色。

7. 我会离家去读大学，对此我从未有过怀疑。

There was never any question in my mind that I would go to a college away from home.

这一句使用了“There be…”结构。

8. 我们必须每天做一些锻炼。It is necessary for us to have exercise every day.

这一句使用了“it”作形式主语。

9. 尽管我期待了好几个月，但我还是没有任何心理准备应付那一天的到来。

Despite months of anticipation, nothing could have prepared me for the impact of the actual day.（Karen Odem *Bittersweet Memories*）

这一句使用了“anticipate” 动词名物化和使役动词“prepare”。

10. 几年后，迫于经济上的困难，我就读过的那所中学关闭了。虽然再去访问母校是不可能了，但是想到我能随时回忆这些特殊的往事，我感到十分宽慰。

Years later, financial difficulty forced my high school to close its doors for good. Although going back is impossible, it's comforting to know I can revisit my special memories any time.（Karen Odem *Bittersweet Memories*）

这一句使用了形容词“difficult”的名词化，动名词短语“going back”作主语，以及“it”形式主语。

11. 许多孩子由于智力高，不愿迎合社会上反知识的观念，而被剥夺了学习足够的社交技能和获得良好交际手段的机会。

Because of their intelligence and refusal to conform to society's anti- intellectual values, many are deprived of a chance to learn adequate social skills and acquire good communication tools.（Leonid Fridman *Nerds and Greeks*）

这一句把形容词“intelligent”名词化，动词“refuse”名词化。

12. 史蒂威是音乐天才也好，他战胜了失明和贫穷也好，突然间都变得不重要了。

Suddenly, it didn't matter that Stevie was a musical genius or that he had conquered blindness and poverty.（Stevie Wonder: *Sunshine in the Shadow*）

这一句运用了“it”形式主语句。

13. 她感到震惊，心情抑郁，甚至惊恐不安。

Astonishment, apprehension, and even horror oppressed her.

这一句主要运用了“动词名词化”技巧。

14. 我们沿着小道不知不觉地朝公园走去，跨过了一座人行小桥。

Somewhat our path took us toward the park and across a footbridge.

实践的“主体”与“客体”对调。

15. 从村广场沿着一条土路，穿过一片高高的树林，几分钟就可以到达海滩。

From the village square a dirt track leads you down through tall trees to the beach in a few minutes.（同上）

16. 走廊的地毯厚厚的。我走在上面，一点脚步声也没有。

The thick carpet on the corridor killed the sound of my footsteps.（同上）

17. 妇女退休后完全过一种家庭生活，她们没有像男的一样感到可怕。

Withdrawal from employment to complete domesticity is a far less threatening experience for a woman than for a man.

这一句把“退休”名词化，译成“withdrawal from employment”，同时把汉语的动词短语“感到可怕”译成“a threatening experience”。

18. 我们早就用不着在生活上极力节约了。

The need for strict economy in our lives has long since disappeared.

这一句使用了“动词名词化”技巧，把“用得着”译成“need”。

19. 我害怕起来了，而且越来越害怕。

Then fear set in and commenced to build up.

实践的“主体”与“客体”对调。

20. 邓小平身体健康，精力充沛，全国人民都很高兴。

Deng's good health and bouncing energy is a source of happiness to people across the land.

把“健康”“充沛”名词化，译成“health”和“energy”。

21. 但人们始终没有也永远不可能忘记文化大革命那可怕的一幕。

But the terrible story of the Cultural Revolution has not been, and may never be, expunged from public memory.

实践的“主体”与“客体”对调，凸显客观事物。

22 大多数人对学生的要求持同情的态度。

There is considerable public sympathy for the students' demands.

使用了“There be…”结构，及形容词名词化结构。

23. 当我得知我通过了入学考试，我有多高兴。

My delight knew no bounds when I learned that I had passed the entrance examination.

使用“拟人”修辞。

拓展学习：李白出生于公元 701 年，被称为中国的济慈。

Li Taibai, “the Keats of China”, had discovered the world in AD 701.

24. 这一情景让格茨比心旷神怡，也符合他此时的心境。在他心目中，黄昏是失意者的时刻。

The scene pleased Gortsby and harmonized with his present mood. Dusk, to his mind, was the hour of the defeated.

通过使役动词“please”的运用，避免了“make+sb.+*adj.*”结构。

25. 林中一个出口让他为之一振，他以为到了教堂旁边的桥了。

An opening in the trees now cheered him with the hopes that the church bridge was at hand.

使用了使役动词“cheer”，避免了“make+sb.+*adj.*”结构。

26. 再者，他们吃不惯公司定量供应的大米，由于他们的故乡根本就不产这种粮食，他们一直无法适应天天吃米。

The rice rations served out by the company did not agree with them, being a food unknown to their land, and to which they could not get used.

通过非人称主语句、分词及定语从句的运用，把汉语几个短句压缩成一个英语复合句。

27. All through luncheon fragments of my conversation with Lord Trimingham kept coming back to me. Two things stood out: one was that whatever happened it was never a lady's fault, and the other, that it might be necessary to kill someone although you didn't really dislike him.

整个午饭时间，我都在回想与特里明厄姆勋爵的谈话片段。突出的有两件事：一是不管发生了什么，错从不在女士，二是尽管你真的喜欢某个人，可能有时还必须要杀死他。

通过非人称主语句的使用，表明小说中的人物是不由自主的想起，并不是主动回忆。

28. 他疲惫不堪，加上气温越来越高，于是他下决心一看到阴凉处就坐下休息。

His weariness and increasing heat determined him to sit down in the first convenient shade.

这一句把形容词“weary”名词化，把短句“气温越来越高”转化为名词短语“increasing heat”，同时运用了使役动词“determine”。

第三章 被动结构

英汉语相比，英语多用被动结构，而汉语少用。前面提到由于英语思维模式受地理环境的影响，往往突出实践的“客体”，可以与英语中非人称主语句对比学习。

第一节 突出信息

英语中的主语通常是上文提到的已知信息，即相对次要而并非侧重的成分。而句末的信息才是新鲜重要及强调突出的信息。在行文中，为了保持上下句的衔接，可以使用被动结构调换主体与客体的位置。

1. The games of the 29th Olympiad in 2008 are awarded to the city of Beijing.

2008 年第 29 届奥运会（主办权）授予北京！

这句话突出的信息是“北京”，所以使用被动结构，把“北京”放在句末。

2. Kissinger was alarmed by China's first atomic blast in October, 1964.

1964 年 10 月，中国爆炸了第一颗原子弹，这把基辛格吓了一跳。

3. The grass-plot before the jail, in Prison Lane, on a certain summer morning, not less than two centuries ago, was occupied by a pretty large number of the inhabitants of Boston, all with their eyes intently fastened on the iron-clamped oaken door. 两百多年前一个夏日的上午，波士顿监狱门前的那块草地万人攒动，众人的眼睛都牢牢地盯着布满铁钉的栎木大门。

4. An object lesson here was taught by an old drug. 一种过去的药物给我们上了一次实物课。

5. 为他们提供了新的行业和职业。

New trades and occupations were revealed to them.

6. 2008 年的奥运会波诺尔如果不参加，将会非常令人遗憾。

Ponor would be sorely missed at the Games.

7.医生和医学院学生务必完成下面两项重要的任务：

Two key tasks required of doctors and medical students are:

这句使用了过去分词，表被动含义。

8. 协议一经签署，接受国中一些权力部门和借出方立刻就提出许多变动，并予以执行，也得到世界银行的默许。

Immediately after the agreement is signed, many changes are suggested and then implemented by both powerful groups in the recipient country and lenders, with the tacit tolerance of the WB.

9. 热情的读者纷纷写信给地方报纸，对上海的城市建设提出各种建议。

Local newspapers have been sprinkled with passionate letters giving various suggestions on the urban construction of Shanghai.

10. 这项合同需要经理签名。This contract should be signed by the manager.

11. Music lessons were given by Miss Temple to some of the elder girls.

一些年龄大一点的女孩的音乐课是 Temple 小姐上的。

12. His first lessons in art were provided locally by Edward Hicks and probably also by Thomas Hicks, Edward's cousin, a portrait painter.

他最初接受的美术教育来自当地画家爱德华·希克斯，可能还有爱德华的堂兄弟托马斯·希克斯（一位肖像家）。

第二节　无须表明动作的执行者

当动作的执行者在信息中无关紧要时，可以使用被动结构，同时省略动作执行者。

1. 困难克服了，工作完成了，问题也解决了。

The difficulties have been overcome, the work has been finished and the problem solved.

2. 要造飞机，就必须仔细考虑空气阻力问题。

Air resistance must be given careful consideration when the aircraft is to be manufactured.

3. 注意看看信的地址是否写对了。

Care should be taken to see that the letter is properly addressed.

4. 近来已注意到本馆存书惊人地减少，此事令人关切。现要求学生不要忘记借还书规则，并考虑其他学生的需要。今后凡借书逾期不还者，必将按章处罚。

It has been noted with concern that the stock of books in the library has been declining alarmingly. Students are asked to remind themselves of the rules for the borrowing and return of books, and to bear in mind the needs of other students. Penalties for overdue books will in the future be strictly enforced.

5. 我们最近查找了卷宗，发现本局并无此信。可以肯定的是，我们于两个月前收到此信，经研究后，已寄还贵处。鉴于以上情况，贵处仍无收信的记录，我们感到遗憾。如果你们找到此信，请即通知本局，不胜感激。

A current search of the files indicates that the letter is no longer in this Bureau's possession. It is noted that the letter was received two months ago, and after study, returned to your office. In view of the foregoing, it is regretted that your offices has no record of its receipt. If the letter is found, it would be appreciated if this Bureau was notified at once.

6. 唯一可见的光线来自某个“维也纳”面包店，早上一点钟的时候，那些需要面包的人可以来这儿领取。The only light visible came from the side of a certain "Vienna" bakery, where at one o'clock in the morning loaves of bread were given away to any who should ask.

7. 侍者用银壶端来咖啡。Coffee was brought in in a silver coffee-pot.

8. 有人向他们小声解释，他们必须立刻出发翻越 Bersund 群山。

It was explained to them in whispers that they must set off at once across the hills to Bersund.

9. 当然没有人尝试介绍/引入。No attempt was, of course, made at an introduction.

10. 19 世纪 20 年代社会生活的各个方面中，被人们评论得最多、渲染得最厉害的，莫过于青年一代的叛逆之行了。

No aspect of life in the Twenties has been more commented upon and sensationally romanticized than the so called Revolt of the Younger Generation.

11. 当然是赌博，而这些也形成了一种恶性循环。

Gambling, of course and a vicious cycle is created.

12. 在美国的黑人历史及在他之后领导人的演变过程中，都可以看到所有这些态度在各个时期的影响。The influence of all of these attitudes at various times can be traced in the history of the American Negro, and in the evolution of his successive leaders.
13. 突然学校安静了下来。Suddenly the hum of the school was hushed.
14. 我以前来过卢克索，记得在依山而建的哈采普苏特陵庙附近有好几条小路通往山上。Having been to Luxor before, I remembered that near Hatshepsut's Temple several trails led up the mountain against which the temples was built.
15. 一个与之竞争的称为 Pelamis 的系统用的是 120 米长、相互铰接的圆筒，已于 4 月在苏格兰实验成功。A rival system called Pelamis, using 120-m-long hinged cylinders, was successfully tested in Scotland in April.
16. 虽然这种历史性的氛围被那些死缠不放的商贩们多多少少地淡化了，但你大可对他们不理不睬。The historic atmosphere is somewhat dampened by aggressive hawkers, but they are easily ignored.
17. 女性所受的教育是要分不同的部位来审视自己的身体，并要对各个部位分别做出评价。Women are taught to see their bodies in parts, and to evaluate each part separately.
18. 不必经历先进的男女平等意识的阵痛，人们便能认识到，教妇女把自己与美联系起来的那种方式，会助长自恋倾向、加深依赖性和不成熟程度。
It does not take someone in the throes of advanced feminist awareness to perceive that the way women are taught to be involved with beauty encourages narcissism, reinforces dependence and immaturity.
19. 国际货币基金组织提出的经济和结构调整政策是为了解决上述各项问题而制定的：消除发展中国家灾难性的金融形势，然后证明这个国家现在符合获取新贷款的条件并且有财力来定期还债。
The policy of economic and structural adjustment suggested by the International Monetary Fund（IMF）was created to solve the above-mentioned problems: to cure the disastrous financial situation of the DC, and then, to certify that the country is now eligible to obtain new loans and has the resources to repay its debt regularly.
20. 然而，心理学家普遍认为，我们绝大多数人没有充分发挥自己的潜力。
However, it is generally accepted among psychologists that most of us fail to do justice to ourselves.（*We are What we think We Are*）
21. 桌子已经收拾得干干净净，只剩下一个煮咖啡的壶，一个杯子和一个茶托。
The table has been cleared of all but a coffee percolator and a cup and saucer.
22. 为什么总把麻烦事推给我呢？Why should all the unpleasant jobs be pushed onto me?
23. 不管老师如何描述这些结构，我们必须记住使用语言不是为了创造一个优美的结构，从而把孤立的语言形式串在一起。In spite of this description of frameworks from the teacher's perspective, it has to be remembered that using a language is not stringing together separate bits of linguistic form in order to arrive at a pleasing design.
24. 需要强调的是，尽管这些作品可以用英文写，（就像这部作品里出现的一样），但它们在文化上或语言上并不仅仅只适用于英语语言环境。
It should be emphasized that although they may be written in English（as are those that appear

in this work）, they need not be intended, culturally or linguistically, to refer only to English-language environments.

25. 语言学家决定不再为语言实践设计新模块，因为已经设计的情景模块能够全面覆盖这些要求。

It was decided to abandon the preparation of modules for the "practical" aspects of the language use, since the situation-based frameworks, already being written, would thoroughly cover the need.

第三节　描述客观事实

在正式的文体中，描述客观事物或事实时，常用被动结构。

1. As oil **is found** deep in the ground, its presence cannot **be determined** by a study of the surface. Consequently, a geological survey of the underground rocks structure must **be carried out**. If it **is thought** that the rocks in a certain area contain oil, a "drilling rig" **is assembled**. The most obvious part of a drilling rig **is called** "a derrick". It **is used** to lift sections of pipe, which **are lowered** into the hole made by the drill. As the hole **is being drilled**, a steel pipe **is pushed down** to prevent the sides from falling in. If oil **is struck** a cover **is firmly fixed** to the top of the pipe and the oil **is allowed** to escape through a series of valves.

因为石油深埋在地下，靠研究地面，不能确定石油的有无，因此，对地下岩层结构必须进行地质勘探。如果认为某地区的岩层含有石油，那就是在该处安装"钻机"。钻机中最显眼的部件叫作"井架"。井架用来吊升分节油管，把油管放入由钻头打出的孔中。当孔钻成时，放入钢管防止孔壁坍塌。如发现石油，则在油管顶部紧固地加盖，使石油通过一系列阀门流出。 这一段话用了十三个被动结构，可见在描述客观事物或事实时，英语倾向于使用被动结构。

2. That concern may be put to rest by the new studies.
以上担忧可能因为一些新的研究成果而得以平息。

3. But my protest was drowned by a commotion in the scullery: rattling, bubbling, and hissing.
我的抗议声淹没在碗碟洗涤处嘈杂声中：卡嗒卡嗒声、咕咕冒泡声、嘶嘶声。

4. The girl, with her back to the viewer, grasps the wrought-iron railings to see the trains below, blanketed in steam.
女孩背对着观画者，手抓锻铁的栏杆，看着下面的火车笼罩在蒸汽之中。

5. Sleep deprivation can also be triggered by depression, anxiety and other mental health issues.
抑郁、焦虑以及其他心理健康问题都可能引发睡眠不足。

6. Florida's rapid growth could be, well, swamped by an increase in its perilously high ground water table. 佛罗里达州的快速发展将会因危险并处于高位的地下水位的上升而覆没。

7. The problem is worsened by unstable governments, lack of political will, and corruption.
政局不稳、缺乏明确的政治意愿及腐败等因素使问题变得更糟糕。

8. Whenever two objects are rubbed together, electrons are transferred from one object to the other. 当两个物体在一起摩擦时，电子便从一个物体转移到另一个物体。

9. Moses says a vehicle is supposed to pass between her village and the clinic once a day, but it

does not come every day.
摩西说每天有一班车从她的村庄与诊所之间经过，但并不是每天都如此。

10. The recently discovered Bolivian titi monkey is now officially named for a Web casino based outside Montreal. 现在，这种新近发现的玻利维亚伶猴已经正式以蒙特利尔附近的一家网络赌场的名字命名了。

第四节　人成为客观事物

我们通常认为人是认识的"主体"，但是人也可能成为被认识的"客体"。

1. Her husband was taken ill with consumption. 她的丈夫患有肺结核。
2. I had been taken suddenly ill in the stomach. 我突然患了胃病。
3. He was given up to his dream. 他进入梦乡。
4. You were more sinned against than sinning, that I admit.
我承认，与其说是你把别人害了，不如说是别人把你害了.
5. His head was sunk in the pillow. 他把头枕在枕头上。
6. As many as 30,000 people were expected to attend the outdoor commencement ceremony.
据估计有 3 万人参加了这次室外的学位授予典礼。
7. A man of known wealth, known integrity, and known ability is largely entrusted with the money of his neighbours.
一个在钱财、人品和能力方面都很知名的人，他的邻居们多把钱托付给他保管。
8. I felt I had been shown the secret of life and why we're here: to be happy and to nurture other life. 我感觉到我窥探到了生命的秘密以及我们生存的意义，那就是快乐地生活同时培育其他生命。
9. Say you are given a choice of two cookies. 假定有两种甜饼干供你选择。
10. I've been tasked with assessing the relative merits of a Vodafone Compass-empowered Blackerry Pearl 8110 against a Navman S50, and this unfortunate experience comes toward the end of my three-day trip.
我接受了评估由"沃达丰罗盘"公司授权生产的"黑莓"珍珠 8110 型与"指路人"S50 型电子指路仪各有哪些优缺点的任务，而这次令人遗憾的体验经过 3 天的行程就要结束了。
11. I was first introduced to the idea of different levels of formality in language for different occasions in seventh-grade English.
在 7 年级的英语课上，我第一次知道了不同场合要使用不同规格的语言。
12. Mill was not given the chance to heal when his tour of duty in Iraq was over.
米勒在伊拉克服役之后并没有得到一个恢复精神创伤的机会。
13 Teachers are not supposed to have favorites in a class. 老师应该平等对待每个学生。
14 I first touched this exotic land in early 1998, when I was awarded a postgraduate scholarship by the New Zealand government and admitted to the master's programme at the prestigious University of Otagao. 在 1998 年年初，我第一次踏上这片异国土地，那时我获得新西兰政府提供的研究生奖学金，并获取在 Otagao 大学攻读硕士的资格。
15. Through a long time of search in the labyrinth of passages and doors he was finally ushered

into a long corridor with a heavy door locked stoutly behind him.
在迷宫般的过道里找了很长时间，最后发现身后是锁得结结实实的大门；前面是通往那个房间的、长长的走廊。

第五节　语篇衔接需要

英语中有时为了句子之间衔接的需要，从而使用被动结构。

1. The Middle Eastern bazaar takes you back hundreds—even thousands—of years. The one I am thinking of particularly is entered by a Gothic-arched gateway of aged brick and stone.

中东集市把你带回到几百年前——甚至几千年——以前。我特别想到的那个集市要从一个用砖石砌成的哥特式的拱形门洞进去，砖石都已年深日久。

第二句中的 “one”指代上一句中的“bazaar”，使用了语篇中的“替代”衔接手段，通过被动结构的运用，不仅避免了人称主语的出现，而且有利于上下句的衔接。

2. “We have seen a huge increase in interest in smaller breeds,” says Daisy Okas, an AKC spokeswoman, who attributes the trend, in part, to Paris Hilton and other high-profile celebs who are photographed with pint-size pooches.

“我们发现，人们现在对小型犬的兴趣大增。”美国养犬俱乐部女发言人如是说。她认为这一趋势在某种程度上是由帕丽斯·希尔顿和喜欢抛头露面的社会名流促成的，经常能拍到他们抱着小型犬的照片。 “who are photographed”是为了语篇衔接需要。

3. **He** wrote also to Napier at once; and as soon as **he** could **he** went to Edinburgh to visit him, where, as **he** was most hospitably received by him. 他还立刻给内皮尔写了一封信，然后他尽早地去了爱丁堡看望他，并在那里受到了最热情的接待。这句使用了“指代”衔接手段，句子中的主语“he”都是指同一个人，所以最后一句需使用被动结构。

4. As if **she** expected their glances, and did not mind gratifying their curiosity, **she** met the eyes of several of her observers by lifting her own, showing these to be soft, brown, and affectionate orbs, a little plaintive in their regard. **She was conducted** out of the gardens, and passed along the pavement till she disappeared from view. 上面几句中的主语“she”都是指同一个人，为了做到句子之间的衔接，最后一句使用了被动结构。

5. She arrived on Saturday afternoon, and was received by assembled family like a very dear friend. 她是星期六下午到的，她被当作一个很亲的朋友一样，受到全家人的列队欢迎。

为了衔接需要，共用一个主语，所以后面需要用被动结构。

6. So I called myself Pip, and came to be called Pip.（同上）

我叫自己皮普，后来别人也就这么称呼我。

7. Wondering what became of John Rabe, Chang was led to his granddaughter.

怀着对约翰雷伯近况的好奇，张女士找到了他的孙女。

因为“Chang”是“Wondering”的逻辑主语，为了使逻辑关系清楚，后面使用了被动结构。

8. I was shown by the waiter to what looked at first like common outhouses at the other end of it, but they turned out to be a suite of rooms.

侍者把我领到院子另一端的房子那儿，初看起来像普通的附属建筑，原来是一套客房。

9. At the first street corner they were joined by the several men who had followed the sheriff.
在第一个街道拐角，几个原先跟着警长的人加入他们中间。

第六节　译成汉语时需加表泛称的代词或省略主语

这类句子在翻译成汉语时，通常使用“有人”“人们”“大家”“别人”“某人”等作主语，或把主语省略。

1. It was proposed to build a hotel in the following spring. 有人提议来年春天建一个旅馆。

2. First of all, it must **be remembered** that the rebellion was not confined to the United States, but affected the entire Western World as a result of the aftermath of the first serious war in a century. Second, in the United States it **was reluctantly realized** by some—subconsciously if not openly—that our country was no longer isolated in either politics or tradition and that we had reached an international stature that would forever prevent us from retreating behind the artificial walls of a provincial morality or the geographical protection of our two bordering oceans.

首先，**值得记住的**是，这种叛逆行为并不局限于美国，而是作为百年之中第一次惨烈的战争的后遗症影响到整个西方世界。其次，在美国，有一些人已经**很不情愿地认识到**——如果不是明明白白地认识到，至少是下意识地认识到——无论在政治方面还是在传统方面，我们的国家已不再是与世隔绝的了；我们所取得的国际地位使我们永远也不能再退缩到狭隘道德规范的人造围墙之后，或是躲在相邻的两大洋的地理保护之中了。

3. It was then presented to him that his servants seemed to have nothing to do in his small family of one. He was stuck with the truth of this representation.

于是有人跟他说，在只有他一个人的小家庭内，他的仆人似乎无事可做，这句话说得合情合理，因此提醒了他。

4. Finally it was decided that it should be baptized Episcopalian and Episcopalian it was.

最后大家决定它应该接受多纳图斯派洗礼，并且使用多纳图斯派过去的仪式。

5. It's decided Rachael should team up for the first shot with Yang Jun.

大家决定由雷切尔和杨俊组队先开第一枪。

6. It should be noted that the great amount of capital always seeking employment where tolerable safety could be insured terribly embittered the competition between capitalists when a promising opening presented itself.

需要注意的是，大量资金总是需要寻找去处，并且能得到最起码的安全保障，当一个有前景的机会出现时，资本家之间的竞争就变得非常激烈。

7. It must be admitted that, of the things we desire, some, though they prove impossible, are yet real goods.

必须承认，我们向往的东西，尽管一些被证明是不可能的，但它们是真实存在的。

8. It was feared an untimely grave might be his portion. 人们担心他可能遭到夭折的命运。

9. But fears were raised immediately that succession battles would bring on a new era of gangland warfare, and scandals that could plague Italy's political elite for years to come.

但人们马上又开始担心：持续的大规模的扫黑行动会引发新一轮的黑帮冲突，更会曝出可能会在未来几年内困扰意大利政界精英的丑闻。

10. Indeed, the short time allowed them for their wine-drinking formed the subject—so it was rumoured—of one of the very few disputes between the Queen and her Prime Minister.

有传言这样说，女王和她的首相的确在这次获批的短暂喝酒时间争吵了，尽管他们很少争吵。

11. It is intended to help them understand polite customs and practices in the Middle East.

旨在帮助他们了解中东的礼貌习俗与行为习惯。

12. It must be seen to that they shall be quartered upon（投胎于）those who are least likely to corrupt them. 必须注意的是，他们将投胎于那些不会腐化他们的人。

13. But the global agricultural system is perilously poised on the assumption that growing conditions will continue to be good in the breadbasket areas of the United States, India, China, and South America. 但是，在美国、印度、中国和南美的主要产粮区将持续保持目前良好种植条件的这种想法的误导之下，全球农业系统的运行岌岌可危。

14. To be called beautiful is thought to name something essential to women's character and concerns.人们认为，被称为美丽意味着具有女性色彩——既有女性特征又为女性关注。

15. Although we practice strictly the punching-card system, everybody must punch card on time. It is stipulated that, anyone who comes in late or leaves earlier by more than five minutes will have one's biweekly pay deducted by one hour. However, there are still some people who can exploit its loopholes.

尽管我们严格地实行上、下班打卡制，迟到早退5分钟以上，就要从他们两周发一次的工资中扣除一小时薪酬，因此打卡十分重要，但有人会钻空子。

16. If Labour decides to dump the beleaguered Gordon Brown, the elder Miliband brother is rumored as a likely replacement. 如果工党决定让陷入困境的戈登·布朗下台，传闻说米利班德哥哥可能会取代他成为下一任工党领袖。

17. Voices were heard calling for help. 有人听见呼救的声音。

18. He was described as impressed by Deng's flexibility. 据说他对邓的灵活态度印象很深。

19. It was widely thought …很多人认为…

20. In about ten minutes a very light tap was heard, the door was opened to the extent of three inches, and a female voice which I readily recognized called to Jack.

大约过了十分钟，听到一个很轻的敲门声，门开了有三英尺的样子，然后我清楚地听到一个女性的声音在喊杰克。

第七节　英语中的被动意义用主动形式表达

在上册中，已经提到英语中一些动词的主动形式表被动含义，为了加深理解被动结构，这里再强调一下。

1. Rockets have found application for the exploration of the universe.火箭已经用来探索宇宙。

可以转换成“Rockets have been applied for the exploration of the universe.”

2. The lack of privacy within the Chinese home finds its extreme expression in many well-to-do families of North China.

中国家庭没有隐私概念，这在北方许多富裕家庭表现得极为明显。

3. Her feelings at last found expression in tears. 最后她用眼泪宣泄自己的心情。

4. The life style has found its growing popularity and acceptance among young people.
这种生活方式已被越来越多的年轻人接受，并受到欢迎。这一句可以转换成“The life-style has become popular and accepted by more and more young people.”

5. This solution finds immediate welcome and acceptance among college students.
这种解决方案立刻在大学生中间受到欢迎。
可以转换成“This solution is welcomed and accepted by college students immediately.”或“This solution enjoyed immediate welcome and acceptance among college students.”

6. While micro blogs are enjoying enormous popularity in China, another form of blogging has sprung up in what is intended to be an innovation in the hottest Internet service in the country.
当微博在中国受到广泛的欢迎之际，另一种形式的博客诞生了，是这个国家最热的互联网服务的一种创新尝试。

7. No city on American soil had known such destruction.
在美国国土，没有一座城市曾经遭受过如此严重的破坏。

8. On Saturdays the village presented a somewhat livelier appearance, and the shade trees around the court house square and along Front Street served as hitching-post for a goodly number of horses and mules.
每到周六，村庄多少有点更加可爱，法院广场周围以及沿前街的遮阴树木会拴上数目不小的马匹或骡子。

9. The hunt for Bigger Thomas served as an excuse to terrorize the entire Negro population, to arrest hundreds of Communists, to raid over labor union headquarters and workers' organization.
追捕比格·托马斯成为恐吓所有黑人，逮捕数百名共产主义分子以及袭击工会总部和工人组织的借口。

10. an area that acts as the main land route into Afghanistan and its capital, Kabul
该地区是通往阿富汗及其首都喀布尔的主要陆上通道

11. The three areas where the project will take place are in the Gao, Koulikoro and Segou regions of the country.
将在这个国家的加奥、塞古和库利科罗三个地区实施这项饮水工程。

12. It came not as a Nixon revelation, but rather as a confirmation of the "New York Times" story. 这不能算是尼克松透漏了什么新东西，而是证实了《纽约时报》的报道。

13. Much of the investment went to the maternity healthcare and services.
许多钱都投到了孕妇的保健与服务上。

14. These problems defy easy classification. 这些问题难以归类。

15. Many questions about prime numbers continue to elude answers.
关于素数的很多问题一直悬而未决。

16. This has led to a substantial improvement of the area's maternal health situation and allowed more than 80 percent of the area's pregnant women to get coverage by 2010.
这不仅使该地区孕妇的健康环境得到实质性的改善，而且到2010年将覆盖到本地区80%的孕妇。

17. The company says the device has been cleared for marketing in the European Union and hopes the World Health Organization will give its approval in early 2012.

该公司说这项设备已获准在欧盟销售，并希望在2012年年初能获得世界卫生组织的批准。

18. Grant has had a huge revival in scholarship in the last two decades.

在过去的二十年，格兰特重新成为学者的热点人物。

19. You will not get the implementation. 这不会执行。

20. As the market gradually opened up, China's trade volume in agricultural products registered sharp growth. 随着市场的逐步开放，中国的农产品贸易量呈现了快速增长。

21. He was instrumental in setting up the meeting. 他参与筹办了这次会议。

22. Li estimated that the light-blogging service in China may see explosive growth as early as next year. 按照李的估计，最早在下一年中国的轻博客业务量会呈现爆炸式增长。

23. Gifts to charities see sharp decline. 慈善机构收到的礼物数量急剧下降。

24. It saw an average growth rate of 80 percent over the past five years, while most Chinese private cosmetics companies struggle to reach double-digit growth.

在过去的五年内，化妆品的平均增长率达到 80%，然而多数中国化妆品私人企业却为达到两位数增长努力拼搏。

25. Some English adverbs function as adjectives. 有些英语的副词具有形容词的功能。

26. The use of knowledge as a countable noun is a rare case.

"knowledge"用作可数名词并不常见。

27. There are two classes of human activities. 人类活动可以分为两类。

28. Lipstick goes into burnables; lipstick tubes, "after the contents have been used up", into small metals" or plastics. Take out your tape measure before tossing a kettle: under 30 centimetres, it goes into small metals, but over that it goes into bulky refuse.

口红归入可燃物类；"口红全部用光后"口红管归入"小金属品"或塑料品类。扔掉一个水壶之前，抽出卷尺量一下：30厘米以下的归入小金属品类，但30厘米以上的就要归入大体积的废品了。

29. There was 38 printings of the book in one year. 这本书一年印刷38次。

30. Consequently, there has been a growing interest in nature food.

因此，越来越多的人对天然食物感兴趣。

汉语中，主语是泛称译成英语时，可以用英语的被动语态、主动语态、非人称主语句或"There be"结构来翻译。

第八节　英语的被动句可译成汉语的被动或主动结构

1. His entire adult life had been consumed by the intoxication and compulsion of gambling away hundreds of thousands of dollars on everything from online poker to sports.

他成年后的整个人生都是在狂赌带来的亢奋和冲动中挥霍掉的，从网上扑克到体育比赛赌了个遍，共输掉了几十万美元。

2. The most recent survey showed Jordanese disapproval dropping to 80 percent, but Pew's

2005 study of global attitudes was still titled "US image up slightly, but still negative".
但是皮尤研究所2005年关于全球态度的研究报告仍沿用了这样的标题："美国形象略有提升，但仍然是负面的"。

3. Not for nothing are they known as one of the most dangerous bears in the country.
它们被冠以国内最危险的野兽之一的名分可不是闹着玩的。

4. The pier, I remember, was accounted a most excellent piece of stone-work, and such I found it." 这句当中，"was accounted"是被动式，也是英文里常有的用法，例如"was recognized""was acclaimed""was acknowledged""was regarded"，可译成"堪称""有……之称""享有……之誉""众人视为"。

第九节 汉语中的存在句型译成英语被动结构

汉语中表示某地有某物的句型，可译成英语的被动结构，或用英语中的名词表示。

9.1 译成被动结构

用被动结构表示物体的位置，能够给人一种动态的感觉。

1. 作为马奈着手绘制的尺幅最大、投入心血也最多的画作，这幅画可以说是记录下了因上述那些翻新改造工程而被迫迁居的人们的众生相：巡游乐师，在他对面以侧面呈现的怀抱婴儿的吉普赛女孩，街头杂耍艺人，淘气的少年，醉汉，还有捡破烂的人——画家很可能在他画室附近仔细观察过这些人。

This painting, the largest and most ambitious Manet had yet undertaken, is a catalogue of the people displaced by these renovations: a strolling musician **flanked** by a gypsy girl and infant, a street acrobat, an urchin, a drunkard, and a ragpicker—individuals the artist might have observed near his studio.

2. 大厅的两侧各有一座高楼。The hall was flanked by two towers.
3. 我们的花园在他们的花园后面。Our garden backs theirs.
4. 窗户前面是大街。Windows front the street.
5. 有窗帘的窗户 a curtained window
6. 石子路 gravelled paths
7. 暴风雪过后，冰冻的道路被撒上了沙。The icy roads were sanded after the snowstorm.
8. I am surrounded by…我周围有……
9 ……还有一位我生平所曾见过最胖的女人坐在一把直背椅上打瞌睡，那简直就像一口袋粮食放在一个火柴盒上一样。…and the fattest woman I have ever seen in my life dozing in a straight-backed chair. It was as if a sack of grain was supported by a matchbox.
10. This is a magnificent stretch of pale yellow sand, overlooked by bamboos and a few trees, which stretches away to the horizon.

在竹林和树木的下方，是一片一望无际的、苍黄的、壮丽的沙滩，一直延伸到天际。

11. Perhaps it's the setting; the city is shrouded in fog along 40 steep hills overlooking glistening San Francisco Bay. 也许是它得天独厚的自然条件所致，这个城市沿着40多座陡峭的山，笼罩在雾中，俯视着闪烁的旧金山海湾。

12. Next to the inn are remains of the abbey garden which is preserved as a part of the national heritage. Surrounded by tall bamboo alive with the musical singing of birds.
紧靠客栈就是古寺院的花园，现已经作为国家文化遗产的保护地之一，周围是高高的竹子，婉转的鸟语回荡其中。

13. Some of the interviews are accompanied by accurate English translations.
一些采访还配有准确的英语翻译。

14. The local snack stalls were found here and there. 风味小吃店遍布各处。

15. Meantime all nature is refreshed; but heaps of flower-petals and fallen leaves are seen under the trees. 此时大自然变得清新如洗；但树下的地上却布满了飘落的花瓣和树叶。

16. Garrick is a delightfully unspoiled village surrounded by fields and woods at the mouth of a river. Yet it's only a short bus ride from the old city of Harburry with its factories, industry, and heavy traffic. 格里克是一个宜人的保持着原始风貌的小村，它位于河口上，周围是田野和树林，此处离工商业发达、交通拥挤的哈伯利古城不远，坐车一会儿就到。

9.2 用名词“home”或“seat”表示

1. But China's countryside, home to 900 million, has energy woes of its own—low tech, but no less important to the nation's development. 但居住着 9 亿人的中国农村，也有其自身的能源难题——低技术，而这里对国家的发展同样重要。

2. The country, home to the World Trade Organization and the International Committee of the Red Cross, has a reputation for trustworthiness stemming largely from banking secrecy rules that date back to the 17th century, when Geneva banks were the lenders of choice for French King Louis XIV.
这个国家，作为世界贸易组织和国际红十字委员会所在地，素以良好的信誉著称，其可靠信誉主要源于可追溯到 17 世纪的银行保密规定——当时日内瓦各家银行是法国国王路易十四优先选择的借贷机构。

3. In Western Europe, the home of traditional US allies, the same trends have been recorded.
在美国传统盟友的老家西欧，也显示了同样的趋势。
拓展学习：a）In 2004, Ireland became the first country to ban smoking in bars, a move copied across Europe. 2004 年，爱尔兰成为第一个禁止在酒吧吸烟的国家，这一做法随之在整个欧洲推广开来。
b）The prohibition amplified a trend toward drinking at home, fueled in part by rising bar prices.
这项禁令使人们在家喝酒的趋势加强了，而酒吧的涨价也是这一趋势加剧的部分原因。

4. Capturing Mumbai in a few sentences is a tall order. Add in its home state of Maharashtra and the bordering state of Goa, and the order becomes taller still.
要用几句话描述清楚孟买是一件很难的事，而如果加上它所在的马哈拉斯特拉邦及其邻邦果阿，那就更难讲清楚了。

5. In 1989, the Utah native had a job at North Carolina State University in Raleigh and wanted to return to his home state.
在 1989 年，这个犹他州的本地人在罗利市的北卡罗来纳州立大学谋得一个职位，但他想回到他家乡所在的州。

6. the artist's native city 画家的出生地

7. It is home to industrial parks, resorts filled with weekend homes, and farms—some of which make Italy the world's leading producer of Kiwis.

这里到处是工业园区，遍布周末别墅的旅游胜地和农场——有些农场使意大利成为世界猕猴桃生产第一大国。

8. Kowloon is also the home to two of the world's most luxurious hotels.

九龙也是世界上最豪华的两家酒店的所在地。

9. It's where the central government resides. 是中央政府所在地。

10. The St.Patrick Cathedral is the seat of the Archbishop of New York.

圣帕特里克大教堂是纽约大主教的住所。

第十节 英汉被动句与主动句结构之间的相互转换

在上册提到了英语中一些动词的主动形式可以表达被动含义，英语中一些形容词结构也可以表达被动含义，还可以通过形容词的名词化或动词的“名物化”来表达被动含义。这里再简单回顾一下。

1. The omniscient narrator is very characteristic of nineteenth century novel.

这位无所不知的作家最能体现十九世纪小说的特点。

可以转换成：The nineteenth century novel is characterized by the omniscient narrator.

2. The reason for not being utterly dismissive of this suggestion is that…

人们没有完全摈弃这个假设的原因是……

3. This letter is significative of her affection. 这封信是她的爱情表露。

4. A baby's cry can be expressive of hunger or pain. 婴儿啼哭可能表示饥饿或感觉不适。

5. All are representative of different versions of that narrative structure.

所有这些都代表了不同版本的叙事结构。

6. Now I myself am reserving judgement on the excellence or importance of this novel, but I will say it is certainly representative of two things.

尽管我本人对这部优秀且重要的小说持保留意见，但不得不说它的确说明了两件事。

7. Is a high forehead indicative of great mental power? 前额高表示智慧高么？

8. His presence is indicative of his willingness to help. 他的出席表明他愿意帮忙。

9. The program is indicative of one of the fastest-growing curriculum trends in U.S. schools: the study of Chinese. 这个项目表明美国学校发展趋势最快的课程之一：汉语学习。

10. All of the items above are free of export restrictions.

上面所列举的所有商品都没有出口限制。

11. At this time of night the streets are empty of traffic. 晚上这个时候，街上没有车辆。

12. I think that's indicative of how she thinks of writing and its access to the past，because writing is continuous with consciousness, understanding of trans-historical

我想这表明她对写作的看法，可以通过作品了解过去，因为写作与意识相呼应，是超越历史的理解。

13. discussions that seem to be productive only of quarrels 似乎只会导致口角的讨论

14. a method productive of results 富于成效的方法

15. Walters said that Chinese parents at Glenwood were supportive of her son's study of their language. 沃尔特斯说，格伦伍德市的中国父母支持她的儿子学习他们的语言。

16. Now they are not supportive of the new programs. 他们现在不支持新计划。

17. They are hopeful of a comeback in 2008, especially the women.
中国柔道运动员，尤其是女子运动员，有望在 2008 年卷土重来。

18. Perhaps such questioning is too reminiscent of what the religious studies teacher has asked.
这些问题使她想起宗教课上老师曾经问过的问题。

19. Your face is reminiscent of your mother. 你的脸使人想起你的母亲。

20. Not only did they disdain science, they found it to be destructive of the human ability to sense and grasp the wonder and beauty of the world.
他们不仅藐视科学，还认为科学会毁灭人类感知和把握世界之神奇和美丽的能力。

21. Such resolutions were in themselves sufficiently provocative of animosity.
这些决议本身足以挑起仇恨。

22. What are the features that mark a great leader? 伟大领袖的特质是什么？

23. An interest in people's deepest feelings characterizes all her writings.
她所有作品的特点是对人内心最深处情感的挖掘。

24. To this end, a variety of drills may be used, and the choice depends on learner preference and **availability** of teaching materials, as well as the teacher's own bias.
要实现这个目标，可能需要使用多种形式的操练，选用何种形式操练取决于学习者以及可以获取的教材，还有教师的喜好。形容词“available”转变成名词“availability”。

25. Gardasil, a vaccine against the virus that causes most cervical cancers, most cancers of the vagina and vulva, and genital warts, won FDA **approval** on June 8, 2006.
2006 年 6 月 8 号，一种针对会引发大多数子宫颈癌、阴道和外阴癌以及生殖器疣病毒的名为 Gardasil 的疫苗，获得了美国食品及药物管理局（FDA）的批准使用。

26. …child abandonment 孩子被遗弃

第四章 移 位 修 饰

在英语中有一种名词性修饰语，从表层结构看似乎是修饰跟在后面的名词，然而在意义上即在深层结构上却是修饰另外的东西，这种修饰现象叫作“转移修饰”（transferred modification）。（章振邦《新编英语语法》）本章对这一概念又做了一定的拓展，把一些与汉语思维模式不一致的修饰语位置变化都称为“移位修饰”。

第一节 地点状语提前用作定语

在英语中，可以把状语用作定语，从而使语言变得简洁。

1.1 把状语中的名词提前用作定语

在这类结构中，可以把用作状语的短语中的名词提前用作定语，例如：“take a cruise on the canal”（在运河上巡航）。可以把状语“on the canal”的“canal”提前，变成“take a canal cruise”。

1. In the real life, he ended an almost 10-year retirement and made his Major League debut in 1999 at the age of 35. 在现实生活中，他结束了将近 10 年的退役生活，在 1999 年 35 岁时复出完成了他在职棒大联盟的处子秀。

2. Looking sideways at Uncle Sam is hardly a New Zealand phenomenon, nor is it new.
斜眼看山姆大叔，恐怕不是新西兰才有的现象，也不是什么新鲜事。
应该是“a phenomenon in New Zealand”

3. This has a lot of real world implications. 这个理论对现实生活有很多启发。

4. successful classroom second and foreign language acquisition 成功的课堂二语及外语习得

5. In an intermediate or advanced class a teacher may encourage groups to prepare a paper drama for presentation to the rest of the class.
在一个中级或高级班里，老师可能会鼓励小组先写出剧本，然后在班里表演。

6. In the United States, proper street behavior requires a nice balance of attention and inattention. 在美国得体的路遇行为是保持注意与不注意间的平衡。

7. The teacher points at meaningless symbols on a wall chart.老师指着挂图上无意义的符号。

8. More than 300 enterprises are Fortune 500 companies.300 多家企业属于财富 500 强公司。

9. an office clerk 一名办公室职员

10. The day before the dance, I found that dress in the right size draped majestically over the living-room sofa.
舞会的前一天，我看到那件服装挂在起居室沙发的上方，端庄高贵，而且尺寸正好合适。

11 the speech bubbles 泡泡中的句子

12 He had a bed bath. 他在床上洗澡。

13 look at herself with the hand glass 用手中的镜子照自己

14. organize a house party 组织别墅招待会
15. His sister is a hospital nurse. 他姐姐是医院护士。
16. campus activities 校内活动
17. He drove a London taxi for 40 years. 他在伦敦开了 40 年出租车。
18. the mechanical teacher/ a computer teacher

机械里/电脑里的老师（节目中的老师），或译成“机械老师/计算机老师”

19. I ordered two book-club copies by mistake. 我从图书俱乐部误购两本。
20. And it isn't as necessary to know anything about an apartment neighbor—or to worry about his judgement of you—as it is about someone with an adjoining yard.

对于同住一座公寓的邻居，你不必去了解他的任何情况，也不必在意他对你的看法，只有屋院相连的邻居才有此必要。

21. Nature constantly yields to man in New York: witness those fragile sidewalk trees gamely struggling against encroaching cement and petrol fumes.

大自然对纽约人总是低头服输。只须看看人行道上那些脆弱的树木迎着四面进逼的水泥路面和阵阵袭来的石油烟气拼命挣扎的样子，就足以说明问题了。

22. lunch box notes 午餐饭盒上的短笺
23. Jim's wife, stood and looked out from the farmhouse's wide verandah at the car purring up the fence track in the fierce noon sunlight. 吉姆的妻子站在农舍宽大的阳台上向外张望，看着小轿车顶着正午的烈日沿着栅栏外的小道呜呜地开了过来。
24. Poussin's main regular job during his Roman years was drawing records of ancient sculpture for a rich antiquarian named Cassiano del Pozzo.

在罗马生活的年月里，普桑的固定工作主要是为一位富有的古文物研究收藏家卡西亚诺·德尔波佐绘制古代雕塑的图画资料。

25. Chinese singer Sa Dingding has just wrapped up her 12-nation tour across Europe, the US and Asia. 中国歌手萨顶顶刚刚结束了她跨越三大洲十二国的巡回演唱。
26. Having toured various countries and featured at the Beijing Olympics, the show also marks the Broadway debut of an original Chinese production and celebrates the Lunar New Year.

在不同国家巡回演出并特别献礼北京奥运会后，这台表演还标志着百老汇上演原汁原味的中国节目的开始，同时也是对中国农历新年的庆贺。

27. A hotel stay may be more comfortable. 住旅馆也许更舒适。
28. a page-10 news story 第十版上的新闻报道
29. Nor did he know about Sun's Penang connection. 他也不知道孙与马来西亚槟城的渊源。
30. Radcliffe offers comfort with a lingering side hug and whispered praise.

雷德克利夫则在旁边安慰她——从侧面搂住了她好一会儿，小声称赞着。

31. Kenyans reacted with spontaneous street celebrations in some cities, although some cautioned that similar deals in previous years ended up in failure.

肯尼亚的一些城市居民自发走上街头庆祝这一协议的达成，尽管一些人警告说以前类似的协议都以失败而告终。

32. NATO foreign ministers offered a show of unity in calling for the departure of Libyan leader Moammar Gadhafi, but they ended their meeting in Berlin still apparently at odds

over ways to add to their Libyan air operation.

北约成员国外交部长在要求利比亚领袖卡扎菲下台的问题上表现了高度的一致，但直到柏林会谈时，在加大对利比亚的空袭行动方式上仍存在明显分歧。

33. Following talks with Secretary State Hillary Clinton, British Foreign Secretary William Hague said the two saw "eye to eye" on what was required in the Libya campaign.

与美国国务卿希拉里·克林顿进行对话之后，英国外交大臣威廉·黑格表示，双方就对利比亚采取行动达成共识。

34. The Chinese, from the highest to the lowest, have an imperturbable quiet dignity, which is usually not destroyed even by a European education. 中国人，从上层社会到底层老百姓，都有一种冷静安详的尊严，即使接受了欧洲的教育也不会毁掉。

35. Former presidential rivals Barack Obama and Hillary Clinton made their first joint campaign appearance Friday in the aptly named town of Unity, New Hampshire.

星期五，曾经是总统竞选对手的巴拉克奥巴马与希拉里克林顿第一次共同亮相于命名贴切的团结之城——新罕布什尔。

36. Thai government personnel were on river patrol. 泰国政府人员在河上巡逻。

37. Chery begins Venzuela assembly. 奇瑞开始在委内瑞拉生产汽车。

38. a wall painting 壁画

39. They have real life application. 他们在现实生活中可以用到。

40. bullet train lunch box 高速列车上的盒饭午餐

41. Chinese artist Li Yu Gang's world tour 中国艺术家李玉刚的世界巡演

42. She sat with five men at a table under an elm tree that shaded them from the hot Kansas City, Mo., sun. 她同五位男士一桌，桌子在一颗榆树底下，树荫为他们挡住了密苏里州堪萨斯城火辣辣的太阳。

1.2 把状语中的名词"形容词化"后提前用作定语

英语中用作状语的成分，可以提前用作定语。例如："the 1912 election across the nation（1912 年全国大选）"，可以把状语中"nation"变成形容词提前，变成"the 1912 national election"。

1. I tried not to laugh but recorded a mental note that I needed to update the user manual I created for my non-computer savvy users to tell them that punching holes into the disk was a no-no. 虽然我尽力不笑出声来，但心里记着，需要升级以前为电脑新手编写的使用手册，告诉他们在光盘上打洞是万万不行的。
2. They don't have outside contacts. 他们与外界没什么接触。
3. She'd never seen my live show. 她从未看过我的现场表演。
4. Its main domestic focus is on education. 在国内它主要关注教育。
5. the national quality watchdog 国家质量监督机构
6. Global automakers in China are more conservative. 全球汽车制造商在中国是保守的。
7. Containing more than 400 old photos about the 1911 Revolution and its impact, the book has been compiled by Pulitzer prize-winning photographer Liu Heung Shing and will have a global release following a cooperative venture with five publishers from across the Taiwan

Straits. 普利策奖获得者刘香成摄影师编著的这本书收录了400多幅关于1911年辛亥革命的老照片，并论及这次革命的影响。随后与中国（台湾）的五家出版商开展了合作，这本书将在全球发行。

8. name derivation, global emphasis in our culture 名字的演变，突出文化的全球化特性

9. The rapid application of these ideas by textbook writers, and equally rapid acceptance of these new principles by British language teaching specialists, curriculum development centers, and even governments gave prominence/priority nationally and internationally to what came to be referred to as the Communicative Approach, or simply Communicative Language Teaching.

教材编写者迅速采用了这些观点，同时这些新的原则还很快得到英国语言教学专家及课程开发中心的认可，这个被称作交际法或者交际语言教学甚至得到国内已及国外政府的重视。

10. Usually the interior is shielded from exterior view only by window curtains or blinds.

即便为了防止外人看到房间内部，通常也只会使用窗帘或百叶窗。

11. Just at this moment a plashy tramp by the side of the bridge caught the sensitive ear of Ichabod. 就在这时，伊卡博德敏感的耳朵听到了桥边的湿地有人行走的响声。

12. launch a foreign war 发动对外战争

13. fight a civil war 打内战

14. no official connection 与官方没有联系

15. In most companies there is an official process for giving someone a job and it is not usual to get a job just because you have some internal relation such as a friend or relative who can help you. 在大多数公司都有一个正式的员工录用流程，通常不会因为你在公司内部有关系，如一个朋友或亲戚帮你，从而得到一份工作。

16. This made me very shy in company, and as a child I had none of the social ease of my lucky grandchildren, who assume unless it is proved to the contrary that grown-ups are their friends. 人多时，我会感到害羞，我小时候不像我幸运的孙辈那样在人群中自由自在。他们认为，大人是孩子的朋友，除非有证据表明并非如此。

17. He had committed social suicide by this step.

他走这一步等于自绝于社会。（意即断送了自己的前程）

18. This is a grand rustic walk through the heart of London, taking in not just endless grass and countless trees but masses of splendid borders, ornamental lakes, bridges, fountains and pagodas, not to speak of wildfowl.

这是一次穿越伦敦市中心的快乐的乡村之旅，跃入眼帘的不仅是无边的草地和数不清的大树，当然还有大片美丽的花坛，点缀其间的湖泊和小桥、喷泉和塔，更不用说飞禽了。

19. Biblical metaphor of Father and Son 圣父和圣子在圣经里的比喻意义

20. Through the book and her subsequent lectures and public appearances, Chang has played an enormous role in forcing the world to remember what happened at Nanjing. 通过书籍和随后的报告以及公开的演讲，张女士在努力使全世界都记住在南京曾发生的一切。

21. There is also a public stereotypes of blacks. 这个也是公众对于黑人的刻板印象。

22. Those are your public presentations of stereotypes.

你们就是这样在公众面前公开表达你们的刻板印象的。

第二节　方式状语提前用作定语

方式状语中的名词可以提前用作定语，例如：a handwritten letter with a pencil（用铅笔写的信），把方式状语“with a pencil”中的“pencil”提前，变成“a handwritten pencil letter”。

1. Today, she mentors a group of young women with the disorder, staying in daily e-mail contact and taking phone calls from them.

如今，她给一群有饮食失调问题的女孩做指导，每天与她们保持电子邮件联系并接听她们打来的电话。

2. make a powerpoint presentation 做一个 PPT 展示

3. We are in radio communication with the spacecraft. 我们通过无线电与太空船联系。

4. make phone inquiries　打电话询问

5. Palm-filled parks are only a quick taxi ride from the business center of the Central District.

乘坐计程车很快就能从中环的商业中心来到棕榈树遍布的公园。

6. Ellis Island is a short ferry ride from Battery Park in Manhattan and is a popular destination for both tourists and schoolchildren. 从曼哈顿炮台公园乘坐渡船可以很快到达爱丽丝岛，对游客和学童来说它是理想的旅游目的地。

7. Yet it's only a short bus ride from the old city of Harbury with its factories, industry, and heavy traffic. 然而它离工商业发达、交通拥挤的古城哈博里并不远，坐车一会儿就到了。

8. Others will make long motor trips with the children bundled in the family car.

其他家庭则会把孩子塞在自家车里做一次长途旅行。

9. Despite lip service to the contrary, most employers want their employees to work long hours, rewarding them with higher pay and better benefits.

尽管嘴上说的一套，但大多数雇主内心想让他的员工工作时间更长，并以更高的薪水和更好的实惠奖励他们。

10. Dad rose to his full height, and pointed his most menacing fingers.

父亲站了起来，用他充满威胁的手指着。

11. She darted at him a severe and menacing look. 她用严肃而又充满威胁的目光瞥他一眼。

12. And she passes but with a slight and contemptuous recognition of him.

当她从他身边经过时，带有一种似曾相识，却又不屑一顾的神情。

13. Adam dropped his bags with an angry thud at the feet of the guard, and stumped off to renew the ticket.

亚当恼了，砰地一声把书包扔在了门卫的脚边，怒气冲冲地跺脚走了，去更换新的图书证。

14. But we all insisted she should, and she gave a doubtful yes.

我们都坚持认为她应该，然后她心存狐疑地答应了。

15. Then she said in a tearful voice. 然后她一把鼻子一把泪地说。

16. take a cheap excursion 进行一次花销不大的旅行

17. He handed her the box and lit a spill for her; and as the flame flashed up into her face she glanced at him with laughing eyes and said: "What do you think of me in a temper?"

他递给她烟盒，并为她点着一片引柴，火苗燃起来照到她的脸上，她两眼笑着瞧了他一眼说：“你觉得我发起火来怎么样？”

18. They came in, the Major and his wife, with their society laugh about nothing（ there was less and less to laugh at）.梅杰和他妻子进来时，尽管没什么可笑的，他们还是出于社交习惯地大笑。

19. their charming opportunist savagery　他们那趁机捣蛋的可爱样子

20. The patients retired sulkily, with an angry scow.

这些病人闷闷不乐地离开，出于愤怒而皱着眉头。

21. She cast towards her friend an eloquent glance. 她寓意深长地对她的朋友看了一眼。

22. with a rather malicious glance at Diana's proportions

颇具恶意地看着帕克尔泰夫人（她因射死老虎而被称为 Diana）的匀称的身材

23. He was paying a pastoral call one day on a woman.

一天，他正以牧师的身份拜访一位女士。

24. Still, she had periodically paid her fairy godmother's visits to Purlieu Villas; she had stood plain godmother to the baby.

她还定期以女恩人身份造访林边别墅；她一直是这个婴儿的平凡的教母。

25. I exchanged polite conversation in the darkness with a man seated in front of me.

黑暗中我与坐在我前面的一个人有礼貌地交谈了起来。

26. The students laughed, and the doctor gave them a circular glance of enjoyment in his joke.

学生们笑起来。医生环视了他们一周，并陶醉于自己开的玩笑。

27. She is smiling, but there is a prohibitive look in her eyes.

她笑了，但她的眼睛中流露出不让谈这件事的神色。

28. He said in a voice of loud and angry complaint.

他说话的声音很大，并带有愤怒的抱怨。

29. As if to emphasize the fact that the world went badly with him the new-comer unburdened himself of an angry and very audible expletive as he flung himself into the seat.

仿佛为了强调世界与他作对，这位新来者怒气冲冲地骂了声“他妈的”，响得使人听得清清楚楚，然后一屁股坐了下去。

30. They thought of the ten drizzling miles to Handleyford.

到达汉德雷福特之前还需在蒙蒙细雨中赶十英里的路程。

拓展学习：山路 ten mountainous miles

31. Nancy looked at Godfrey with a pained questioning glance.

南希用带着痛苦和质询的目光扫了戈弗雷一眼。

32. They are our tomorrow and they carry with them their flat, video-game consciousness.

他们是我们的未来，带着他们那种单调的通过电脑游戏培养出的意识。

33. We（Chinese）never had the vinyl generation. We went from the cassette generation to the CD generation. 我们（中国人）从来没有形成过黑胶唱片的一代。我们从听磁带的一代发展到了听光盘的一代。

34. This consists of looking over a new dialogue and its native language translation and discussing any issues of grammar, vocabulary, or content that the teacher feels important or that students are curious about. 这包括仔细阅读一个新对话以及它的译文，并讨论语

法、词汇或老师认为重要的内容，或学生好奇的内容。

35. The television generation grew up in the insistent presence of hype, delights in much of it, and has no scruples about practicing it. 电视的一代是在强烈的广告刺激的环境中成长起来的一代。他们也很欣赏这种广告刺激，并且毫不犹豫地去亲身实践。

36. a threatening fist 具有威胁意味的拳头

37. I gave her a despairing look. 我绝望地看了她一眼。

38. By doing what we're doing today you avoid the headline risks that are going to come for people who did not do anything. 通过我们今天所做的这些努力，可以避免即将被当作什么都没做的坏典型大肆宣扬的危险。

39. It was a cash purchase. 这是用现金购买的。

40. That includes credit card payments, travel tickets, photos and much else.
包括信用卡支付、旅游订票、拍照，还有其他许多功能。

41. A circle was formed so that everyone had visual contact with each other and all were within easy reach of a tape recorder microphone. 围成一个圆圈，这样每个人都可以与其他人进行目光接触，而且大家都可以轻松够到录音机的麦克风。

第三节 结果状语提前用作定语

表示结果的状语，可以把状语中的名词或形容词等提前用作定语。

1. Two ducks make **a rippled landing** near our dock, while a loon skims along the edge of a nearby island, hunting its morning food. 两只鸭子在我们所在的船坞附近上岸，**引起水波荡漾**；一只潜鸟在附近的岛边滑翔着寻觅它的早餐。

2. He had been frequently conscious of her **soft presence** in the room.
他时常感到由于她的存在，房间里会**添上一丝柔和的感觉**。

3. But did you know that in the days after the assassination, Booth's friends and（especially）lovers hurriedly burned or hid his letters（one paramour, Isabel Sumner, kept her mash notes secret from the world for an astonishing 62 years）?但你知不知道，暗杀行动之后的那些天里，布斯的朋友和（尤其是）情人们曾经匆匆地将他的信件烧毁或藏匿（其中一位情人伊莎贝尔·萨姆娜竟能将这些秘密藏了 62 年之久，实在令人惊讶）？

第四节 目的状语提前用作定语

目的状语中的名词提前用作定语，例如："a seating plan for the guest coming to dinner（晚宴客人的座位安排）"可把"dinner"提前，用作定语："a seating plan for the dinner guest"。

1. I read this morning in the *Times* that the mayor is a dinner guest this evening at the White House. 我今天上午阅读《泰晤士报》时，得知市长今晚做客白宫晚宴。

2. Around 1840, he took a study trip to England and the Continent, where he spent two years in Rome. 1840 年左右，他前往英格兰和欧洲大陆游学，在罗马待了两年。

3. breakfast cereal 作为早餐的麦粥

4. The Major meanwhile had also been looking for something to do, and, wandering to the other

end of the studio, saw before him my breakfast-things（早餐用具）neglected, unremoved.

5. Mrs. MachIntyre reached up and laid a comforting hand on his shoulder.
麦克恩泰尔太太伸出手去放在他的肩上以示安慰。

6. Cokane comes sympathetically to him and puts an encouraging hand on his shoulder.
Cokane 充满同情地走向他，并把一只手放在他的肩上以示鼓励。

7. "May I come in?" said the Prime Minister, with a vote-catching smile.
首相说"我可以进来么？"时，带着一种争取赢得选票的微笑。

8. Several vacationers at the luxurious Richelieu Apartments there held a hurricane party to watch the storm from their spectacular vantage point.
住在该镇那座豪华的黎赛留公寓度假的几位旅客为了观看飓风组织了一次聚会，从有利的位置观赏飓风的壮观景象。

9. have a parting word with him 与他道别

10. take a long and parting draught 出发前的痛饮

11. big-game animals 只供狩猎的大型动物

12. Robbins followed at a respectful distance. 罗宾跟在后面并保持适当的距离。

13. The latter was sitting at the back, a revolver in each hand, his face toward the group, which at sight of him trailed after at a respectful distance. 他坐在后面，每只手都拿着一把左轮手枪，脸朝向尾随在他后面处于视线之内并与他保持适当距离的那群人。

14. In response to her farewell wave, Irene put her hand to her brow, and, turning slowly, shut the door…为了回应她的挥手告别，伊琳她的手放在眉毛上，并慢慢地转身，关上门……

15. a nostalgia trip 怀旧之旅

16. a honeymoon trip 蜜月之旅

17. The California state parks program, which reaches about 20,000 students a year designed the elephant seal trip around the seventh grade curriculum on evolution.
加州州立公园项目每年能够惠及大约 2 万名学生，该项目围绕 7 年级的进化课程内容设计了观测海象的校外考察旅行。

第五节 时间状语提前用作定语

这种用法在汉语中也比较常见。

1. It was half-term weekend. 在学期正中间的一个周末。

2. post-imperial China 后帝制时期的中国

3. Good Labor Day afternoon 劳动节下午好

4. a summer job 一份夏季工作

5. The young man sat a few moments by the roadside, applauding himself greatly, and thinking with how clear a conscience he should meet the minister in his morning walk.年轻人在路边歇了一会儿，对自己大加赞赏。寻思明天早上碰到牧师散步，该何等问心无愧。

6. her rheumatic flannel 一块患风湿病时曾用过的法兰绒破片

7. But her childhood library visits searching encyclopedias and history books turned up little on the carnage.

但童年时她到图书馆翻阅了百科全书和历史书，却未曾发现有关此次大屠杀的记载。

8. Despite the immense goodwill of a grateful nation, Miller has slumped into struggle and despair. Then came the news that he and his childhood sweetheart, Jessica, were getting divorced.

尽管国家感激他，对他表现了极大的善意，但米勒还是陷入了挣扎和绝望。接着传出消息说，他和青梅竹马的妻子杰西卡要离婚了。

9. childhood home 小时候的家

10. He was on his afternoon stroll. 他下午在散步。

11. Cyril and I had an evening together. 晚上我和西里尔在一起。

12. The sheriff sent Polly to the house for cloth, and bound up the prisoner's wound with a rude skill acquired during his army life.

警长让波莉去屋内拿块布，然后用他在部队服役时学到的粗糙技术给犯人包扎伤口。

13. make a Thanksgiving Day journey from the coast of Miami to the tropical shores of Hawaii
感恩节的旅行横跨迈阿密海岸到夏威夷的热带海滨

14. The full Rose waxed in the warm June air. 花蕾在六月的暖风中长得浑圆。

15. The family had an early supper. 这一家人早早吃了晚饭。

16. So we convince these distributors to give us the parts on next 30 days credit.

我们说服批发商赊给我们零件，30 天后还款。

17. At the fall meeting of the American Geophysical Union in San Francisco last December, Zoback gave a new perspective on the quake and its aftermath.

去年 12 月，在旧金山召开的美国地球物理学联合会秋季会议上，佐巴克就这次地震及其后果提出了一个新的看法。

18. One day, on her lunch break, she was so tired she sought out a couch and napped.

有一天，在午餐休息时，她觉得太累了，就找了个躺椅小睡了一会。

19. A 2005 survey by the National Sleep Foundation, a Washington D. C., nonprofit foundation that focuses on sleep and public health, found that 26% of adults get a good night's sleep only a few nights a month or less.

国家睡眠基金会是位于首都华盛顿的一个关注睡眠和公众健康的非营利性组织，它在 2005 年所做的一项调查发现：有 26%的成年人每月只有几夜（或更少）高质量睡眠。

20. In a Nov. 15 report, the government acknowledged that enforcing the ban on use of the cross isn't feasible, and said it would propose changing the law to allow both the emblem and "made in Switzerland" to be used for any product or service that is legitimately Swiss.

在 11 月 15 日的一份报告中，政府承认禁止使用瑞士十字是不可行的，并称要建议修正法律，允许任何合法的瑞士产品或服务使用其国徽和“瑞士制造”字样。

21. Evening dog walks do not serve merely for recreation, as the lay people think.

狗晚上出来散散步可不像外行人想的那样仅仅是为了消遣。

22. A noblewoman who married a prince, a teenage mother and a friend of a monarch, Princess Dashkova seemed to have nothing in common with Franklin, an elderly self-made man of the New World and enemy of Geoge III.

达什柯娃亲王夫人出身贵族家庭，嫁给了一位亲王，十几岁就做了母亲，并成为沙皇的朋友；而富兰克林在新大陆靠个人奋斗取得了成功，人过中年，是乔治三世的敌人——这两人看上去毫无共同之处。

23. A horizon-obscuring arch built by the English at the edge of Mumbai's harbor, it commemorates the 1911 arrival in India of England's King George V and Queen Mary.

一座遮挡视野的拱形建筑，它位于孟买港的边上，是英国人为了纪念 1911 年英国国王乔治五世和玛丽王后的到来而修建的。

24. set a 2011 deadline for removing American combat forces

美国战斗部队人员撤离的最后期限定在 2011 年

25. I can't take a fall walk without thinking about the gentle miracle of the leaf.

我秋天散步时，总会想到那柔软而又神奇的树叶。

26. Its post-2008 recovery has been slow, and some observers fear that Europe's financial problems could tip the US and world economy into a second recession.

2008 年之后，经济一直缓慢地恢复，一些观察家认为欧洲的财政问题可能会使美国及世界经济陷入二次危机。

27. In the process, football changed irrevocably from a gentleman's weekend exercise to the greatest spectator sport in the history of human race. 在这个过程中，足球不可逆转地在人类历史上从一项绅士的周末运动发展成为最伟大的群众运动。

28. On one occasion we were all in the country, staying in a cottage which was to be the scene of many later holidays, and my father had a terrible job to find us.

有一次我们都在乡下，住在一间茅舍里，这也是我们后来多次度假的地方，我的父亲费了九牛二虎之力才找到我们。

29. in the 1998 book　在 1998 年出版的这本书中

30. Breakfast TV is like a chat show and a news programme rolled into one.

早餐时间的电视就像是访谈节目和新闻节目的综合。

31. a cradle convert　从婴儿时改信教

32. college friends　大学时期的朋友

33. Meanwhile Mr. Bronson was talking about their experiences on a weekend trip to Moscow.

其间布朗森先生正在谈论他们周末去莫斯科的经历。

34. Blacks held a very public 4th of July celebration in 1875.

黑人们在 1875 年 7 月 4 日举行盛大公共庆典。

35. Her account of nodding daffodils beside Ullswater, after an idyllic spring 1802 walk, inspired her brother's most famous poem.

在 1802 年春天，她在厄尔斯沃特湖畔田园诗般的的漫步之后，记录下了那些舞动的水仙，这为她哥哥创作著名的田园诗提供了灵感。

第六节　表示频度的词提前用作定语

这种用法在汉语中并不常见。

1. Take cheap holidays here and also the local intensive television watchers.

在这里度假花费不高，还有当地人非常喜爱看电视。

2. These and other signs indicate the difference between the person who takes an occasional trip to Atlantic City and someone with a real problem.
这些以及其他一些迹象表明，偶尔光顾大西洋城的人和真有问题的赌徒之间是有区别的。

3. The thrill of seeing my **first** hummingbird in my garden has never left me—the sight of seeing this unbelievably tiny creature with dazzling plumage flitting boldly from flower to flower. 我从未忘记第一次在我的花园里看到一只蜂鸟时的那种心跳的感觉——一只披着炫目的羽、小得令人难以置信的生灵正勇敢地在花丛中飞来飞去。

4. tickle an **occasional** trout 偶尔抓到一条鳟鱼

5. And if truth be told an **occasional** cup of wine. 偶尔还酒后吐真言

6. There were **occasional** tape recordings, usually of audiolingual drills.
偶尔会有录音，通常是关于听说练习的。

7. We spent **occasional** holidays in Berkshire. 我们偶尔到伯克郡去度假。

第七节 分词用作定语或逻辑谓语时的移位

分词用作定语或逻辑谓语时，可以前移用作定语。

1. founding fathers of the nation 国父

2. I identify myself as one of critical lovers and loving critics of the United Nations.
我自认为我既是一个批评联合国的爱护者，又是一个爱护联合国的批评者。

3. As powerful as the digital age is, the loss of data through the transition to new forms of media storage makes me wonder how much valuable history and other defining characteristics of our civilization will be lost over time.
尽管数字时代非常强大，数据在新型媒体存储器之间转移过程中的丢失让我想到多少有价值的历史以及其他能够反映我们的文明特征的东西会随着时间流失。

4. And here we have the not only promising entry of George Washington on to the colonial militay scene.
我们这里有的是，不是很有前途的乔治·华盛顿进入殖民地的军事力量（领导层）。

5. Now in his late 60s, he had mastered the skill of sightless tourism, using his remaining four senses to create pictures in his mind. 在他接近 70 岁时，他已经掌握了这项无须视力的旅游技能，他用余下的四个感官感受美景。

6. For developing Asia's two largest countries—China and India—Goldman Sachs lowered respectively its 2008 growth forecasts to 10 per cent from 10.3 per cent and to 7.8 per cent from 8 per cent.
就亚洲两个最大的发展中国家中国和印度的发展来说，高盛公司将其对这两国 2008 年经济增长率的预测分别从 10.3% 和 8%降低到 10%和 7.8%。

第八节 介词的宾语提前用作定语

这一部分在上册的组词规律已经提到过了，这里简单提一下。

1. And there's an extraordinary Yale-London collaboration of a decade.

耶鲁和伦敦展开了十年的非凡合作。

2. I've got a dentist appointment this afternoon. 我已经约好下午去看牙医。

3. Almost all major African American poets in the 20th century attempted their John Brown poem. 在20世纪，几乎所有的美国非洲裔诗人都试图写写关于布朗的诗。

4. no other constructional change　没有其他建筑布局上的变化

5. conversational particpants　参与谈话的人

第九节　形容词用作定语时的移位

形容词用作定语时，位置不是固定的。例如，“a happy group of people（一群快乐的人）”，也可以说“a group of happy people”；有时显然不是修饰紧挨着的词，例如：“the architectual materialization of this concept(这一设计理念的具体化)”,其中“architectual”应该修饰“concept”。

1. For a gathering of people from around the world, we laid out quite a surprising spread of Chinese dishes. 我们为这群来自世界各地的人摆上了令人惊讶的中国菜。

2. The cabman blundered up and downstairs with trunks, and saluted Sophia's haughty generosity, and then there was quietness.

车夫搬着行李跌跌撞撞地上楼下楼，并向索菲娅傲慢地慷慨致敬，然后一切归于平静。

3. There was a surprising flash of violent emotion within him, as if in the presence of something undreamt-of, dangerous, and final. 仿佛由于某种没有想到的、危险的、不可改变的东西，他的内心突然产生一种让人惊讶的剧烈情感。

4. a surprising piece of news　一则让人惊讶的消息

5. a tangled mass of water-weeds　一堆乱草

6. The only other thing I remember about my life upto the age of five was getting into a temper and cutting a hated pair of knickers to pieces.

我唯一记住的一件事就是在我五岁时发脾气把一条我讨厌的灯笼裤剪成了碎片。

7. We had an interesting day's play in the cricket match.

我们玩了一天有趣的板球比赛。

8. a lazy afternoon　让人懒散的下午

9. an easy mistake　难免的错误

10. Any living creature that ventured within his chain-radius was apt to have a busy minute or two, and the unhappy fowls, who often strayed within reach, were grabbed instantly.

任何犯险进入它的以链条为半径的领地的家禽，为了逃命都会挣扎一到两分钟，而经常那些误入它的势力范围的不幸家禽会被立刻捕获。

11. He always spoke to me as he washed before eating his dinner, told me tales of his own childhood and let little drops of moral tuition fall into my lap.

他在饭前洗手时经常会跟我聊天，告诉我他儿时的故事，让琐碎的人生道理流入我的心扉。

12. They were her country-women; and the beef and ale of their native land, with a moral diet not a whit more refined, entered largely into their composition.

她们是那位女王的同胞乡亲，家乡的牛肉和麦酒，以及丝毫没有经过加工的精神食粮大量地进入她们的躯体滋养助长。（丝毫未经提炼的精神食粮指所受的道德教育和影响极为粗劣。）

13. The faces of the sisters expressed an embarrassed anxiety.
这对姐妹的脸上流露出尴尬的焦虑神情。

14. She was much older than the ordinary servant, and she had acquired a partial moral dominion over Constance, though Constance would have warmly denied it.
她比这个普通的佣人大得多，她在道德方面能够部分地影响康丝坦斯，尽管康丝坦斯极力地否认这一点。

15. The fabric is sound; the work in wood and plaster tells of a more leisurely and a more honest age than ours. 说明那个时代的人比我们现在清闲、诚实得多。意即房子的质量比现在粗制滥造的要好得多。

16. with a fair show of resolution　清楚地表明决心

17. To lose a hotel and a cake of soap on one afternoon suggests willful（故意的）carelessness.
在一个下午，先是找不到住的旅馆，接着丢失香皂，你的粗心可就有点存心的味道啦。

18. Prime Minister remarked in a heavy, rheumy(因感冒多稀粘液的)voice, as he plodded out.
首相一边拖着沉重的脚步往外走，一边用低沉、浑浊的声音这样评论道。

19. shed sad /grateful tears 伤心落泪/感激涕零

20. As an excited member of the beginners' chorus line, I was aware of my lowly status.
加入初学者的歌舞队行列让我既兴奋又自卑。

21. Heyward, perceiving that their guides now set about their repast in sober earnest, assisted the ladies to alight, and placed himself at their side, not unwilling to enjoy a few moments of grateful rest after the bloody scene he had just gone through.
海沃德看到他们的向导认认真真地停下来准备吃饭，于是就扶姐妹俩下了马，自己也在她们身边坐了下来，乐得趁此休息一下，消除经历这场血战之后的疲劳。

22. Mr. Warbuton was elaborately courteous, and it may be that he found a slightly malicious amusement in the embarrassment which he thereby occasioned in his companion.
沃伯顿先生温文尔雅，也许是因为他对由此而使他的同伴产生窘困的心情感到一种略带恶意的好笑的情趣。

23. The Bastable catering was of the kind that is classified as a rude plenty, which Clovis translated as a plenty that gives rise to rude remarks. 巴斯塔布尔夫人的伙食可以归入量多而粗劣这一类，而克洛维斯把它说成是量多而引起粗话。

24. Clovis said suitable things in highly unsuitably manner, and proceeded to make punitive expeditions among the breakfast dishes. 克洛维斯用极为不合适的方式说适当的事情，并对早餐菜肴进行了惩罚性的征伐（即大吞大嚼）。

25. And she gave her insolent blackmailing stare. 她不仅无礼而且带有恐吓地盯着她。

26. Here he coolly seated himself, and after taking a long and apparently a grateful draught, he commenced a very strict examination of the fragments of food left by the Hurons which had hung in a wallet on his arm.
他静静地坐了下来，慢慢地、舒舒服地把水喝完，然后放下挽在胳臂的袋子，打里面掏出休伦人留下的食物，仔细地查看起来。

27. There was an eloquent pause after the story had been told.
故事讲完以后，他意味深长地停顿一下。

28. He simply sat in it, and the dog after a painful effort to jump on his knee, relinquished that aim, sat with head thereon, and gazed with the sense of relief at his master, that one has at the end of a long journey, when one is home again amongst familiar thing.

他径直坐到里面，然后那只狗为了跳上他的膝盖挣扎了一番，最后放弃了努力，昂着头坐在那儿，带着释然的感觉注视着主人，那是一种长途跋涉到达终点后的释然，回到家后看到熟悉事物的释然。

29. The couple had an indefinable air of prosperous thrift.

这对夫妇有一种让人说不出的感觉，既有钱又节俭。

30. She looks at her friends, and their eyes, in some private permission, meet.

她看了看她的朋友，当她们的目光相遇时，眼里有一种私下许可的神情。

31. That she longed rather to behold all those rigid countenances contorted with scornful merriment. 使她宁可看到那一张张僵刻的面孔露出轻蔑的嬉笑来嘲弄她。

第十节　修饰语与被修饰位置调换

这种用法，汉语中也会出现，但没有英语中那么普遍。

1. the industrial west　西方工业社会
2. It's an administrative headache to do it.　划分小组是件很头疼的管理工作。
3. knowledgeable others 其他有学问者
4. carved porcelain 瓷雕
5. a carved relief 浮雕
6. While embracing some of the production of ethnical others,
同时阅读其他种族作家的作品，
7. The possessive female was aroused in Annie. 激起了安妮心中的女性占有欲。
8. agricultural futures 未来的农业（农业的未来）
9. rural south 南部农村
10. verbal economy 语言简练（简练的语言）
11. Peninsular Italy 意大利半岛
12. agrarian south 南部农业
13. suburban New York 纽约郊区
14. rural Voment 佛蒙特乡村
15. white Europeans /Americans 欧洲/美国白人
16. So California passed a water package in November.
11 月加州通过了一揽子水利计划。
17. miss American 美国小姐
18. protestant Americans 美国清教徒
19. in corporate America 在美国的公司
20. herbaceously tranquil 平静的绿地
21. I like to lie calmly in its herbaceous tranquility, gazing up at the skyline of dwellings stretching from the Ritz to Spencer House.

我喜欢躺在宁静的绿地上，注视着从利兹酒店延伸至斯潘塞府邸的那片天空。

22. This system generates both wealth and employment and has been proved a conservation success. 这一制度取得了创造财富和就业机会的双丰收，而且业已证明它可以成功地保护野生动物。

23. And as he watched the feast being readied he would hear a jovial conversation blend of family news, comments on the weather, political views and compliments on the attractive table decorations. 在饭前的快乐交谈中，他会听到一些有关家事的交流、天气的评论、政治见解和对精美的桌上装饰的称赞。

24. His speech to the staff was a judicious blend of optimism and caution.
他对员工发表的讲话中所表现的乐观与谨慎是明智的。

25. From Frankfurter to dachshund sausage to hot dog, this all-American favorite is a delicious blend of cultures!
从法兰克福香肠到狗香肠再到热狗，这种最受欢迎的纯美国食品是混合各种文化的美味。

26. With his characteristic blend of shrewdness and spontaniety he was not above tapperckating his own physical appearance. 他个性尖锐，变幻莫测，不会承认自己的外貌缺陷。

27. the gentle miracle of the leaf 树叶那神奇的柔软

28. So how does an ordinary cotton bandage accomplish such healing magic?
那么一种普通的棉制绷带是怎样完成这种愈合奇术的呢？

29. Primo Angeli's studio in a fashionable district of San Franisco has the look of a pop art joke. 普利莫·安吉利的工作室位于旧金山一个豪华时尚街区，看起来像一件滑稽有趣的流行艺术品。

30. significant others 其他重要的

31. in addition to my daily animation fix 除了我每天固定要看的动画片

32. She looked into the shopping basket: individual fruit pies, small salad cream, yogurt, tomatoes, cat food and a chicken quarter.
她发现购物篮里有：一份水果馅饼、小份的沙拉奶油、酸奶、西红柿、猫食和一夸脱鸡。

33. Ancient Greek society—the prototypical Western society was characterized by individualistic activities, such as hunting, fishing, and small-scale farming. 古代希腊社会——西方社会的原型——主要特征是个体行为，如狩猎、捕鱼和小规模农业耕作。

34. Two-year community colleges are still an educational bargain.
两年制社区大学教育仍然很划算。

35. Cash-strapped consumers turn to less expensive dining options.
经济拮据的消费者开始选择不那么贵的食物。

36. He seemed to understand that the honor was in having a whole new life-form named after you, not necessarily what its eating preferences are.
他似乎理解，能够以自己的名字——而不一定是以他们爱吃的东西——来命名一类全新的物种是一种荣幸。

37. The president says he knows Americans are concerned about their economic future, with the challenges of higher energy prices and a falling housing market slowing growth.
布什总统说，他知道由于能源价格上涨和房地产市场下滑使经济增长放缓，美国人对未来的经济感到担忧。

38. People dislike grandstand playing with one person trying to seize all the glory and honor for himself. 看台上的观众不喜欢队员试图把所有的辉煌与荣耀揽在自己头上。

39. Analysts say McCain is taking a huge political risk by choosing a relative political unknown, in contrast with the Democratic vice presidential candidate Joe Biden, a Washington veteran who has extensive foreign affairs experience.

分析家说麦凯恩选择一位名不见经传的人作为副手，是政治豪赌。相比之下，民主党的副总统候选人乔·拜登是华盛顿的老牌政治家，拥有丰富广泛的外交经验。

40. national minority / ethnic minorities / minority nationality 少数民族

41. volunteer students 学生志愿者

42. student youths / young students 学生青年

43. a baby girl 女婴

44. lecture series 系列讲座

45. Open a sushi joint nearby. 在附近经营一家寿司连锁店。

46. narrative repetition 反复叙述

47. a composite thing existing in a spatial simultaneity, synchronically

空间上同时存在的一个组合体

48. Limited library hours, fragmented by long lunches and breaks, preclude the extended stints of research and concentration so crucial for formative collegiate minds.

图书馆开放时间本来就有限，又被长时间的午饭和休息所打断，这一切阻碍了学生想做研究的尝试，妨碍了他们的注意力，而这种注意力对于学术心理的养成至关重要。

49. formative story for Lincoln 关于林肯性格的形成

50. formative political ideology 政治形态的形成

51. He wasn't even president of rotary club. 他甚至不是俱乐部的轮值主席。

52. hawk designer watch fakes 兜售仿制的名牌手表

第十一节 介词短语中的名词副词化

英语中的一些副词在翻译成汉语时，可翻译成汉语的介词短语或句子，因此可以把它们理解为英语介词短语中的名词副词化。

11.1 表示原因

表示原因的介词短语或句子中的名词可以变为副词，从而使语言变得简洁、抽象。

the only gravitationally round asteroid 一颗因受重力控制而呈圆球状的小行星

11.2 表地点

表示方位的介词短语中的名词副词化。

1. Most of the workers were hired locally. 大部分工人都是从当地雇的。

2. Since ammonia can be domestically produced from a variety of energy sources it provides a

path to reduce dependence on imported petroleum.

由于国内可从各种能源中生产氨，这就为减少对进口石油的依赖提供了一条出路。

3. But for years, atmospheric scientists generally assumed that pollutant aerosols worked locally or regionally.

然而，多年来大气科学家普遍认为，污染性浮质只在当地或局部地区发挥作用。

4. Google disagrees and brings a missionary zeal to its library project, partly because it falls directly within the company's mission: "to organize the world's information and make it universally accessible and useful."

谷歌公司并不这么认为，而且对其图书馆数字化抱有传教士般的狂热。部分原因是，这项计划与公司的发展宗旨直接吻合——"整合全世界范围内的信息，使信息在全球范围内都触手可及，为人们利用。"

5. The Federation of the Swiss Watch Industry urged the government to insist that at least 80 percent of a mechanical watch, or 60 percent of an electronic one, must come from Switzerland for it to qualify as locally made.

瑞士钟表业联合会敦促政府要坚持机械表至少有 80%的零部件——或电子表的 60%——必须来自瑞士才有资格称之为本地制造。

6. Adapting new safety features internationally isn't always straightforward, either.

适应一些新的安全性能在国际上也不总是一番风顺的。

11.3 表 方 式

表示方式的介词短语中的名词副词化。

1. Perhaps 15 percent of women and girls in parts of the north of CAR have been abused sexually in the past months.

在过去的几个月内，在 CAR 北部部分地区，大概有 15%左右的妇女和小女孩遭到性虐。

2. HPV is a sexually transmitted disease（STD）. HPV 是一种性传播疾病。

3. But Michael Flickinger, 54, founding director of the University of Minnesota's Biotechnology Institute, had found a way to make hydrogen—then electricity—from genetically engineered bacteria embedded in the adhesive latex polymer particles that form the basis of most paints.

但是明尼苏达大学生物技术研究所的创始人和所长、54 岁的迈克尔·弗利金杰，已经发现了一种由基因工程生产的细菌制取氢——然后发电——的方法，而这些细菌是被加入构成大多数油漆底料的沾性胶乳聚合物颗粒中去的。

4. genetically modified crops 转基因作物

5. Engineers have been recording information magnetically and reading it out electrically since the dawn of the computer age, but as they have endeavored to pack more and more data onto their machines, they have been forced to use smaller and fainter magnetic inscriptions and thus more and more sensitive read-out devices.

自从进入计算机时代，工程师们一直在利用磁力来记录信息并通过电流将它读出，但是因为他们竭力想把越来越多的数据挤压到他们的机器中，所以他们不得不使用更小、更微弱的磁性记入，这样一来，越来越灵敏的读出磁头就出现了。

6. Scott also wants to sell more organically grown food and cotton clothing, partly because it's good for the planet, partly because he believes he can get prices down and boost sales to low-income customers.

斯科特还想销售更多有机食品和棉布服装，一方面因为这样做对地球有利，另一方面他认为，他可以降低商品价格，从而提高对低收入顾客的销量。

7. A lens that has developed a cataract can be removed surgically and replaced by an artificial one. 已发展为白内障的晶状体可通过外科手术摘除，换一个人工的。

8. Researchers turned their efforts toward the ultimately failed chemically powered lasers.
研究人员将努力转向以失败告终的化学激光器。

9. The fact the Aztecs mathematically calculated areas has been known since 1980s, but until now there was little understanding of they did it.

自 1980 年以来人们就知道，阿兹特克人用算术来计算土地面积，但直到现在，我们对于阿兹特克人是如何进行计算的仍然知之甚少。

10. The images are captured electronically. 电子成像。

11.4 用作逻辑宾语或逻辑主语

介词短语中的名词副词化，用作逻辑宾语。汉语中的名词可以译成英语的副词，作逻辑主语。这种用法在上册已经提到，可以对比学习。

1. The key finding of this research was that those who engage in "deep" acting seem to find jobs which demand high levels of emotional labour more personally rewarding.

这一研究的重要发现是，那些从事“深层”表演的人似乎发觉需要高层次情感劳动的工作对个人更有益。

2. socially integrated 融入社会

3. privately-owned companies 私人企业

4. These aesthetically driven expats from all over the world, most in their early 30s, gather in cultural clusters.

这些受美学观念驱动的外国侨民来自世界各地，多数在 30 出头，并以文化群体聚居。

5. In a life marked by personal tragedy and artistic triumph, Edith Piaf (Marion Cotillard) grows from a child born in poverty to an internationally acclaimed singer.

爱迪丝·皮雅芙（玛丽昂·哥迪亚饰）的一生既因个人生活的悲哀不幸引人瞩目，又因艺术生涯的辉煌成就光芒夺目。她是从一个出身贫寒的小女孩成长为一个享誉世界的歌手。

6. All people speak a language according to a set of generally accepted rules, for otherwise their speech would be all topsy-turvy and unintelligible.

大家说话当然要根据一套公认的法则，否则大家随便乱讲，彼此无从互相了解。

7. The system illustrates how a renewable resource, publicly owned and managed, can be exploited to create a job-sensitive manufacturing and service industry worth more than 70 billion dollars annually in the United States and Canada.

这一制度揭示了在公有制和公共管理下如何利用可再生资源开发与就业问题密切相关的制造业和服务业，而且这项制度每年给美国和加拿大带来了 700 多亿美元的收入。

8. His talent was publicly acknowledged for the first time when at just 7 years old he insisted on performing spontaneously at the annual Rochester Dickens Festival.

他的歌唱天赋第一次得到大家的承认是在他刚刚 7 岁时，当时他自告奋勇，坚持要在一年一度的“罗切斯特狄更斯节”上表演。

9. It is hidden because unlike, say, mainlining heroin, gambling is generally a socially acceptable behavior.

说隐蔽，因为赌博同（比如说）静脉注射海洛因不一样，是一种社会一般还可以接受的行为。

10. Lifestyle is expensive monetarily and personally, because it costs a great deal to keep up appearances and do what you think is socially acceptable.

生活方式无论在经济上还是精力上都代价高昂，因为你要付出很多去保持光鲜的外表，去做你认为在社会上很体面的事。

11. Add artificially triggered climate change to the volatility already initiated by globalization, and the next few decades may see previously unthinkable levels of economic upheaval, in which fortunes are won and lost based as much on the physical climate as on the business climate.

已经由全球化引发的动荡不安的局势再加上人类活动导致的气候变化，在接下来的几十年内，我们可能会经历经济剧变（其剧烈程度是从前无法想象的），而在此剧变过程中，自然气候对财富得失所起的作用和商业环境所起的作用一样大。

11.5 其他类似结构

1. “I can be a bit of a know-it-all,” admits the Vassar and New York University-educated Hathaway, who caught the acting bug from her theatrically trained mother.

“我对表演多少也可以算是个百事通吧。”先后在瓦萨学院和纽约大学进修的海瑟薇承认，她是在接受过表演培训的母亲的影响下迷上表演的。

2. At that point, it wasn’t just my family and friends who had been reinforcing my belief that I was mechanically hopeless. And it wasn’t just the Army test, either. I was the one who kept telling my self, “You can’t do this!”

从这一点上说，不断强化我在机械方面完全无能这一信念的不只是我的家人和朋友，还有那次军队的考试。是我在不断告诫自己：“你做不了这样的事！”

3. Yes, admittedly it has been historically spread by the British Empire over the past couple of hundred years.

是的，这是无可否认的历史事实，在过去的几百年里，英语被大英帝国广泛地传播开来。

4. They are conceptually simple, even if occasionally technically complicated.

从概念上来讲很简单，尽管有时从技术上来讲却很复杂。

5. A little light seeps（渗出）in dustily between cracks in the boards, secondhand from a cobwebbed window somewhere across the cellar. 一丝充满尘埃的光线从有隙缝的板墙里透过来。这光线间接来自地窖某处一个结满蛛网的窗户。

6. “It is made mostly of cashmere and a little wool, exactly like an Armani coat,” said one shop assistant pointing out a stylishly cut grey coat in Lilanz, a branded shop run by China Lilang,

a local Jinjiang company which raised HK$1.06bn（US$136m）in November through a Hong Kong stockmarket listing.

“它的面料主要是山羊绒和少许羊毛，与阿玛尼外套完全一样，”一名利郎专卖店的店员指着一件剪裁时髦的灰色外套说。经营这家专卖店的是晋江本土公司中国利郎（China Lilang），于今年11月在香港上市，融资10.6亿港元（合1.37亿美元）。

7. In reality, this was an elaborate, small-scale model filmed in a studio by a specially designed camera.

事实上，“飞船”是一个精致的小模型，是用一台特别设计的摄影机在摄影棚里拍出来的。

8. Sand dunes and water waves are superficially similar in shape.

沙丘和水波表面看来形状相像。

9. The world's first commercially available bionic hand took many hands many years to develop. 世界上第一款商用仿生手是积多人多年的努力才开发出来的。

10. It is so ecologically out of balance that if it goes on this way, it will kill itself.

这里的生态平衡被破坏得如此厉害，若是任其发展，整个生态系统就会自我毁灭。

11. They are physiologically different. 他们有着不一样的生理特征。

12. The blueprint must be dimensionally and proportionally correct.

蓝图的尺寸和比例必须正确。

13. Certainly people in the enterprises must be mathematically informed if they are to make wise decision. 当然，企业管理人员要想做出明智的决策，就必须懂得数学。

14. Do you think in English when you speak English, translate mentally?

当你说英语时，是用英语思考，还是需要有一个翻译过程？

15. Is it possible to help the students not to think competively in the academic field and yet to have excellence in his studies, his actions and his daily life? 有没有可能帮助学生在学术领域里不再想着竞争，但在学习、行动和每天的生活中依然保持优秀？

16. vote affirmatively　投赞成票

17. write them down mindfully　用心记下

18. I was doing well socially, academically and relationally.

我擅长社交，学习成绩优异，与身边人关系融洽。

第五章 定　　语

关于定语的用法，英汉思维模式有一致的地方，也有差异，本章把重点放在有差异的地方。

第一节 前置定语

定语放在被修饰部分的前面与汉语思维模式是一致的，容易理解和使用。

1.1 名词加“of”构成的定语

这种用法在上册已经提到过，在这里再回顾一下。

1. long years of crisis　漫长的危机
2. It may eventually be the first of a new class of anti-aging drugs.
它可能会成为新一代抗衰老药物的先驱。
3. ten dollars worth of stamps　价值 10 美元的邮票
与名词所有格进行对比（two hours' walk）
4. thousands of pound's worth of damage　价值数千磅的损失
5. discussion type of article　讨论型文章
6. The latest generations of men will find new meanings in Shakespeare, new elucidations of their own human being. 最近几代人会对莎士比亚有新的理解，并重新认识人类。
7. Not surprisingly, first generation Asians in America, hailing from nations that still stress academic fundamentals, score the highest on Amercian educational tests.
不足为奇的是，生活在美国的第一代亚洲人，他们来自那些重视学术基础的国家，他们在美国的考试中成绩是最高的。
8. older generation Indian Chinese　老一代的印度华人
9. Thus, even before we entered the war, death had become a familiar and compelling subject for the new generation of American writers.
因此，甚至在我们参战之前，死亡已经成为新一代的美国作家熟悉的、感兴趣的话题。
10. a few weeks of quiet and solititude　几周的安静与焦虑
11. many years of education　多年的教育
12. a whole day of watching parades　看了一整天的游行
13. Along one typical 100m stretch of one street, there are 34 shops all selling different domestic branded products.
在一段典型的百十米长的街道两侧，有 34 家出售各种本土品牌产品的商店。

1.2 名词短语用作定语

1. The **management consultancy** Mckinsey has predicted that the luxury business could be

worth $27 billion annually within four years, almost triple the current estimated figure.

麦肯锡管理咨询公司预测在四年内奢侈品行业规模可能会达到 270 亿美元，几乎是目前市场估值的三倍。

2. **American *Vogue* editor-in-chief** Anna Wintour 美国 *Vogue* 杂志主编安娜·温图尔

3. ***A Map of the World* author** Jane Hamilton 《世界地图》作者简·哈密尔顿

4. at twenty metres distance 在 20 米距离

5. our next door neighbour 我们的隔壁邻居

6. It was all phony: the accent, the **$ 10,000 a year salary** he was supposed to be earning, the contracts in the United States and Britain.

一切都是假的：口音，他可以挣到的 1 万美元年薪，以及在美国和英国的合约。

7. Many philanthropic activists are propelled in their work by what authors Cheryl and Jim Keen and **wife/husband** Sharon Daloz Parks and Larry Parks Daloz describe in their book, *Common Fire: Lives of Commitment*, as "experience of the other".

《共同的激情：奉献的人生》是谢丽尔和吉姆·基恩以及莎伦·达罗茨·帕克斯和拉里·帕克斯·达罗茨夫妇所写的一本书，书中描述的“另一种体验”是很多慈善活动家从事慈善事业的动力。

8. cradle to grave system 终身制度

9. first-time readers of *Paradise Lost* 第一次阅读《失乐园》的读者

10. hand-to-hand combat 贴身搏斗

11. In his recent book *Satisfaction*, Emory University psychiatrist Gregory Berns points to extreme endurance athletes who push themselves to their physical limits for days at a time.

埃莫利大学精神病学家格雷戈里·伯恩斯在他的近作《满足》中指出，极限耐力运动员每次训练都要使自己的身体连续数天处于极限状态。

12. *Prada* director David Frankel《普拉达》的导演大卫·弗兰科尔

13. The 2008 Berlin International Film Festival awards have been announced.

2008 年柏林国际电影节各个奖项的归属已尘埃落定。

14. That *Economist* review called Goodman's latest book, *Intuition*,"exciting""exotic".

《经济学家》所刊登的那篇书评称赞古德曼的新作《直觉》“激动人心”“充满异国情调”。

第二节 后 置 定 语

汉语中的定语多数是前置，放在被修饰语前面，而英语中定语位置相对灵活，可以前置或后置。

2.1 “of”短语用作后置定语

英语中为了表达需要，可以用“of”短语作后置定语。

1. What is worse is that I literally kill my computers within two years of purchase, such that I have gone through more hard drives in my lifetime than I have new pairs of shoes.

更糟糕的是，不夸张地说我弄坏了我买了不到两年的电脑，以致于我一生更换的硬盘比买的新鞋还要多。

2. They might do like my mother did and make a picture of a giant shinny fish using the disks that I have thrown out over the years.

他们可能会像我妈妈一样把我多年扔掉的光盘拼成一个巨大的闪闪发光的鱼形图。

3. She and two other students represented their class of 13 at the conference in Boston, where the team was given an award from NAIS for their work.

她与另外两个同学代表她们班 13 名同学出席了波士顿的会议——在会上，全国独立学校协会因她们工作出色，向她们颁了奖。

4. the morning of our trip to the San Juans 圣胡安之旅的那天早晨

5. the best writer of the year 年度最佳作家

6. my husband of only one year 结婚才一年的丈夫

7. his friends of many years 他多年的朋友

8. English wife of 20 years 结婚 20 年的英国妻子

9. It has a population of 390 000 people and an area of 1200 square kilometers.

拥有 390 000 人口，面积 1200 平方公里。

10. I came upon a little lad of perhaps ten years old. 我碰到一个大约 10 岁的少年。

11. It is a day of the gathering of the family—to give thanks for the year's blessings.

这是一个家庭聚会的日子——感恩上帝一年的保佑。

12. I have ordered that a lunch of bread and cheese shall be served to all.

我已经吩咐给大家准备了面包和乳酪当点心。

13. on a day of indescribable glory 在一个辉煌无比的日子

14. like many women of her background 像许多具有她这种背景的人一样

15. a group of some 20 people 一个 20 人左右的团队

16. a girl of Indian parents 一个女孩，其父母是印度人

17. Ford relays matter-of-factly the tragedy of his early life: born Leslie King Jr. in Omaha, Neb., son of a doting mother and an abusive father.

福特以平淡的口吻讲述了他早年的坎坷经历：出生于内布拉斯加州奥马哈市，原名小莱斯利·金，有一个过分慈爱的母亲和一个暴虐的父亲。

18. In August, she moved back home to New Jersey, with her father, an engineer, and mother, a school teacher. 8 月，她与当工程师的父亲和当教师的母亲一起搬回新泽西州的家中。

2.2 名词短语用作后置定语

1. Allegra Goodman, the novelist **daughter of two professors,** oversees one brainy household.

阿莱格拉·古德曼是当代美国女小说家，其父母都是大学教授。在她管理的小家庭里，每个成员都很聪明。

2. Only if the learner's interlanguage has reached a stage **one step before the acquisition of the structure to be taught**.

只有当学习者的中介语离习得所学的结构一步之遥时。

3. There is a world **shortage of fuel**. 全世界都缺少燃料。

2.3 表“方位”“距离”“大小”短语用作后置定语

这部分也是名词短语用作后置定语。

1. people **east of Suez** 苏伊士以东的人

2. the land **just south of the Tiber River** 就是台伯河南边那块地

3. the school **two hours north of Barcelona** 学校在巴塞罗那以北两小时的车程

4. There was also another dwelling place some distance away from the buildings.
在离交易站的房子不太远的地方，另有一个安身之处。

5. Sons and daughters away at colleges use their four-day holiday to go home, and employees take extra days from their work to be able to make the trip.
在外求学的儿女们利用四天的假期回家，在外工作的人们会额外请几天假以够路途往返。

6. Tell the boy to carry them to the house three doors away.
告诉男仆把它送到隔壁第三家。

7. kids next door 隔壁家的孩子

8. a forest the size of Wales 一片如威尔士大小的森林

9. In *Star Wars*（1997）, a spaceship the size of a small city cruises effortlessly through space.
《星球大战》（1997）里面，一艘宇宙飞船在空间轻松地穿行，这飞船足有一个小型城市那么大。

10. Then everyone took his own pancake to a tent half the size of a football ground to slowly enjoy it.
大家端着饼到有半个足球场大的帐篷里去慢慢享受。

11. From the driver's seat, Jim grinned down at the trio, a round-eyed twin **each side of Grandpa**, holding a hand apiece.
吉姆坐在驾驶座上,瞧着这祖孙三人,咧嘴笑了——眼睛圆圆的双胞胎分别走在爷爷两侧,各自拉着爷爷的一只手。

2.4 形容词短语用作后置定语

形容词短语用作定语时，通常放在被修饰语的后面。

1. The teachers' language shared many of the features of the mechanical question-and-answer drills **characteristic of audiolingual classroom**.
教师的语言具有许多听说课堂上机械的问答操练的特征。

2. I would never make a mistake **this stupid** and jeopardize everything we've built.
我从不会犯这么低级的错误，并危及我们所建造的一切。

3. And this resulted in a relationship of linguist to teacher **reminiscent of a family tree**. Let us take the Audiolingual Method as an example.
语言学家和教师的关系让人想起家族关系。以“听说法”为例。

4. An institution for testing people's attitudes found that a good vocabulary is the only characteristic **common to successful people**.

一家民意测试机构发现拥有丰富的词汇是成功人士唯一的共性。

5. On average one American died of heart disease attributable to smoking.

死于心脏病的美国人通常是因为吸烟造成的。

6. The director was a man ruthless and efficient, who at times, but very imperceptibly indulged in grim humor.

主任是一个狠毒、干练的人，时常纵情欣赏自己的极为微妙的残酷的幽默。

7. this place devoid of Chinese people 这地方没有华人

8. Some towns rich in producing maple syrup started to hold Maple Syrup Festivals, one after another.

一些盛产枫糖的市镇都纷纷举办枫糖节。

9. The number of Americans 65 and older will double in the next 25 years to about 72 million, according to government census data. By then, seniors will account for nearly 20 percent of the population, up from just 12 percent in 2003.

根据政府的人口普查数据，在未来 25 年内，美国 65 岁及以上人群将成倍增长，达到大约 7200 万。到那时，老年人将占人口总数的近 20%，而这个数据在 2003 年只有 12%。

10. Not my love, or Paula's love or the love of strangers on a banana boat, but a love so all-encompassing it will take a lifetime to grasp.

不是我的爱，不是波拉的爱，也不是香蕉船上那些陌生人的爱，而是如此包罗万象的一种爱——他要用一生去理解。

11. a policy obstructive to our plans 妨碍我们计划的政策

12. It's an abstract painting suggestive of a desert landscape.

这幅抽象画展示了一幅荒凉的景色。

13. Hawthorne's literary world turns out to be a most disturbed and problematical one possible to imagine. 可以想象霍桑的文学世界是最令人不安和问题不断的。

14. in every way possible 千方百计

15. the people nearest to me 离我最近的

16. possibilities open to females 面向女性的机会

17. the organization responsible for local government in a town 对当地镇政府负责的组织

18. person responsible for his death 对他的死负责的人

19. responsible manner 负责任的方式

20. a word unfamiliar to you 一个你不熟的单词

21. a woman unable to give birth in the normal way 一个不能正常分娩的妇女

22. bacteria capable of producing oil 可以产油的细菌

23. the president elect 被选出而尚未就职的总统

24. jobs open only to woman 限招女性的工作

25. the dog opposite 对面的狗

26. the couple downstairs 楼下的夫妇

27. the house opposite（to）mine 我对面的房子

28 words pregnant with meaning 富有意义的言辞

29 with the prettiest look of surprise imaginable 可以想象到的最漂亮的惊讶表情

30. We tried every imaginable means / every means imaginable.
我们尝试了各种可以想象出来的办法。

31. That level of fascination made sense in the days before telescopes could observe details in planetary atomospheres, before space probes had explore Mars and bulldozed into a comet, and before we understood the history of asteroid and comet collisions, linking celestial bodies **large and small**. 在望远镜能够观测到行星大气之前的时代，在太空探测器探索火星、穿入彗星之前，以及在人类了解小行星历史和彗星碰撞、把大小天体联系起来考虑之前的时代，人们被行星序列的魅力所迷惑是讲得通的。

32. Peers **past and present** have certainly influenced Buffett's strategy.
过去和现在的慈善家们肯定对巴菲特的慈善战略造成过影响。

33. the present situation 现在的情形

34. a story **much funnier than that** 比那有趣多的故事

35. secretary-general 秘书长；总书记

36. within the city proper or in the suburbs 在市内或郊区

37. a winter climate similar to the best of summers 与夏日最好天气媲美的冬天气候

38. Buy one, get one free. 买一送一。

39. Shop fronts were piled up with all sorts of foods and gifts appropriate for the New Year's holiday. 商店堆满了各种食物和礼物，这是为新年假期准备的。

40. a home education program appropriate for her son's talents
适合她儿子天赋的家庭教育计划

41. plants native to America 原产于美洲的植物

42. Kangaroos are indigenous to Australia 袋鼠产于澳大利亚

43. with payment proportional to the work done 报酬与工作量成比例

44. compensation proportional to his injuries 得到的赔偿与他受的伤成比例

45. anyone untrustworthy 任何一个不值得信任的人

46. The car broke down when we were still five miles short of our destination.
当我们离目的地还有 5 英里时，车坏了。

拓展学习：I puzzled about it for a moment then realized how totally engrossed I was in the wonderful display of unconditional love not more than an arm's length away from me.
我一时有些困惑，然后忽然意识到，就在不到一臂远的距离里，我是多么全神贯注地在观看着这场无条件的爱的美妙展示。

47. My father was only a year short of fifty when I was born.
当我出生时，爸爸还差一岁就 50 了。

48. a dark, cloudy night with no stars visible to（the naked eye）
一个漆黑、多云，看不到星星的夜晚

49. Those **younger than 50** will only gain a maximum of $ 21,000.
而那些年龄未满 50 岁的最多只能得到 2.1 万美元。

50. After a few moments of an agony frightful and absurd, he decided to go and meet his doom.
经历了片刻可怕而又荒唐的痛苦，他决定去面对自己的命运。

51. Incidentally he reflected that the fellow dead there had been a noxious beast anyway.

他突然发现死在那儿的家伙其实一直就是一个道德败坏的畜生。

52. The heavy work lay with the horses, for they had to go far and pick their way clear of habitations.

这些马匹的任务繁重，因为它们不仅要走很远的路，而且还要选择远离居民区的道路。

53. With step solemn and slow, he ascended the pulpit.

迈着庄重而又迟缓的步伐，他走上讲道坛。

54. To my astonishment, I perceived that it had grown to a pallor truly fearful.

令我惊讶的是，我觉得它已经变得苍白，着实让人害怕。

55. Certainly the miracle chip will affect American life in ways both benign and productive.

神奇的集成电路芯片必然会以既有益又有效的方式影响美国生活。

56. The research was carried out among 132,271 Jewish children **born in Israel** in the 1980s by Dr. Abraham Reichenberg, from the Mount Sinai School of Medicine in New York, and colleagues from the Institute of Psychiatry in London.

该研究是由纽约西奈山医学院的亚伯拉罕·雷钦伯格博士和伦敦精神病学研究所的同行们，在以色列 20 世纪 80 年代出生的 132 271 名犹太儿童中进行的。

57. with only 250 available to care for a population of 20 million

58. They can gather information or clues not available to human beings with their extraordinary senses of smelling and hearing.

他们可以使用自己非凡的嗅觉和听觉搜集人类无法获取的信息或线索。

59. One of my responsibilities was designing custom database solutions for those individuals not skilled in using computers.

我的任务之一就是为那些不擅长使用电脑的人设计自定义数据库解决方案。

60. Those in the rear, **unable to read the placard**, surged forward, a sense of bitter disappointment clutching at their hearts.

在后面的那些人，由于看不清海报，向前涌来，结果大失所望。

61. Checklists were prepared, in order to gather authentic documents **representative of the kinds of texts** commercial officer have to be familiar with and to carry out interviews to identify aspects of the language the learners would want to master.

2.5　定语与被修饰语分开

定语有时太长，为了避免“头重脚轻”，可以把定语与被修饰语分开。

1. Photographs are usually taken of the bride and bridegroom and their families and friends.

通常会为新郎和新娘以及他们的家人和朋友拍照。

2. When I awoke on the morning of Sunday, the 22nd, the news was brought to me of Hitler's invasion of Russia.

当我在 22 号星期天早上醒来时，我获悉希特勒入侵俄国。

3. Few vestiges are now left of the old expressway that once separated the city's financial district from one of the oldest ethnic neighbourhoods in the nation: the Italian North End.

曾经将城市金融区和美国最古老的少数民族裔聚集区——“意大利北区”——分割开的那

条旧高速公路如今已遗迹难觅了。

4. These permit the generalization and incorporation into the course design of learners' needs, wants, and desires.

这些使得我们可以总结学习者的需要、所求及意愿并把它们融入课程设计。

2.6 形容词与名词作定语时的区别

名词作定语强调职能，形容词作定语强调属性，但并不是绝对的。

1. Food and Agricultural Organization of the United Nations 联合国粮农组织
2. European agriculture minister 欧洲的农业部长
3. Environmental Protection Agency 环境保护局
4. a wild animal protection center 野生动物保护中心
5. national security team 国家安全团队
6. the homely environment 家居环境
7. After studying **home science** at Otago University in the South Island of New Zealand, she won a scholarship to do her masters' degree in maternal and child nutrition at Kansas State University, in the US, in the late 1970s.

长期以来，罗宾对营养均衡一直情有独钟。在新西兰南岛的渥太哥大学学习家政后，20 世纪 70 年代晚期罗宾获得奖学金在美国堪萨斯州立大学攻读产妇和婴儿营养学的硕士学位。

第三节 形容词用作定语时的翻译

英语中的形容词用作定语时，有时与汉语的思维模式一致，译成对应的形容词，有时与汉语思维模式并不一致，需要在学习时注意总结。

3.1 与汉语思维模式一致的形容词

这样的形容词有很多，在理解和翻译上，没有多大困难，在此列举部分形容词。

1. visionary president 有远见的总统
2. accessible books 通俗的书
3. an easy woman 放荡的女人
4. He is a difficult man to get on with. 他是个不易相处的人。
5. It's a handy source of information. 第一手的资料。
6. a wide and gentle slope 宽阔而舒缓的山坡
7. rimless/ boundless sea 无边的大海
8. the old-time circus masters 这位资深的马戏团老板
9. instrumental use 工具性用途
10. brotherly love 兄弟般的爱
11. Your focus should be on building a foundation of solid and complete work.

你们的重点应该是建立一个扎实和完整的工作基础。

12. Hot dogs are known as an all-American food.

大家都知道热狗是一种纯美国食品。

13. princely state 诸侯国
14. You are really overqualified for the job. 太屈才了。
15. fatal/deadly shock 致命打击
16. a responsible guy 一个负责任的人
17. heavy metal 重金属
18. heavy marketing investments 大量市场营销投资
19. The late show was even worse. 晚场的表演更糟。
20. One night passed uneventfully. 一夜无事。
21. On New Year's Day France hands over the rotating European Union presidency to the Czech Republic, ending one of the most eventful six-month tenures ever as head of the 27-member bloc. 新年这一天法国把欧盟轮值主席一职交给捷克，结束了作为27国集团首脑为期六个月的任职，这也是事情最多的任职期之一。
22. You won't want your clothes look horribly, hopelessly inappropriate.

很显然谁也不想穿得不论不类、俗不可耐。

23. The tragic death of Michael Jackson has shocked the world, and messages of grief and appreciation have poured in from his family and close friends in Hollywood and around the globe. 迈克尔·杰克逊的不幸故去震惊了世界，他的家人以及他在好莱坞和世界各地的密友知己纷纷表达了哀伤之情并给予了他很高的评价。
24. His story, with many variations, illustrates the trajectory of most pathological gamblers: a period of exhilaration and great windfalls—punctuated by a little dishonesty here and there—ending in misery, financial ruin, and shattered personal relationships.

他那跌宕起伏的经历展现了多数病态赌徒的生活轨迹：有一个时期兴奋不已，大发横财——在某些方面不时有点小小的欺骗行为——最后落得个痛苦不堪、倾家荡产、众叛亲离的下场。

25. sticky problem 棘手的问题
26. Factories that show Wal-Mart they're cutting air pollution will get preferential treatment in the supply chain.

那些让沃尔玛看到他们正在减少空气污染的工厂将在供应链上得到优惠待遇。

27. And the unhappy Geoff—a sorry picture of grease and dust in an old T-shirt

倒霉的杰弗穿着沾满油污和尘土的旧T恤的那副狼狈样

28. The answer is very strong obvious. 答案明显具有说服力。
29. I have sketchy memories of kindergarten. 对幼儿园的记忆已经模糊了。
30. Spanning for months in the midst of the Nazi occupation, the film kicks off with a haunting recreation of the Nazis parading down the ChampsElysees, goose-stepping in front of the Arc de Triomphe.

影片讲述了纳粹占领期间4个月内发生的故事，开篇就是让人难以忘记的纳粹党人沿着香榭丽舍大道的狂欢游行，在凯旋门前正步走。

31. The Chinese lag behind the world's best in the demanding sport but still expect their best-yet result in Beijing.

中国队在这个要求极高的项目上落后于世界最好的水平，但是他们仍然期待在北京奥运会上创下自己最好的成绩。

32. Through the clouds, at the extreme left, emerge ghostly images of buildings that the second painter depicted on a gentle hillside.

在画面的左上角，透过云层，隐约浮现出第二位画家绘制在一个缓坡上的几座建筑物的模糊图像。

33. This and other promising findings about the life-changing effects of crises are the province of the new science of post-traumatic growth.

诸如此类有关危机改变一生的发现有着客观的研究前景，这正是创伤后成长这一新兴学科的研究领域。

3.2 充当逻辑主语或逻辑宾语

关于形容词充当逻辑主语或逻辑宾语，在上册已经提到了，这里简单提一下。

1. As you can see, the distribution of parental age of concern is very broad.

你会发现，父母开始关注时，孩子的年龄分布是广泛的。

2. students' question of discussion 学生讨论的问题
3. technical updating 技术升级
4. developmental delay 发展迟缓

3.3 介词宾语提前

对一些名词后面的介词短语，有时会把这个短语中的名词提前变成形容词充当定语。前面已经提到这种用法，这里回顾一下。

1. a contemporary relevance 与当代有关
2. That rat in fact had mental maps. 实际上那只老鼠有心理地图。
3. nationalistic reading of Quixote 堂吉诃德的民族主义解读
4. intravenous drug use 静脉注射吸毒
5. grammatical obscurity 语法上的晦涩
6. There is also methodological limitation. 还有方法论上的限制。
7. the very beginning of the literary reception of John Milton

弥尔顿刚在文学领域为人所知的时候

8. I could give you a technical reason. 从专业角度解释。
9. It is a kind of allegorical place. 寓言中才会出现的地方。
10. There are reasonably philosophical or scientific grounds for worrying about each one of the premises. 我们对每一个前提的怀疑都有合理的哲学或科学依据。
11. A woman could be considered and should be considered as excellent a creature as a man, that women might actually be as ontologically valuable as men. The scriptural account of the priority of the sexes, the Genesis story of Adam and Eve established no such thing.

从存在论上来说，女人实际上应有和男人一样的价值。圣经中关于男性先于女性的论述，上帝创造亚当和夏娃的故事并不能证明性别地位一说。

12. a common sense biological understanding of the world 常识性生物知识

13. Many languages do have a standard form—particularly on paper—and this is what we learn, but they probably also have a variety of regional dialects and social styles, and many are the products of the historical mingling of other languages.
许多语言都有规范形式，特别是书面语，这也是我们要学习的，但它们也可能有许多方言以及多种社交语体，许多是与其他语言混合的历史产物。

3.4　译成汉语的状语

英语中形容词作定语，在译成汉语时，可以译成方式、原因、地点、时间状语等。

1. He spends those years after college in studious retirement at his family house.
大学毕业后那些年，他一直在家闭门读书。

2. go to a random person　随机找一个人

3. I would like to take this opportunity to extend your formal invitation.
我利用这个机会正式邀请你们加入。

4. The nation is about to get a big lesson in African-American history.
美国准备大张旗鼓地学习非洲裔美国人历史。

5. The Baptist minister at last told the lady about his accidental killing the little dog.
牧师最后告诉这位太太，是他无意间害死了那只小狗。

6. She is not adventurous in terms of face scanning. 她在观察别人时不会探险似地乱瞄。

7. His conclusion was that the answer was "No", which he backed up by a thorough review of China's rural development over the previous 15 years.
他通过对中国此前 15 年农村发展的全面回顾，从而得出结论，答案是"不"。

8. For couples with children who are tying the knot, the biggest challenge is creating an instant family. 对于带着孩子结合的伴侣来说，最大的挑战是要迅速组建一个家庭。

9. SearchWiki is a tough sell because most of us are already trained to surf the Web quickly.
SearchWiki 的推广有一定难度，因为我们大多数人经过磨炼已习惯于快速搜索。

10. Manus, who could not be contacted because he was applying for his Cuba visa, and teammate Suriya Prasathinphimai（75kg class）, will lead to the Carribbean island later this month before joining six of their compatriot in the US for the worlds, with the likely inclusion of 32-year-old fly-weight Somjit Jongjohor.
马努斯因正在申请去古巴的签证，故联系不上。他和他的队友苏里亚·普拉萨丁菲迈（75 公斤级）2007 年 7 月晚些时候将前往这个加勒比海岛国，然后他俩与美国的 6 位同胞（可能包括 32 岁的特轻量级拳击手颂吉特·永友荷）一起参加拳击世锦赛。

11 With the possible exception of track and field（athletics）, wrestling is the most ancient sport known to have been continuously practised competitively.
可能除了田径运动以外，摔跤是自古以来连续不断举行竞技性比赛的最古老的运动项目了。

12. He has become the public face of shell-shock.
他成了尽人皆知的炮弹休克症的患者。

13. One of the great joys of reading reference books is the chance distraction thrown up by the strictly alphabetical organization of information.

阅读参考书最大的乐趣之一是严格按字母顺序排列的信息会偶尔让你分神。

14. Sixty years later, the city-state has both gained territorial independence, and managed to bootstrap its way to wealth in spite of a lack of water and energy.

60 年后，这个城邦国家不仅获得了领土独立，而且在水资源和能源匮乏的情况下，千方百计使自己富裕起来。

15. He had a nervous breakdown. 他精神崩溃过一次。

16. your conversational partner 你的谈话伙伴

17. They'd done everything together in the intervals of paying numerous diplomatic attentions to mother. 在礼仪周全地向母亲大献殷勤之余，他们什么事都一起做。

18. Manet's stylistic discoveries 马奈在绘画风格上的一些发现

19. He was on the editorial staff of *The New Yorker* magazine. 他是《纽约客》杂志的编辑。

20. press a correct button 不要按错键

21. Treated wastewater made its public debut. 处理过的污水首次公开亮相。

3.5 具有动作意义的形容词

这类形容词可以译成汉语动词并在其后加一个“的”。

1. Penalties for overdue books will in the future be strictly enforced.

未来将严格执行对借书逾期不还的处罚。

2. Psychologists believe that constantly hiding the deep dislike you feel for colleagues and **difficult** patients is stressful enough but if combined with forcing false positive emotions pushed you nearer to “burnout”.

心理学家认为，经常掩饰自己内心对同事和爱挑剔的病人的厌恶感，压力本来已经够大了，如果再强颜欢笑，就会把人逐步推向“心力交瘁”的状态。

3. He continued forging his legacy with strong adaptations of **difficult** novels, *The Talented Mr. Ripley*（1999）and *Cold Mountain*（2003）, both of which earned critical kudos and numerous award nominations.

他再度为观众奉献两部佳作——《天才雷普利》（1999）和《冷山》（2003），这两部影片把不易改编的小说做了精彩的编排，因此获得了评论界的一致好评和众多的奖项提名。

4. The idea of fraudulent labeling became important.

假冒商标的行为开始受到重视。

5. his other sweaty works 他的其他费劲心力之作

6. The theories become very trendy. 这些理论已广为接受。

第四节 过去分词用作定语时的翻译

英语中的过去分词用作定语翻译成汉语时，可以译成定语、表语、状语、谓语、名词等。

4.1 译成定语

过去分词可译成对应的汉语动词并在其后加上“的”用作定语。

1. They were wanted criminals, drug smugglers, money smugglers, illegal immigrants—and, yes, a few were suspected terrorists.

他们是通缉犯、毒品走私犯、金钱走私犯、非法移民——而且，一点不假，有几个是恐怖分子嫌犯。

2. In 1950, as Joseph McCarthy（R-Wis.）raged against supposed widespread Communist infiltration of the U.S. government, the authorities revoked Qian's security clearance.（In 1950, it was supposed that as Joseph McCarthy（ R-Wis）raged against ...）

1950 年，约瑟夫·麦卡锡激烈地反对假想中的共产主义在美国政府中的广泛渗透，当局撤销了对钱学森的涉密许可。

3. deeply discounted items 高折扣商品

4. the spent fuel 用过的燃料

5. the confirmed cases 确诊病例

6. In the current polarized domestic political debate, charges of insufficient patriotism have become common.

在当前两极化的国内政治辩论中对缺乏爱国主义的指责已经变得非常普遍。

7. The vast majority of polled women loved wearing heels, even though a good half of them had either fallen off them or wrenched their ankles.

调查了大量喜欢穿高跟鞋的妇女，甚至多一半人都因穿高跟鞋摔过跤或扭伤过脚踝。

8. The old man looked down in amazement at Tessa's upturned face.

老人惊讶地低头看着特莎上扬的小脸。

9. I think there are a lot of unanswered questions because Diana said different things to different people. And she was different things to different people—I think that's what makes her endlessly fascinating.

我认为还有好多未解之谜，因为戴安娜对不同的人说了不同的话。当然她在不同的人的心目中的形象也不尽相同，我想这也是她永远令人着迷的原因。

10. When paid a dollar they said，Well, I don't want to be a donkey.

拿到一美元的人说，我不想当个吃力不讨好的家伙。

11. It is an accomplished fact of life. 生活中的一个即成事实。

12. Semantics is about the relation of words to reality—the way speakers commit themselves to a shared understanding of the truth.

语义学是研究词汇与现实的关系——即说话者与其他人对客观事实达成共识的方式。

13. Militants opposed to Indian rule of the disputed Kashmir region attacked the Parliament here in 2001, pushing the two neighbors to the brink of another war the following year.

2001 年反对印度对克什米尔争议地区控制的激进分子袭击了这儿的议会，第二年把这两个邻居推向另一场战争的边缘。

14. In the 1500s, European explorers marveled at the potential this protected body of water had as a seaport and trading center.

在 16 世纪，欧洲探险家对这片有着天然屏障的水域作为海港和交易中心的潜力感到惊奇。

15. There isn't a search engine on the planet that can keep up with my huge quantities of disorganized media and data.

世界上没有一个搜索引擎能跟上我的量大而又杂乱的存储媒介和数据增长的步伐。

16. Drivers of General Motors 1978 Cadillac Seville will also be able to punch a button and find out the miles yet to go to a preset destination and the estimated arrival time.

驾驶通用汽车公司 1978 年产的卡迪拉克牌塞维利亚型轿车的司机也享有类似的便利：只要按一下控制键，就能知道离预定的某个目的地尚有多少里程以及预计到达目的地的时间。

17. the densely populated parts of India 印度人口稠密地区

拓展学习：in dense urban areas 人口密集城区

18. a promised call 承诺（给某人）打的电话

19. a drowned man 一个淹死的人

20. one of the aliens referred to in the recording 录音中提到的外星人

21. added value 附加值

22. Williams, Brown, and Jones, the above-mentioned will attend the course.

刚才提到的威廉姆斯、布朗，还有琼斯可以参加这门课程的学习。

23. the preferred animals 喜爱的动物

24. the closed door 关着的门

25. escaped criminal 逃犯

26. an interested audience sufficiently informed on all these

感兴趣的听众对这些事物相当熟知

27. mutual and partaken bliss 相互的、共享的快乐

28. a district devoted to jokes 一个人们热衷于说笑话的地区

29. Obama said this must be accompanied by mutually agreed land swaps to ensure secure and recognized borders for both states under any future agreement.

奥巴马总统说，在这一过程中，可进行双方认可的领土交换，以便在未来达成的任何协议中为两国建立安全并得到认可的边界。

30. speaking with forced playfulness 不自然的玩笑（嬉闹）

31. He said Africa was at risk of, "becoming the forgotten continent in the context of the fight against climate change."

他说："在抗击气候变化的斗争中，非洲大陆有被遗忘的风险。"

32. Report your agreed place to the class.

把你们商议好的地方（旅游目的地）向班级汇报。

33. a written application 书面申请

34. fabled village 传说中的村庄

35. a retired receptionist 退休前是一名接待员

36. unexercised 未实行的

37. a road with flown sand 沙土飞扬的道路

38. Adam, his hand already on the swinging door, halted and looked with astonishment and hurt pride at the doorkeeper, who grinned and pointed to a notice requesting all readers to show their cards that day.

手已经放在旋转门上的亚当停了下来，觉得没面子，吃惊地看着门卫，门卫微笑着，指着要求所有借阅者出示证件的公告。

39. shared apartments 共享公寓
40. feathered farmers 享受补给的农民
41. take targeted measures 采取有针对性的措施
42. perform at the challenged level 有困难做某事
43. a prolonged visit 长期逗留的访亲
44. improved medical care 改善的医疗服务
45. a finished product 成品
46. The four years passed at college were，for his purposes，wasted. 大学四年为了他荒废了。
47. At the longed-for moment when our elders ceased eating their peaches and began to look about them instead of showing off to each other（grown-up conversation always seemed to me a form of showing off）

在这盼望已久的时刻，当我们的长辈不再吃桃子，开始看着他们而不是相互炫耀（成年人的谈话总是对我来说似乎是一种炫耀）

48. an informed opinion 有把握的见解
49. aged parents 年迈的父母
50. Could she be their intended victim? 她会是他们计划中的受害者么？
51. paid vacation 带薪假期
52. For a city fed by ocean commerce, it struck many as a travesty.

对于一座靠海洋贸易为生的城市来说，这条路在许多人眼里显得不伦不类。

53. the computerized glint of sunlight on car metal 电脑制作的汽车金属上闪烁的阳光
54. a night spent with my family 和家人一起度过的晚上
55. In research presented at the American Academy of Neurology's annual meeting, scientists pointed to the prefrontal cortex, that part of the brain responsible for decision-making and impulse control, as being impaired in pathological gamblers.

在美国神经病学会年会上发表的研究报告中，科学家门指出，病态赌徒的额叶前部皮层——即用于决策和冲动控制的大脑部分——正受到损害。

56. Presented with his research, local officials were surprised at the portrait of pollution that emerged. 当地官员对他提交的研究报告揭露出的污染现状感到震惊。
57. Using this figure, the cost of the nearly 4,000 American troops killed in Iraq adds up to some $28 billion. 按这样计算，在伊拉克战场上阵亡的近 4000 名美国士兵需得到的赔偿累计要达到约 280 亿美元。
58. a Jinjiang company listed on the Shenzhen stockmarket 一家在深圳上市的晋江公司
59. unmarried people 未婚的人
60. a married daughter 已婚的女儿
61. China currently ranks 31st on the tax burden list among the documented 209 countries and regions around the world.

在全世界 209 个备案的国家和地区当中，中国当前的税费负担排名 31 位。

62. East Asian countries such as Vietnam and China are worried about the increased risk of animal-related diseases during the lunar New Year holiday next month, when travel from one region to another and poultry consumption rise rapidly.

越南和中国等东亚国家担心在下个月农历新年期间会有更多与动物有关的疫症爆发，因为在节期内人们从一个地区到另一地区的旅行更加频繁，而且食用的鸡鸭数量也大大增加。

63. Taking a guided tour is the only way for visitors to see the inside of UN Headquarter.

游客只有在导游陪同下，才可以参观联合国总部内部。

64. Although the specifics of Joe's rant are localised, the anti-American sentiment expressed is worldwide.

尽管乔的激情演讲中某些细节是具有地方性的，但其中表达的那种反美情绪却是全球性的。

4.2 相当于介词短语的中心词提前

这种用法，在前面已多次提到，可对比学习。

1. The wall had a penciled message in an anonymous hand: i think of you.

不知道谁用铅笔在上面写着：我想你。

2. the walled city（the city with walls）有城墙的城市
3. the chaired lady（the lady on the chair）坐在椅中的女人
4. a veiled woman 带面纱的妇女
5. near the curtained window 靠近挂窗帘的窗户
6. barbed wire 带刺铁丝网
7. There was a wooded area on the northern part of the island.

在这个岛的北部有一片林地。

8. wooded mountains 树木繁茂的山
9. bearded men 长胡子的男人
10. the leafed darkness 树叶下的浓荫
11. Get benched. 坐冷板凳。

4.3 译 成 状 语

1. The quake and subsequent fires destroyed about 28,000 buildings, causing an estimated property loss of $524 million dollars. 地震和随之而来的火灾摧毁了大约 2.8 万座建筑物，据估计，由此所造成的财产损失达 5.24 亿美元。

2. An estimated 2,000 locals work on the tuna boats and hundreds more in processing plants.

估计有 2000 名当地人在金枪鱼捕捞船上工作，另有数百人在加工厂工作。

3. An estimated 114 million workers in China now are migrants, and roughly 15% work on construction sites throughout the country, usually far from their home villages.

据估计，中国现在有 1.14 亿流动人口，其中大约有 15%在全国各地的建筑工地上做工，他们通常都来自遥远的农村。

4. An **estimated** 20 billion hot dogs are eaten in the United States each year!

据估计，在美国每年有 200 亿只热狗被吃掉。

5. An estimated US$ 2 billion is harvested annually in the region.

该地区的金枪鱼年捕捞量估计价值有 20 亿美元。

6. Other studies have shown links between brain problems and repeated exposure to extreme

conditions. 其他的研究结果证明了大脑问题和身体反复暴露在极端环境中的联系。

7. The study authors noted that the results "are more likely to be due to progressive, subtle brain insults caused by repeated high-altitude exposure".

该研究的作者指出，这些测试结果“最有可能来自渐进的、细微的脑部损伤，而这些损伤是由于它们反复暴露在高海拔区域所引起的”。

8. Therefore did Mrs. Packletide face the cameras with a light heart, and her **pictured fame** reached from the pages of the *Texas Weekly Snapshot* to the illustrated Monday supplement of the *Novoe Vremya*.

于是帕克尔泰德夫人轻松愉快地接见了许多新闻摄影师，她的照片给她带来的名气从《得克萨斯每周画报》一直传到俄国的《新时代》星期一增刊插图。

9. She shuddered as she remembered that once, during **a drunken rage**, he had threatened to chop her body into little pieces and feed her to the sharks.

每当想起有一次他**醉酒后发怒**，威胁要把她砍成碎片喂鲨鱼，她就浑身发抖。

10. For a moment Yusef seemed about to sink again into **drugged sleep**.

有一会儿，**由于药物的作用**，尤塞夫似乎又将睡着。

11. In the garden the cats, not susceptible to fears about taking root, closed their drugged eyes again.花园中的猫，没有害怕生根的忧虑（作者借此烘托诺拉不能行走的恐惧心理），它们在麻药的作用下又闭上了眼睛。

12. Rural Affairs Minister Eamon O'Cuiv is proposing a bus service to shuttle people to and from country bars as a crackdown on **drunk driving** threatens pubs that are the traditional meeting places in many communities.

由于（政府的）严惩**酒后驾驶**行动威胁到乡村酒馆业的生存，而乡村又是许多社区的传统聚会场所，因此爱尔兰农村事务部大臣埃蒙·奥奎夫提出开通公交车服务接送那些往返于乡村酒吧的人。

13. Given these stereotypes, it is no wonder that beauty enjoys, at best, a rather mixed reputation. 由于存在这些老套的思想，美的名声至多不过是毁誉参半就不足为奇了。

14. While she sat there in her usual relaxed majesty there came at the door a knock which I immediately recognized as the **subdued appeal** of a model out of work.

当她坐在那儿，带着平日里放松后的威严，刚有人敲门，我立马听出，原来是一位失了业的模特儿怯生生地想找活干。

15. As English was largely a northern language, the forced application of Latin grammar to its analysis ended inevitably inadequacies and frequent exceptions to rules.

大体讲来，英文本是一种北方的语言，强行用拉丁语法去分析英文，其结果当然不免要有一些牵强，更随时要遇到例外。

16. When paid a dollar, they said: 付了他们一美元后，他们说：

4.4 译成表语

虽然汉语中没有表语，为了更好地理解这种用法，套用英语的语法，称作表语。

1. What is within my competence to dispute is the perceived need for carrying drinks into

aeroplanes.
首先我能够说的是，那种要把喝的东西带上飞机的需要是可以理解的。

2. It seemed to be an understood thing. 这件事情仿佛是不言而喻的。

4.5 译成谓语

这种结构可以用来翻译汉语的连动结构。

1. She was pursing a writing career that had already resulted in one published biography.
她潜心于自己的写作，并在其间出版了一本传记。

2. You could say he was a success: He was a published author, an accomplished musician, fluent in German and American Sign Language 你可以说他是成功的：他是一个作家并出了书，一个颇有成就的音乐家，一口流利的德语，而且懂美国手语。

3. I'd say that there are three issues involved in our supposed deprivation through the water-ban. 我想说的是，我们之所以认为禁水令剥夺了我们的某些权利，这里涉及三个问题。

4. Previously, the little-understood fall had been estimated at 40 to 250 meters.
此前人们对海平面的下降了解甚少，对海平面下降幅度的估计是 40 至 250 米。

5. They support the continued spread of democracy and liberalism.
他们支持继续传播民主和自由主义。

6. Missorting was easy to spot, given the required use of designated garbage bags.
由于要求使用指定的垃圾袋，错误分类的垃圾很容易识别。

7. an increase in suicidal thoughts and attempted suicide 企图自杀或自杀未遂的增多了

8. According to one movie critic（ a woman ）who is a declared Robert Redford fan, it is having that cluster of skin-colored moles on one cheek that saves Redford from being merely a "pretty face".
一位自称是罗伯特·雷德福德的影迷的影评家（一位女性）认为，正是他一面脸颊上那几颗肉色的痣拯救了雷德福德，否则他只是个彻头彻尾的"小白脸"。

9. This is probably due to the fact that the cell phone, E-mail as well as the telephone are preferred means of communication. Few people care to give thoughts to improving the postal service. 这也许是因为电子邮件、手机以及电话已成为人们青睐的通信工具，因而无人重视邮政服务的改善了。

10. Medvedev has called for continued consultations.　梅德韦杰夫呼吁继续协商。

11. She did not hear the story as many women have heard the same, with a paralyzed inability to accept its significance.
她没有像许多女人听到同样的消息那样，无法接受而呆若木鸡。

12. In the United States, social skills programmes now concentrated on teaching unpopular children to smile with the required degree of warmth. 在美国，社交技能项目主要教那些不受欢迎的孩子学会微笑，并要求微笑时要带有一定的热情。

13. They advanced towards him with their spears raised. 他们举起长矛向他走来。

14. The UN itself doesn't have an agreed definition of "sustainability".
联合国本身对"可持续发展"的定义没有达成一致意见。

15. I am not sure when a bottle of clear fluid first became a lifestyle accessory, but has travelled hand in hand with the supposed discovery of dehydration as a public-health crisis—a discovery made not by the science community but by the bottled water industry.
我不能肯定一瓶清澈的液体第一次成为一种生活方式的附属品是在什么时候，但它是伴随着"脱水是一种公共健康危机"这种假想而传播开的。
16. A fancy bike came equipped with a "tank" mounted between the upper-frame bars.
一辆漂亮的自行车骑过来了，在自行车前后杠之间装有一个"水箱"。
17. I went to Rome for the first time at age 16, and, armed with a magazine picture in my hand.
十六岁那年，我第一次去罗马，手里拿着一张杂志图片。
18. Electrically powered cars have been designed at many different times but have always stumbled because of perceived lack of performance and range.
在许多不同时期人们曾设计过使用电力的汽车，但总是因为运动性能和行驶里程上感到不足而搁浅。
19. The clouding of the lens—or cataract—forces an image to travel through a distorted medium, resulting in diminished vision.
晶体状浑浊——或白内障——使得图像从一种发生了畸变的介质中穿过，导致视力下降。
20. with her backpack slung on one shoulder 肩上背着背包
21. with broad fields like open hands stretched out to receive the sun
宽阔的田野像张开的手伸出去迎接太阳

4.6 过去分词的逻辑主语及逻辑宾语

类似用法在上册书已经提到，可以对比学习。
1. In September 1642 Poussin returned to Rome and remained in his adopted country permanently. 1642 年 9 月，普桑返回罗马，终老在他的第二故乡。
其中"his"是"adopt"的逻辑宾语。
2. "I think it is sending a message that, in this time of significant challenge internationally, the continuity that Bob Gates brings to the Pentagon and his good judgment, his good sense, his demonstrated performance is absolutely critical for this moment," said Senator Reed.
议员里德说："我认为这传递了一个信息，在面临国际挑战的这个重要时刻，鲍勃·盖茨带给五角大楼的连续性，他精准的判断能力、清晰的思路以及他过去的表现在此时都是至关重要的。"
3. Seou's military faced severe criticism for its perceived slow and weak response last year.
去年首尔军方由于被认为反应迟缓与软弱而遭到猛烈批评。
"its"是"perceived"的逻辑宾语。
4. AFP said Putin's expected return to the presidency will likely give a further boost to ties.
AFP 说期待普京当选总统后会进一步加强联系。
"Putin"充当"expected"的逻辑宾语。
5. My eyes must have betrayed my horror at the sight of what amounted to my first battered child. 当我看到那个等同于被我打的孩子时，不用说我的眼睛一定流露出惊恐的神情。
"my"是"battered"的逻辑主语。

6. His changed attitude suggested that what had done was rather foolish.

"his"是"attitude"的逻辑主语。

7. It would guarantee essentially the status of Paradise Lost as scripture itself, as something divinely authorized or perhaps even divinely authored.

同圣经一般被神圣的权威化或者是出自权威之手般的地位。

4.7 标题中的过去分词

1. Assassination Plot Exposed 暗杀阴谋曝光
2. Suspect Wanted 通缉犯
3. Jewel Theft Sought 追捕珠宝大盗
4. A wanted criminal 通缉犯

第五节 兼有状语功能的定语从句的翻译

英语中的定语从句翻译比较复杂，这里主要探讨一下定语从句兼有状语从句的功能，在意义上与主句有原因、目的、让步、假设等关系。目的是为了与前面的形容词、过去分词用作定语时的功能进行对比，加深对英汉思维模式转换的理解。

5.1 译成表示"原因"的分句

1. The ambassador was giving a dinner for a few people whom he wished especially to talk to or to hear from.

大使只宴请了几个人，因为他特地想和这些人谈谈，听听他们的意见。

2. The mother couldn't trust big-city traffic where the rest of her children were concerned.

母亲不再相信大城市里的交通状况了，那可关系到她剩下的孩子们。

3. We know that a cat, whose eyes can take in many more rays of light than our eyes, can see clearly in the night.

我们知道由于猫的眼睛比我们人的眼睛能吸收更多的光线，所以猫在黑夜也能看得很清楚。

4. We must deal here, on both sides of the fence, among whites as well as blacks, among workers as well as employers, with men and women in whose minds there loom good and bad of such height and weight that they assume proportions of abnormal aspect and construction.

在这里我们必须两面讨好，白人与黑人，工人与雇主，男人与女人，因为在这些人的头脑中，对善恶的分量看得非常之重，简直达到了反常的程度。

5. The neighbors who, when someone lay drunk in the street, moaning and groaning in that typical French ivresse that you were propaganded to believe did not exist, would open their windows and the murmur of talk.（Ernest Hemingway: *The Snows of Kilimanjaro*）

由于宣传，你不再相信有那种典型的法国式的酩酊大醉，可当夜里有人烂醉如泥，躺在街上呻吟不已，邻居们就会打开窗子，议论也随之而出。

6. There is a great deal to be done: longer working in return for more, and more powerful,

legislation to outlaw the ageism that blights the working lives of many in late middle age.
要做的还有许多：工作越久应该回报越多，同时还需要更强有力的法律禁止年龄歧视，因为这种年龄歧视缩短了中老年人的工作寿命。

7. Every here and there, a doorway gives a glimpse of a sunlit courtyard, perhaps before a mosque or a caravanserai（ a big inn）where camels lie disdainfully chewing their hay.
到处都可以从门洞瞥见阳光普照的院子，院子后面可能是清真寺或一家大的客栈，因为有骆驼傲慢地卧在院子里，咀嚼着干草。

8. Besides, Nancy, used all her life to plenteous circumstances and the privileges of "respectability" could not enter into the pleasures which early nurture and habit connect with all the little aims and efforts of the poor who are born poor.
enter into: sympathize; be able to understand and appreciate
另外，由于南希一生享有优越的环境和受人尊敬的特权，不能体会出身贫穷的人由于从小所受的教育和养成的习惯在那些卑不足道的目标和努力中享受到的那种乐趣。

5.2 译成表"结果"的分句

1. There was something orginal, independent, and heroic about the plan that pleased all of them.
这个方案富于创造性，独出心裁，很有魄力，所以他们都很喜欢。

2. He had a smile and scowl that were equally effective in tyrannizing over both his mother and Horace. 他的一喜一怒在对他的母亲和霍勒斯横行霸道时起着同样的作用。

3. I told her it was a burning coal but that she couldn't move to take it off.
我当时告诉她，那是一块她不能伸手拿掉的燃煤。

4. Tom had a remarkably smooth, soft voice, and a habitually respectful manner, that had given Legree an idea that he would be cowardly, and easily subdued.
汤姆的声音非常平缓、温柔，并且习惯性地毕恭毕敬，这在莱格里看来，是懦弱的表现，容易驯服。

5. There are so many troubles—crime, the murderous soullessness that seems to be taking over the lives of many young people…
我们正面临许多问题：犯罪、灵魂的空虚似乎正夺走许多年轻人的生命……

6. Manet's stylistic discoveries, such as "there are not lines in Nature", which led to his abandoning of the conventional outline and his shaping the forms by means of color and subtle gradation of tints, decisively influenced the Impressionists, but their representation of light and optical reactions to color were different.
马奈在绘画风格上的一些发现——诸如"大自然中没有线条"——使他摒弃了传统的轮廓，而是用颜色和色调精细的层次变化来塑型。他的那些发现对印象派画家产生了决定性的影响，但他们在表现光和对色彩的视觉反映的方式是不同的。

7. As he delves into the facts behind the multimillion dollar lawsuit at the center of the conflict, Michael finds himself making moral and ethical decisions that will place his life in danger.
在他深入研究了处于这场冲突中心的那桩百万美元诉讼背后的种种事实时，他发现，如果自己基于道德良心做出决定，那么他的生命就将被置于危险的境地。

8. It was a humble motion, almost a bow, that instantly struck him as absurd and betraying of all his weakness.

这是一个恭谦的举动，几乎是个鞠躬的样子，那一瞬间对他的打击就像是对他所有的虚弱的鄙视和背叛。

9. The rice rations served out by the Company did not agree with them, being a food unknown to their land, and to which they could not get used.

再者，他们吃不惯公司定量供应的大米，由于他们的故乡根本就不产这种粮食，他们一直无法适应天天吃米。

5.3 译成表“让步”的分句

1. President Calderon has made some real steps that were tough for him to make in order to confront organized crime within his country. 为了打击国内有组织犯罪，卡尔德龙总统已经采取了一些实质性措施，尽管对他来说并不容易。

2. He insisted on building another house, which he had no use for.

他坚持要再造一座房子，尽管他并无此需要。

5.4 译成表“目的”的分句

1. So my chance of getting to revolutionary China are pretty slim, although I have not given up my efforts to get a passport, that will enable me to visit the countries of Socialism.

因此，我到革命的中国来的希望相当小了，虽然我并没有放弃努力来争取一张护照，以便访问社会主义国家。

2. They were a logical extension of the highway systems that attempted, in part, to keep the country's post-World War II suburban sprawl and its older cities somehow connected.

过去的高架路是高速公路体系的一种合理的延伸，部分原因是为了把该国第二次世界大战后不断扩张的郊区和旧城区连接起来。

5.5 译成表“条件”、“假设”的分句

1. He would be a short-sighted commander who merely manned his fortress and did not look beyond. 谁如果只守城堡而不往远处看，那他就是一个目光短浅的指挥员。

2. There are limits beyond which repressed emotion become dangerous.

克制感情是有限度的，超出限度就会发生危险。

5.6 表 示 转 折

1. She found Jose there pacifying the cook, who did not look at all terrifying.

她看到约瑟正在安抚厨师，但厨师看起来和颜悦色的。

2. Even the course of infectious diseases which doesn't seem to have anything to do with food can be affected by how well-fed people are.

甚至与食物似乎没有任何关系的疾病传染过程，都可能会受到营养好坏的影响。

第六章 非谓语动词的翻译

非谓语动词是指在句子中不是谓语的动词，主要包括不定式、动名词和分词（现在分词和过去分词），即动词的非谓语形式。过去分词的翻译在前面已经提到，这里主要探讨一下不定式与现在分词的翻译。

第一节 不定式的翻译

1. Who are you to think? 你以为你是谁？

2. Who am I to complain if I got a few bad ones thrown in as well.
如果我还有许多不尽如人意的日子，我该向谁抱怨呢？（凭什么抱怨）

3. Who are we to be the "big brother" who attempts to dictate our notion of a superior way of life to others against their will?
我们凭什么充当"老大"，把我们所谓的更好的生活方式的观念专横地强加给他们，而不管他们的意愿呢？

4. I have no reason not to believe you. 没有理由不相信你。

5. Love is too strong a term to be sure. 喜欢倒说不上。

6. It will be very interesting to know. 了解一下会很有趣。

7. I found jewelry to be a better buy here. 我发现在这里买珠宝更划算。

8. Bliss was it in that dawn to be alive, but to be young was very heaven.
幸福不仅仅是天亮时我们还活着，更是保持年轻的心。

9. So to speak. 可以这样说。

10. She can stay here in the hotel, in the finest suite, to be paid by Zetrov, of course.
她可以住这儿的宾馆，并且是最好的套间，当然由泽特鲁夫买单。

11. You are hard to miss. 你是可造之材。

12. You are hard to forget. 很难忘记你。

13. much to be desired 很多不足之处

14. Christ was born to save. 基督是为了拯救而生的。

15. wrong man to ask 问错人了

16. The fruits of our labor was never really ours to begin with.
我们的劳动果实从一开始就不是我们的。

17 That was to come later. 这是以后的事了。

18 It takes time to be considered. 要考虑时间。

19. The time comes to pay. 报应到了。

20. Your life was mine to take. 你的命运掌握在我的手中。

21. The job is mine to do. 这份工作是我的。

22. the question to be answered 需要回答的问题

23. The first thing to notice is… 首先需要注意的是……

24. Vezzali then went one better in Sydney, stamping her dominance to capture both gold.
维扎利后来在悉尼奥运会表现出胜人一筹的实力，获得了个人和团体两块金牌，标示出她的霸主地位。

25. To take a measure of our progress, *Discover* offers a look in that mirror as we analyze the 25 greatest steppingstones in robotics, points in time where science fiction meshes with science fact.
为了估量我们的进步，《发现》杂志与大家一起回顾了机器人科学发展的 25 个最重要的台阶，并及时指出了科学幻想与科学事实在哪些地方实现了相互融合。

26. Mozart had the single-mindedness of genius. He seemed born to create music.
对音乐特别有天分，他似乎为音乐而生。

第二节　现在分词的翻译

这一节分两部分探讨现在分词的翻译。

2.1　现在分词译成汉语的谓语动词

把这一节与前面提到的过去分词译成汉语谓语对比，并注意与汉语"连动结构"的转换。

1. A dog ambles around wagging its tail. 一条狗摇着尾巴，走来走去。

2. He watched Spielberg films growing up. 他看着斯皮尔伯格的电影长大的。

3. He shuddered, remembering. 他想起来就全身战栗。

4. A swan came swimming. 一只天鹅游过来。

5. Jacob, recognizing the spot and the game, rushed forward barking, and then back to plant a warm lick on Shaun's eager face.
雅各布认出了这地方，记起了那游戏，他叫着冲向前去，然后又奔回来在肖恩急切的脸上热乎乎地舔了舔。

6. While walking Mr. Kapala to my car, my heart was pumping fast, doubting he can do it.
我领他走到我的车旁。我的心跳加速，心中也半信半疑。

7. The boy's mother, Sophia of Mecklenburg, died giving birth to him in 1503.
男孩的母亲是梅克伦堡的索菲亚，1503 年生下他就去世了。

8. He had been terrified, but his love for Shubijaya had kept him there, standing trembling, his eyes rolling from the sheikh's face to that of the political officer.
他心里很害怕，但对舒比贾亚的爱让他坚持留在了那儿，他抖抖索索地站着，眼睛在村长和那位政府官员的脸上来回转动。

9. Mama arrived panting at the tail of the procession, just in time to see the happy end of the chase. 老伴最后一个赶到，气喘吁吁，却正好看到这场追捕的圆满结局。

10. Next morning, boats from all over the sparkling bay came clustering to the Prince of Wales for church services. 第二天上午，一艘艘轻舟快艇越过波光粼粼的海湾，从四面八方云集到威尔士亲王号周围做礼拜。

11. He was the admiration of all the negros; who, having gathered, of all ages and sizes, from

the farm and the neighbourhood, stood forming a pyramid of shining black faces（他们站在一起，闪着光的黑色面孔堆成一座金字塔）at every door and window, gazing with delight at the scene, rolling their white eye-balls, and showing grinning rows of ivory from ear to ear.

12. He generally sat up till twelve or one o'clock reading, before he went to bed.
他一般都要看书学习到 12 点或 1 点，然后才上床睡觉。

13. The heron came flapping over the water. 那苍鹭鼓动着翅膀从水面上飞来。

14. At the same time her face had an almost set smile, as though she had said to herself: "I will die smiling（笑着死）."

15. starting on Jan 1 next year 从明年一月一号起

16. I was a big comic fan growing up. 我从小就是一个漫画迷。

17. At last he reached us and received welcoming hugs.
最终，他找到了我们，并受到欢迎与拥抱。

18. Enjoy welcoming beer. 欢迎品尝啤酒。

19. It was already growing dark when at last he opened the door, and stood listening. Not a sound! A milky twilight crept about the landing below. He had turned back when a sound caught his ear.
当他最后打开门时，天已经变黑了，站那儿，听了一会。没有任何声音！乳白色的光照射在下面的楼梯平台上，这时他听到一个声音，便转过身去。

20. Winston Churchill came to the Augusta at eleven o'clock, which saw the dramatic handshake of Roosevelt and Churchill at the gangway（舷梯）. They prolonged the clasp for the photographers, exchanging smiling words.
11 点钟，温斯顿·丘吉尔来到“奥古斯塔”号。就在这个时刻，人们看到罗斯福和丘吉尔在舷门戏剧性地握手。他们延长握手时间，微笑着互相问候，以便让摄影记者拍照。

21. She stood looking at them. 她站在那儿看着他们。

22. She was rising（nearly）eighteen now, and charming. 她现在快 18 岁了，长得迷人。

23. Stepping out the front door on my way to get the Sunday newspaper, I glance to my left, toward a birch tree at the lawn's edge.
走出前门去拿星期天报纸的时候，我向左边草坪边沿的一株白桦树瞥了一眼。

24. The old man halted, his heart suddenly singing.
老人停了下来，他内心突然唱起了歌。

2.2 现在分词与所修饰的名词有逻辑主谓关系

现在分词可以用作形容词做定语修饰名词，因此部分现在分词已经被称作形容词，还有部分被称作介词。过去分词也有这种倾向。

1. ending piece of music 结尾曲
2. setting sun 落日
3. falling star 坠落的星星
4. walking dead 行尸走肉

5. parting genius 逝去的天才
6. his undying fame 不朽之名
7. That's a good question and there are still innumerable, often competing answers to that question. 这不仅是个好问题，而且还有无数的答案，且这些答案经常是相互矛盾的。
8. This is by far the most learned and most demanding lyric poem.
这是目前为止弥尔顿所写过的，最博学读起来也最吃力的一首抒情诗了。
9. This will be the working assumption that I bring to my reading of this poem.
这是我个人对于诗歌的理解之中极为有益的一点假设。
10. talk about ageing population 讨论人口老龄化问题
11. an ageing population 老龄化人口
12. expressing views of population ageing（动名词）发表关于人口老龄化的观点
13. conflicting reports 前后矛盾的报道
14. the lecturing guide 滔滔不绝的导游
15. falling fertility rate 下降的生育率
16. increasing life expectancy 寿命不断延长
17. rising median age 平均年龄上升
18. After a while I punched the button on my talking watch: "The time is nine forty-five."
过了一会儿，我按了按我那个语音报时表的按钮："现在是 9 点 45 分。"
19. All the others had seemed full of holidaying families.
其余的包间似乎都坐满了一家家外出度假的人。
20. flying dust 飞尘
21. a flowering maple 一棵开花的枫树
22. He dashed like an escaping hawk out through the French window.
他像一只逃脱的鹰一样从落地窗冲了出去。
23. Then "You've no proof of anything," he countered, looking at the smiling daffodils
他看着那些灿烂的水仙花反驳说："你们没有任何证据。"
24. There is a kind of fear growing up amongst us that we shall one day be short of work.
在我们中间有一种恐惧在加深，担心我们有一天会没有工作。
25. There was something wrong going on. 错误正在上演。
26. There was a pause, then a cry of surprise, and then a voice shouting from the houses.
屋内先是片刻的安静，然后一声惊呼，再接着传出一声喊叫。
27. I noticed several bare branches near the top, their black twigs scratching the air like claws.
我发现靠近树梢的地方有几根光秃秃的枝丫，上面黑乎乎的小枝像鹰爪一般伸向天空。
28. He, Kayerts, was a thinking creature. 他，凯尔茨，是一个会思考的生物。
29. Sophia was downstairs first, and Constance found her looking at the blank wall beyond the door leading to the kitchen steps.
索菲亚先到了楼下，康斯坦茨发现她看着通往厨房台阶的门外的空白墙。
30. He looked at the stream of sunlight flowing in by the door, left open to give air to a room hot with the breath of children and teacher.
为了给室内孩子和老师热气腾腾的气息换换气，门是开着的，他看着太阳光线从门照射进来。

31. in a revealing chat 在一次透露内情的聊天中

32. This is a cultivation of the actual living disease bacteria.
这是培育出来的真正的、活的病菌。

33. Dapple was a slight sleeper. The sound of the two men talking would wake her.
达普是一个睡眠少的人。 两个人说话的声音会吵醒她。

34. Rainfall changes could also cause skyrocketing prices for commodity crops, something the global economy has rarely observed in the last 30 years.
由降水变化带来的农业减产可能会导致农产品价格的暴涨，这在过去 30 年的全球经济中是很少见的。

35. You know that you live in a happening city when you find Brooklyn boring,
当你意识到自己居住在一个新鲜事物不断产生的城市时，就会觉得布鲁克林区枯燥乏味了。

36. Straining to locate my friend among the passengers deplaning through the jet way, I noticed a man coming toward me carrying two light bags.
正当我盯着刚下飞机从出境过道走出来的乘客，望穿秋水地找朋友时，我发现一个男子提着两个轻便的行李朝我走来。

37. We do have some tantalizing tips, though, about what makes things hurt.
不过，我们确实发现了一些让人感兴趣的有关疼痛产生的原因。

38. I made two stick figures holding hands, one taller than the other, and at the bottom I wrote, "Mommy loves Haley." 我画了两个火柴棍状的小人儿，手拉手，一个人个头稍高一些，并在底下写道："妈妈爱哈莉。"

39. This fledgling field has already proved the truth of what once passed as bromide: What doesn't kill you can actually make you stronger.
这一新兴领域已经证实了曾经被视为老生常谈的一个真理：大难不死意志弥坚。

40. It turns out that some of the people who have suffered the most, who have been forced to contend with shocks they never anticipated and to rethink the meaning of their lives, may have the most to tell us about that profound and intensely fulfilling journey that philosophers used to call the search for "the good life".
事实证明，一些遭受苦难最多的人——他们被迫全力应付他们未曾料到的打击，并重新考虑他们生活的意义——或许对那种深刻的、给人以强烈满足感的人生经历（哲学家们过去称之为对"美好生活" 的探寻）最有发言权。

41. He is a symbol of pain and suffering and the enormous problems endured by veterans returning home.
他是回国退伍军人所承受的痛苦、不幸以及诸多严重问题的象征。

42. He rolled the chair over opposite the door, his hand resting on the edge of the drawer.
他把座椅转过去面朝门，一只手放在抽屉边。

43. But instead of simply recommending that polluting farms and factories be shut, Professor Berger specializes in creating new ecosystems in severely damaged environments.
但伯格教授并不是简单地建议关闭污染环境的农场和工厂，而是专门研究在被污染严重破坏的环境中创造新的生态系统。

2.3 现在分词与所修饰的名词有逻辑动宾关系

1. the resulting fire 引起的火灾
2. hurting pubs 遭到打击的酒吧业

第三节 分词短语译成一个句子

现在分词与过去分词短语在译成汉语时，都可以译成一个句子。其中一些分词已具有介词功能。

1. His book is a volume of outrage, not apologized for by the impulse of a moment, but cherished through a space of ten months.

这并非可加以辩解的一时冲动，而是蓄在心中长达十个月之久的仇恨。

2. Microsoft initially responded — with a certain cheek, given its own record as a monopolist—by objecting to the DoubleClick deal on antitrust grounds, arguing that Google was becoming “dominant”.

微软的最初反应是以反垄断为由抗议 Google 收购 DoubeClick 的这项交易，称 Google 正取得“统治地位”——考虑到微软自身作为垄断者的经营记录，它这样的反应有些厚脸皮。

3. Born to a British mother, Tanya Streeter was brought up in the Carribbean.

坦雅・斯特里特在加勒比海长大，她的母亲是英国人。

4. I felt myself getting sleepy, lulled by the plane’s subtle motion.

飞机的微微颤动使我平静了下来，觉得自己有了睡意。

5. This is a great tribute to the way other languages have populated the space, led by the Japanese with an astonishing 37% of all blogs.

这正是其他语言如何占据博客圈空间的一个绝好佐证。日语博客高居榜首，占了所有博客总数的 37%，令人吃惊。

6. Nor do we see any basis for holding that this jury verdict, affirmed in a thoughtful decision by Oregon’s highest court, is a denial of Philip Morris’s due process rights.

并且我们也没有任何依据认定俄勒冈最高法院经过深思熟虑后所支持的陪审团的这一裁定剥夺了菲利普・莫里斯烟草公司的正当法律程序之权利。

7. Growing up on a farm, she and her brother spent hours messing around on their bikes in England’s Worcestershire countryside.

因为在农场长大，她和她哥哥经常骑自行车在英国沃西斯特郡的乡下闲逛，一逛就是几个小时。

8. Astronomer Clyde Tombaugh had found Pluto through a dogged search for a long-suspected Planet X beyond Neptune, and everyone initially assumed he had found something large.

长期以来人们一直猜测在海王星公转轨道外存在一颗未知行星，通过坚持不懈的搜寻，天文学家克莱德・托姆伯发现了冥王星，所有人最初都以为他发现了一个大家伙。

9. Take Nokia Corp. Given its No.5 ranking, it may seem crazy to consider the Finnish giant a comeback story.

以诺基亚公司为例。考虑到该品牌排行第五，把这家芬兰的大企业想成是一个品牌复兴的故事也许听着很古怪。

10. Rather than turning us into flesh puppets who can be posed at will once mastered, heels given women an extra dimension.
高跟鞋并没有把妇女变成一旦受人控制就成了任由摆布的肉身玩偶。

11. Clandestine premarital intercourse, if discovered and proved, brings severe punishment on both man and woman.
未婚前男女如被发现有私通行为，双方均受严重的惩罚。

12. Failing that, commodities such as furs or wood might be shipped home.
倘若不能成功，还可把毛皮、木材等物品装船运回国内。

13. Before moving, we filled out an address change form and sent it to the post office, requesting all our mail be delivered to our new address beginning the day we moved.
在搬家之前，我们填写了新家地址，通知邮局，要求它从我们搬走之日起把我们的所有信件该送到新址。

14. There was a scream, drowned immediately in a louder murmur of voices, fading into far-off laughter. 忽然听到一声尖叫，立刻又被更嘈杂的人声淹没，化为渐渐远去的哈哈大笑。

第四节 动名词的翻译

动名词放在名词前面，说明事物的性质或表示原因等，还有一些动名词已经用作名词了。

1. Hence the importance placed by food experts on the eating of whole-wheat bread and more fresh vegetables. 因此食物专家强调吃全麦面包和较新鲜的蔬菜。
2. his growing up 他的成长
3. drinking buddies 酒友
4. It was crucial to his becoming a writer. 对他成为作家起到关键作用。
5. No killing babies. 不杀婴儿。
6. running shoes 跑鞋
7. But her wondering doesn't change how she feels or what she wants.
但是这种想法也改变不了她的感觉和她想要的。
8. They do the breeding there. 他们在那里繁殖。
9. Learn feeling words like angry, sad. 学习情绪词汇，如：生气、忧伤。
10. This is one of the greatest social happenings of this entire period.
这是整个这一时期巨大的社会变化之一。
11. This is a weighing house. 这是过磅处。
12. one of enduring works written in 1922 创作于 1922 年，流传很久的作品之一
13. bottling plant 瓶装工厂
14. thrashing machine 脱粒机
15. adding machine 加法机
16. driving licence 驾照
17. the Japanese ageing suit 日本研发的可以让人体验老年生活的服装
18. a walking stick 拐杖
19. planful growing of food 有计划地种植食物
20. There's five Russian restaurants in walking distance of your apartment.

在你住处附近有五家俄罗斯饭店。

21. the qualifying matches　资格赛

22. That deal set off a round of panic buying. 那笔交易引发了一轮抢购。

23. The summing up of the judge was admirable. 法官的总结让人钦佩。

24. He had assumed that her leaving home was the point at issue, that everything turned on that, and that the sole alternative was obedience, and she had fallen in with that assumption until rebellion seemed a sacred principle.

他以为她的出走是问题的症结所在，一切事情都取决于此，而顺从就是唯一的解决办法，原先她的想法也是这样，但现在叛逆已成为神圣的原则。

25. with the coming home of the generals, colonels, or even captains

将军、上校甚至船长都回家了

26. a smacking family　打骂孩子的家庭

27. logging companies　伐木公司

28. a wooden folding chair　一张木制折叠椅

29. firing squad　行刑队

30. Some predict that the world will face a wave of "aging recession".

有人预测，世界将面临"因老龄化而衰退"浪潮。

31. get a dueling scar 留下决斗伤疤

32. To have a better understanding of adolescent children, modern parents are advised to learn some educational psychology.

要想更好地了解青春期的孩子，建议现代家长学习一些教育心理学。

33. An understanding of the prerequisites to preparing a language course includes a grasp of certain theoretical issues.

34. a formal understanding　一份正式备忘录

35. He and his father walk back to the inn where they are staying. He writes down this four-to-five minutes composition note for note in just one sitting.

他和父亲回到了他们住宿的旅馆后，他逐个音符地写下了这首长达 4 至 5 分钟的作品，并且是一气呵成。

36. In the unfolding of the novel, that there is a mystery here to be told, and then we get the telling of that mystery.

随着小说情节的发展，将要讲述一个神秘的故事，然后我们就读到了这个神秘的故事。

37. Indeed, the bringing together and initial cutting up and organizing of the materials is about 90% of the actual preparation.

事实上，汇总、初步的删减及材料的组织大约占了实际准备工作的 90%。

38. Being grateful meant assuming that you were in charge of children and laundry and running out of toilet paper.

感激就意味着你要负责照顾孩子，洗衣，要注意洗手间里的卫生纸用完了。

39. Setting up a new course implies a skillful blending of what is already known about language teaching and learning with the new elements that a group of learners inevitably bring to the classroom.

拓展学习：It is a blend of theory and practice.

第七章　存在句型与主谓句型的转换

表示“某地有某物”的存在句型或“某人（物）有某物”句型可以转换成“主谓结构”，在翻译时可以相互转换。

1. There is no consulting of the boy.　没人征求这个男孩的意见。

2. Was there ever?　曾经有过么？

3. They are characterized differently.　他们具有不同特征。

4.（There is）No talking to your neighbor.　不要与邻居说话。

5. There are rumblings. 传言纷纷。

6. There is an accident with John. 约翰发生了一次事故。

7. There is not much support for his theory. 他的理论没有多少证据支持。

8. But there is a lot of evidence that similarity above and beyond proximity has an effect on attractiveness and on liking.

但有很多证据表明，相似性远不同于邻近性，前者会影响吸引和喜欢。.

9. There is some evidence for…有证据……

10. The general story of why we can't in general is because there's no surprise, there's no mock aggression, and also there my be a general deadening of self-stimulation.

为什么大部分人不能咯吱自己，是因为它在我们意料之内，没有打闹，通常这种引自己笑的念头都会嘎然而止。

11. There is no guarantee that… 不能保证

12. There is no easy definition. 不容易定义。

13. The driveway passed under a portico. 柱廊下面有一条车道。

14. A huge granite rests on a tower of stale doughnuts.

在高高的一摞炸面圈上，有一块巨大的花岗岩石。

15.The coral reefs surrounding the tiny island **teem with** colorful fish and the other sea life. 这个小岛周围的珊瑚礁有大量的彩色鱼类和其他海洋生物。

16. A five-foot sausage gazes at you from a wall-painting.

壁画上一个五英尺高的香肠在凝视着你。

17. In front of them the broad path diverged into a series of tracks that twined away between the houses.宽阔的乡村道路岔成条条曲径，在房舍中间蜿蜒伸展远去。

18. Just below Manawaka, where the Wachakwa River ran **brown and noisy** over the pebbles, the scrub oak and grey-green willow and chokeberry bushes grew in a dense thicket.

就在马纳瓦卡镇下方的瓦卡库阿河的**褐色**河水在小圆石上**哗哗**流过的那个地方，矮橡树、灰绿色柳树、野樱桃混杂的灌木丛长势茂密。

19. There are other more subtle problems concerned with the creation and absorption of text on screen. 关于剧本的创作和理解也存在其他一些微妙的问题。

20 There was in her manner a suggestion of reluctance to begin the task ahead.

她的态度表明她不愿意开始眼前的任务。

21. There is considerable public sympathy for the students' demands.
大多数人对学生的要求持同情的态度。

22. No matter what the context, there is general agreement that the provision of a useful and stimulating approach to second language learning is desirable. 无论在何种情况下，人们普遍认为有必要提供对第二语言学习有帮助和能够激发学习者的方法。

23. There was no doubt of Clarissa's determination to keep in touch.
克拉丽莎决心保持联系毫无疑问。

24. He says there is recognition that investment in agriculture in developing countries has been neglected for a very long time.
他表示承认，发展中国家农业投资已经被忽视了很长时间。

25. There were indications President Bush wanted to visit Ukraine several years agc.
有迹象表明几年前布什总统想访问乌克兰。

26. There is a steady stream of visitors. 参观者络绎不绝。

27. There is a prohibitive look in her eyes. 她眼睛中流露出不让谈这件事的神色。

28. Post-industrial societies have workforces which are moving from manufacturing to service oriented work.
在后工业社会中，劳动力正在实现从生产制造向以服务业为导向的工作转移。

29. There are limits beyond which repressed emotion become dangerous.
克制感情是有限度的，超出限度就会发生危险。

30. You can have the same item that you engage intellectually or psychologically in radically different ways. 对于同一首曲子，在理智和情感上会产生极端不同的反应。

31. You have what's called a rule-outs. 这里还有一些需要排除在外的因素。

32. You have my full support. 我完全支持。

33. My father had a terrible job to find us. 父亲费了九牛二虎之力才找到我们。

34. He adds that one of the wounded had serious leg injuries. 他补充说，一名伤者腿伤严重。

35. Cyril and I had an evening together. 晚上我和西里尔在一起。

36. We've got 95% abstentions. 95%的人弃权。

37. I am sorry to say that these dear children, with whom I had no previous acquaintance, were very naughty. 这些可爱的孩子（我以前不认识）太淘气了，我很抱歉这么说他们。

38. She has a detailed knowledge of this period. 她对这一时期有详细的了解。

39. I have no conception/idea of what you mean. 我不知道你什么意思。

40. You have my full permission to… 我完全同意……

41. She has visions of starring in a movie that requires her to become an expert in something, like marathon running or horseback riding.
她期待自己能主演一部要她成为某方面——像跑马拉松或者骑马——高手的电影。

42. There couldn't have been a worse place for Arabella to have a puncture—right in front of the entrance to the church.
阿拉贝拉扎破胎的地点不可能还有比这儿更糟糕的了——恰好在教堂的入口处。

43. There was no telling how quickly the fire would spread. 很难说那火势会蔓延多快。

44. There is no telling. 不得而知（无可奉告）。
45. There are five Parliaments. 召开了五次国会。
46. Spring brings warm weather and flowers. 春暖花开。
47. We tend to get cold winters and warm, dry summers in this part of the country.
在我们这个地区，冬天往往很冷，夏天则温暖而干燥。
48. There's something enticing and invigorating about the restaurant experience. Be it the atmosphere, quality of food, entertainment, meaningful conversation or…the service.
到餐馆就餐的体验有富于诱惑力、令人心旷神怡的特点。可以是氛围、餐饮质量、娱乐消遣、富有意义的谈话或是……餐厅的服务。

第八章　英汉句子成分转换规律

英汉句子成分的转换比较复杂，因为同一个意思有多种表达方式，但通过这种研究，我们可以找到一些常用的转换规律。

第一节　英汉主语在翻译时的转换

英汉互译时，汉语的主语不一定译成英语的主语，同样英语的主语也是如此，它们可以译成汉语的表语、宾语或谓语等。

1.1　主语与表语转换

英语的表语转换成汉语的主语。

1. Matter is anything that occupies space. 凡占有空间的都是物质。
2. The rotor is a well-designed structure. 这个转子结构设计精巧。

1.2　主语与宾语转换

汉语的主语可以译成英语的宾语，英语的主语可以译成汉语的宾语。

1. The earth has the shape of a spheroid. 地球的形状是椭圆形的。

拓展学习：a stage shaped like a giant glove/in the shape of

2. The road has an ascent of five degrees. 这条路的坡度为五度。
3. The engine has given a consistently good performance. 发动机的运转一直平稳。
4. He has blue eyes. 他的眼睛是蓝色的。
5. This anodyne(平淡的)definition of well-being leaves out the better half of the story, the rich, full joy that comes from a meaningful life.

这种对幸福的平淡定义忽略了问题的主要方面——一种富有意义的生活所带来的那种丰富、完整的愉悦。

6. Hydrogen is found in many compounds. 许多化合物中都有氢。
7. As the match burns, heat and light are given off. 火柴燃烧时就发出光和热。

1.3　主语与谓语转换

英语主语可以译成汉语谓语或谓词性主语，同样汉语的谓语可以通过“动词的名物化”译成英语的主语，可以参考上册“动词名物化”章节中的例句。

1. A repeat of the 1906 quake would be as devastating to the Bay Area as Hurricane Katrina was to New Orleans. 如果像 1906 年那样的大地震再次来袭，它对湾区就会像卡特里娜飓风对新奥尔良一样造成毁灭性的破坏。
2. The doctor’s extremely quick arrival and uncommonly careful examination of the patient

brought about his very speedy recovery.

医生迅速到达，并非常仔细地检查了病人，因此病人很快康复了。

3. Even the pressure of her cheek on the pillow was almost unbearable.

即使连脸颊压在枕头上也几乎难以忍受。

4. His studies of people who have endured extreme events like combat, violent crime or sudden serious illness show that most feel dazed and anxious in the immediate aftermath.

他对那些经历了诸如搏斗、暴力犯罪或突患重病等极端事件的人群进行了研究，结果表明，在刚经历不幸后大多数人都会感到茫然和焦虑。

5. The announcement of her engagement generated a media tornado. Implicit in her decision to marry the Prince, who was famously private, was a rejection of the acting industry.

她随后宣布订婚，引起了一场媒体风暴。她毅然决定嫁给这位以低调著称的王子，其中隐含着对演艺界的拒绝。

6. He caught every disease that happened to be about, and nearly died of each one. His latest acquisition had been scarlet fever.

每一种可能发生的疾病他都患上了，而且几乎死于每一种疾病。 他最近患的是猩红热。

7. Clare turned at hearing her footsteps, but his recognition of her presence seemed to make no difference in him, and he went on over the five yawning arches of the great bridge in front of the house.

克莱尔听见了她的脚步声，转过身来，虽然他知道是她来了，但是似乎没有改变态度，又继续往前走，走过屋前那座有五个拱洞的大桥。

8. Her exit from the Pension Frensham struck her now as poignantly pathetic, in its quickness and its absence of ceremonial. 她从 Pension Frensham 离去，此刻让她伤心至极，因为这件事来得之快，并且没有任何解释。

9. general conception of a farm 通常意义上的农场。

10. The worship of Force, to which Carlyle and Zietzsche and the creed of Militarism have accustomed us, is the result of failure to maintain our own ideals against a hostile universe.

凯雷、尼采崇尚武力和对军国主义信仰让我们习以为常，那是因为我们不能坚持与充满敌意的宇宙斗争的理想而造成的。

11. National opposition to a government policy 全国人民反对政府的政策

12. Englihs rule of Hong kong 英国统治的香港

13. natural formation of their island 他们的岛屿是自然形成的

14. The popular idea of an English village is of one in a valley.

人们印象中的英国村庄位于山谷内。

15 And withdrawal can be punishing, with terrible headache, irritably and anxiety.

洗手不干则可能经受惩罚性的折磨，如剧烈的头痛、易怒和焦虑。（谓词性主语）

16. The hunt for Bigger Thomas served as an excuse to terrorize the entire Negro population, to arrest hundreds of Communists, to raid labor union headquarters and workers' organizations. 把追捕比格·托马斯作为借口，恐吓所有黑人，逮捕数百名共产党人，袭击工会总部和工人组织。（谓词性主语）

17. His haunts are not confined to the valley, but extend at times to the adjacent roads, and

especially to the vicinity of a church at no great distance. 对他的搜寻不只限于山谷，有时还扩大到临近的路上，特别是离此不远的教堂附近。（谓词性主语）

18. Although bombing and military action in the Middle East inflamed opinions, Uncle Sam's response to the Asian tsunami worked wonders for public diplomacy.

尽管在中东的狂轰烂炸和军事行动激起了民愤，但是山姆大叔对于亚洲海啸的反应在公共外交方面创造了奇迹。（谓词性主语）

19. A couple of hours drive took him to the town and without very much effort he located the officers of the solicitors whom he had been informed were responsible for the sale of the cottage in the absence of the owner. He stated his business at the outer office and was ushered into in the presence of the senior partner.

他驱车几个小时来到镇上，很快找到中介人员，在这之前他已经打听到是这家中介机构负责代理不在当地的产权人出售那所小屋。他在事务所外间说明来意，被引到里面见到了事务所的资深合伙人。

1.4 主语与状语转换

英语中的主语可以译成汉语中的状语或状语性主语，同样汉语中的状语可以译成英语的主语。

1.4.1 英语主语与汉语地点状语转换

英汉语中，都可以用地点作主语，也称为“状语性主语”，在互译时，可以把主语转换成状语。

1. Recreation centers couldn't find enough indoor space for playing.

娱乐活动中心没有足够的室内场所供这项活动的开展。

2. The street was running with people. 街上很多人在跑。

3. The next slide takes us to a blow up of this.

从下一张幻灯片我们可以看到它的放大图像。

4. The children's playground rang with happy shouts. 儿童游乐场上回响着快乐的叫喊声。

5. The school was now thudding with activity and I could see boys streaming out of the assembly hall and into classrooms.

校内响起孩子们活动时乒乒乓乓的声音，我看见男生从大礼堂蜂拥而出，继而进入了教室。

6. Jin Xing Dance Theatre Shanghai will present a modern dance performance for its seasonal finale. 在上海金星舞蹈剧院将上演现代舞蹈作为季节性大结局。

7. Her eyes were blazing with fiery. 她的眼睛里闪烁着怒火。

1.4.2 英语主语与汉语原因状语转换

1. Within days, panic buying emptied store shelves.

没有几天的工夫，由于抢购，商店里货卖光了。

2. To most housewives, a shopping trip often serves as an escape from housework as well as an relief from boredom.

大多数家庭主妇常常逛商店，这样她们既不用劳作家务，还可解解无聊。

3. Shortness of time has required the omission of some places of natural beauty and of historical

interest. 由于时间不够，他只能放弃去一些风景点和名胜古迹地方。

1.4.3 **英语主语与汉语时间状语转换**

1. Friday started with a morning visit to the modern campus of the 22000-student University of Michigan in nearby Ann Arbor, where the Chinese table tennis team joined students in the cafeteria line for lunch and later played an exhibition match.

星期五那天，中国乒乓球队一早就到安伯亚附近去参观拥有22 000名学生的密执安大学现代化校园。他们和学校学生在校内自助餐厅排队取午餐，然后举行了一场表演赛。

2. The years 1770 to 1773 were largely occupied with traveling in Italy, studying, learning, observing, absorbing, and giving concerts.

1770到1773这几年主要在意大利旅游、做研究、学习、观察、理解等，并举办音乐会。

3. The CORE day is filled with physical fitness programs, therapy sessions, education sessions and chores.

在“康复中心”，每一天都被健身训练、心理治疗课、教育课和其他琐事排得满满的。

4. March 1940 found me working in a small construction firm.（J. Austen）

1940年3月，我在一家小型建筑公司工作。

5. Ten years make little difference in the appearance of these remote Southern towns.

十年来这些偏远的南方城镇的外观几乎没有变化。

6. Ten years have brought no change. 十年过去了，都没有变化。

7. This century has witnessed dramatic changes in two key factors that define the physical reality of our relationship to the earth: a sudden and startling surge in human population, with the addition of one China's worth of people every ten year.

这个世纪，我们目睹了由两种因素造成的戏剧性的变化。它反映了我们与地球关系的物理现实。人口突然的剧增，每十年相当于增加了一个中国的人口。

8. Post-industrial societies have workforces which are moving from manufacturing to service oriented work.

在后工业社会中，劳动力正在实现从生产制造向以服务业为导向的工作转移。

9. The melting of winter snow traditionally sees Kurdish rebels crossing over the mountainous border into Turkey to launch an offensive against Turkish forces.

冬天雪开始融化时，按照传统库尔德反叛分子会越过山区边界进入土耳其，对土耳其部队发动攻势。

10. A U.S. government scientific report concludes that future decades will see significant climate change in the United States, caused primarily by human activity.

美国政府的科学报告得出结论，未来几十年美国气候将发生重大变化，主要由人类活动引起。

11. The first three decades of the twentieth century brought massive waves of Italians to the United States. 20世纪的前30年，掀起了意大利人移民美国的热潮。

12. We judged that three nights more would fetch us to Cairo.

我们断定，再有三个晚上，我们就会来到开罗。

13. The following season saw her weight rise as she tried to reach a happy medium between

starving her body and overfeeding it. 在接下来的演季里可以看到她的体重在增加，这是因为她努力在挨饿与饮食过量之间找到一种适当的平衡。

1.4.4 用作状语的介词短语中的名词与主语转换

英语中，用作状语的介词短语中的名词可以转换成主语；汉语中，用作状语的介词短语中的名词可以转换成英语的主语。

1. If you go along this road you can reach the new residential area.
沿着这条路走，你就会到新居民区。
变成：This road leads to the new residential area.

2. A survey placed the company 13th for achievement.
调查显示公司业绩排第 13 位。

3. The picture showed us an entire view of the town from high above.
通过这张照片，我们可以看到整个城镇的鸟瞰图。

4. The camera gave us a bird's eye view of the golf course.
透过相机，我们可以鸟瞰整个高尔夫球场。

5. Big windows give a wonderful view of the swimming pool and the sea.
透过大窗户可以看到美丽的泳池和大海。

6. A knife could have cut the tension during the seemingly endless trip back to the plantation.
在返回种植园的似乎无穷无尽的征途上，空气紧张得似乎可以用刀子切割。

7. Every here and there, a doorway gives a glimpse of a sunlit courtyard, perhaps before a mosque or a caravanserai（ a big inn）where camels lie disdainfully chewing their hay.
随处都可以从门洞瞥见阳光普照的院子，院子后面可能是清真寺或客店，因为有骆驼傲慢地卧在院子里，咀嚼着干草。

8. And a door left agar（半开着）gave him a peep into the best parlor.
透过一扇半开着的门，他可以瞥见里面最好的客厅。

9. The comb felt as if it was raking my skin off. 觉得好像梳齿就要把我的头皮耙掉了。

10. The chateau overlooks fields of corn and olive trees.
站在城堡上，可以俯视玉米地和橄榄树林。

11. America has shown us too many desperately worried executives dropping into early grave.
在美国，有多少走投无路的经理过早跌进了坟墓。

12. The door stood open onto a scene of boyish pandemonium.
教室的门敞开着，但见男孩们把教室弄得一片混乱。

13. A careful comparison of Li Bai's poems with those of Du Fu will show their difference.
仔细比较李白与杜甫的诗歌，你会发现不同之处。

14. My conscience told me that I deserved no extraordinary politeness.（J. Asuten）
凭良心讲，你待我礼貌有加，我却受之有愧。

15. The Nobel citation said Dr. Fert and Dr. Grunbeg's work also heralded the advent of a new even smaller and denser type of memory storage called "spintronics".
诺贝尔评委会在赞词中说，费尔博士和格林贝格博士的工作还宣布了被称作"自旋电子器件"的一种更小和更密集型的新的记忆储存器的出现。

16. Cities across the world see rallies against corporate greed.
在世界各地的城市都出现了反对企业贪婪的集会。

17. Money prints your bible. 印刷圣经需要花钱。

18. Under his feet a pear-shaped hole framed a patch of grey light.
外面的光线通过脚下梨型的树洞照射进来，并在脚下形成一片微弱亮光。

19. Activities are the place where you can introduce new projects, track a to-do list, brainstorm new solutions, and more.
在活动中，您可以引入新的项目、跟踪任务列表、集体讨论新的解决方案以及更多活动。

20. The system illustrates how a renewable resource publicly owned and managed, can be exploited to create a job-sensitive manufacturing and service industry worth more than $70billion annually in the United States and Canada.
美国和加拿大通过这一制度的实施不仅有效保护了公有的可再生资源，而且开发了与就业相关的制造业和服务业，其市场规模每年超过 700 亿美元。

21. This paper is 250 names. 这张纸上有 250 个名字。

22. Bars and hotels hang pictures of Marlon Brando as Don Corleone from the *Godfather* films of the 1970s. 那里的酒吧和饭店里挂着马龙·白兰度在 20 世纪 70 年代的电影《教父》中扮演唐·克莱奥内的剧照。

23. A thin white moon hung high in the fine autumn sky over the valley.
宜人的夜空悬挂着一轮苍白的秋月，清辉倾洒在山谷之上。

24. A silver of brilliant red crests the top of the shadowed forest. It silhouettes our mother on the lake shore, the first light catching the soft red of her hair. 阴暗的丛林顶端露出一抹灿烂的红霞。衬托出母亲站在岸边的轮廓，第一缕阳光照在她柔和的红发上。

25. Hues of lavender, rose and amber begin to pulsate in the sky.
天空中开始闪烁着淡紫色、玫瑰色和琥珀色。

26. High above, in the soft blue, a lone star still sparkles. Silver mist rises gently from the lake.
高处，一片柔和的蓝色中，一颗孤星仍在闪耀。银色的雾霭从湖面上缓缓升起（湖面上缓缓升起银色的雾霭）。

27. A grated iron door gave entrance from the passage to each of the four cells.
过了这道铁栅栏门，有一条通往四间牢房的过道。

1.4.5 汉语中状语性主语

汉语中状语性主语句型译成英语时，一般译成被动结构或使用存在句型。

1. 昨晚抓住了三个小偷。Three thieves were arrested last night.
2. 今天开会。There is a meeting today.
3. 校园东头盖了一座楼。A building was built at the east end of the campus.
4. 四川上个月抢救了两只挨饿的大熊猫。

Two starving pandas were rescued in Sichuan last month.

5. 到处都是广告。

There aer advertisements almost everywhere.

Advertisements are seen everywhere.

6. 每天都有英语节目。

There are English programmes everyday.

English programmes can be seen everyday.

7. 我们的宿舍能住六人。

Six people can live in the dormitory.

Our dormitory can sleep six people.

1.5 介词宾语译成主语

1. He is strong of will. 他的意志坚强。

2. With the introduction of the new method, the products decreased in cost.
引进了新方法，产品的成本降低了。

3. When water freezes, it becomes larger in volume instead of smaller.
水结冰后，体积变大而非变小。

4. The trust is lacking in the relationship. 爱情中缺失信任。

5. Friciton can be reduced and the life of the machine prolonged by lubrication.
润滑能减少摩擦，延长机器寿命。

1.6 主语与定语转换

与上一节“介词宾语译成主语”对比学习。

1. Various substances differ widely in their magnetic characteristics.
各种材料的磁性特性有很大的不同。

2. The development of scientific research in China is characterized by the integration of theory and practice.
我国科学研究发展的特点是理论联系实践。

第二节 谓 语

谓语在英汉语中作为句子的主干成分，翻译时也相对复杂。

2.1 谓语与宾语转换

这里包括英语的宾语转译成汉语的谓语，英语的谓语转译成汉语的宾语。

1. Physical changes do not result in formation of new substances, nor do they involve a change in composition. 物理变化不生成新的物质，也不改变物质的成分。

2. The following provides a brief account of how the human body is built.
下文简要说明人体是如何构成的。

3. In the early dawn, the guard towers were silhouetted against the sky.
黎明时，天空映出了瞭望塔的轮廓。（英语谓语译成汉语宾语）

4. The mountain was clearly defined against the sky.
山巅被天空衬托得轮廓格外分明。（同上）

5. Her experiences were damagingly printed in the details of a feature.
她的经万被以专栏的形式做了特别详细的报道。

2.2　谓语与定语转换

英汉之间谓语与定语的转换比较抽象，与前面提到的过去分词译成谓语进行对比，并总结。

2.2.1　英语中用作定语的形容词译成汉语谓语

1. The design calculations will serve as an illustrative application of the theory of semi-conductor device. 这些设计计算可用来说明半导体器件理论的实际应用。

拓展学习：(1) Once again, the computer revolution has served as an illustrative case study. 我们再次以计算机革命为例来说明这个问题。(2) Here's a more sophisticated illustration of the same point. 有个更复杂的例子能够说明这个观点。

2. Some methods require the instructional use of existing materials.
一些教学法需要说明如何使用现有材料。

3. AE monitoring has been studied for diagnostic applications such as leakages in pressure boundaries. 人们已经研究把音频发射用于诊断例如压力边界的泄露。

4. I identify myself as one of critical lovers and loving critics of the United Nations.
我自认为我既是一个批评联合国的爱护者，又是一个爱护联合国的批评者。

5. IQ tests are after all a male invention of dubious validity.
智商测试毕竟是男人的发明，是否有效值得怀疑。

6. our readerly experience of these two lines 我们阅读这两句诗的体验。

7. Its limited thickness and youthful age are other discoveries.
它厚度有限，年代短，这是另外两个发现。

8. Limited library hours, fragmented by long lunches and breaks, preclude the extended stints of research and concentration so crucial for formative collegiate minds.
图书馆开放时间本来就有限，又被长时间的午饭和休息所打断，这一切阻碍了学生想做研究的尝试，妨碍了他们的注意力，而这种注意力对于学术心理的养成至关重要。

9. He is a published writer. 他已经有作品问世。

10. Emma Thompson is battling a rare affliction. It's a condition for which there are no known doctors or ominous-sounding Latinate names.
艾玛.汤普森正在与一种罕见的痛苦进行斗争。这种疾病连医生都无可名状，也没有听起来别扭的拉丁学名。

11. There is no known cause for idiopathic autism, a rare single gene disorder.
先天自闭症的成因还不为人知，它是罕见的单一基因病症。

12. **Many** factors affect equipment reliability. 影响设备可靠性的因素很多。
我们力求通过扩大我们之间的经济、文化、科学、技术及人员交往来加深双方的相互理解。

13. We seek a **better** understanding through multiplication of our economic, cultural, scientific, technical, and human ties.

14. She had seen the dictionary, flying over the pavement of the little garden, fall at length at the feet of the **astonished** Miss Jemima.（*Vanity Fair*）

她眼看字典飞过小花园的甬道，最后掉在吉米玛小姐的脚边，吓了她一大跳。

15. American movie star Angelina Jolie is making her directorial debut with a film set during Bosnia's civil war in the 1990s.

美国电影明星安吉丽娜·朱莉（Angelina Jolie）正在拍摄她执导的首部电影，故事以 20 世纪 90 年代的波斯尼亚内战为背景。

16. Now Foster is ready to get behind the camera for the third time since her 1991 directorial debut, *Little Man Tate*.

现在福斯特准备退居幕后，自 1991 年导演处女作《神童泰德》以来第三次执导影片。

拓展学习：Beginning with her memorable **big-screen debut** in Garry Marshall's klutz-turned-swan family comedy, six of Hathaway's eight films have been either G- or PG-rated affairs. 她在加里·马歇尔那部丑小鸭变天鹅的家庭喜剧中初登大银幕，从那次令人难忘的首演开始，海瑟薇参演的 8 部影片中有 6 部都被划为了 G 级或 PG（parental guidance）级。

17. It was a fateful call. 这个电话改变了我的命运。

18. Boucher's delicate, lighthearted depictions of classical divinities and well-dressed French shepherdesses delighted the public, who considered him the most fashionable painter of his day. 布歇对古希腊罗马诸神和穿着考究的法国牧羊女的描绘不仅细腻，而且轻松愉快，为公众带来愉悦的享受，布歇也因此被认为是那个时代最时尚的画家。

拓展学习：fashionably dressed 装扮入时的

19. sent provocative telegram 发电报寻衅滋事

20. Research and anecdotal evidence suggest that distant analogies lead to new ideas—like when a heart surgeon bounces things off an architect or a graphic designer.

研究成果及一些传闻轶事表明，将相去甚远的事物进行类比能促成新的想法——譬如，一位心脏外科医生能从一位建筑设计师或一位图表设计师那儿得到启发。

21. She is almost two generations distant from Robert Frost.

她几乎与罗伯特·佛罗斯特差了两代人。

22. There is not a single adequate text. 没有任何一个单独的文本足以阐释这门课。

2.2.2 英语中用作定语的现在分词译成汉语谓语

1. Scientists are reporting an unusually high number of starving whales.

科学家们报告称，有数量多得异乎寻常的鲸在挨饿。

2. We heard wailing sirens and roaring engines and then squealing tires. The fire trucks arrived.

我们听到警报器尖啸、引擎轰鸣、轮胎嘎吱的声响。消防车到了。

3. the sagging dollar 美元贬值

4. a patch of flowering tobacco 一片开满花的烟草地

5. While this was happening, a baby girl（perhaps one or one-and-a-half）was squirming excitedly in her mother's arms, never once taking her little eyes off the wonderful sight of her returning father.

在这过程中，一个小女孩（1 岁或者 1 岁半的样子）在她妈妈的双臂间兴奋地扭来扭去。从看到归来的父亲那一刻起，她的小眼睛就一直盯着父亲，兴高采烈。

6. He crashed down on a protesting chair. 他猛然倒在一把椅子上，椅子被压得吱吱响。

7. She was last seen in public on Jan 14, 2006, at a dinner marking the Martin Luther King Jr, holiday, where she received a standing ovation from the 1,500 people in the crowd.

人们最后一次在公众场合看到她是在 2006 年 1 月 14 日马丁·路德·金纪念日晚宴上，前来集会的 1500 人起立鼓掌，向她致意。

8. look forward to a standing ovation 期待着人们起立鼓掌

9. The drive to get drunks off the road is dividing a nation whose tourism board advertises it as a place to enjoy welcoming pint of stout.

爱尔兰旅游部门将该国宣传为欢迎游客前来享受一品脱烈性黑啤酒的地方，而政府消除酒后驾车行为的举措正使国民分裂为对立的两派。

10. His achievements are now more important than ever—especially as the Chinese economy moves relentlessly toward front and center on the world stage. Hence the continuing relevance of this very old man.

现在，他的成绩比以往都更重要——尤其是当中国的经济不可阻挡地迈向世界舞台的前沿和中心时。因此，这位老人的影响仍在继续着。

11. Despite her fading hopes of winning the nomination, Senator Clinton continues to argue that she would be the stronger Democrat to run against the presumptive Republican nominee, Senator John McCain.

尽管赢得提名的希望越来越渺茫，克林顿仍然坚持她是在与共和党对手麦凯恩的竞争中更有胜算的候选人。

12. The rising moon arouses birds to sing. 月出惊山鸟。

13. And the United Nations is predicting rising food prices over the next decade.

联合国预测未来十年粮食价格上涨。

14. And ethnic unity became part of the founding declaration of the nation.

民族团结成为建国宣言的一部分。

2.3 汉语谓语译成英语表语

汉语谓语译成英语表语这种现象比较常见，与前面第六章“存在句型与主谓句型的转换”对比学习。

1. It's an anticipation of a very thought-provoking talk. 期待一场发人深省的报告。

可以转换为被动结构：A very thought-provoking talk is anticipated.

2. He was the admiration of all the negros.

3. They are an expression of basic assumptions about life itself.

他们是中国人基本生活态度的反映。

4. Evil is an inheritance. 邪恶是可以遗传的。

5. There is no easy answer to that question. 这个问题回答起来可不容易。

6. This is a brief mention. 这里简单提一下。

7 If the neighbors I've met are any indication, many people will still drive into town rather than commute on a crowded train.

如果可以拿我遇见过的邻居们做代表的话，那么，许多人今后仍然会开着私家车进城，而不会去乘坐拥挤的城铁上下班。

8. If my overstuffed e-mail in-box is any indication, this game of planetary enumeration remains a deep concern of elementary school students and the mainstream media.

如果我的被邮件塞得满满当当的电子邮箱能表明什么的话，那就是这种数行星游戏仍然还是小学生和主流媒体都非常感兴趣的事。

9. It's always a concern. 这总是一个考虑因素。

10. He said that the move is further proof that Volkswagen is bringing advanced technologies to China. 他表示，此举进一步证明了大众汽车将先进技术引入中国。

11. I am living proof that is true. 我是活生生的例子证明那是对的。

12. The US economy's sustainability has also attracted Chinese people's attention. Rapid increases in deficits worry other countries and the response of the international financial market to the recent downgrade of US sovereign credit is a manifestation of this kind of concern. 美国经济的可持续性也吸引了中国人的关注。急剧增加的赤字，让其他国家担心，国际金融市场对近期美国主权信用评级下调的回应是这种担忧的表现。

13. With the recent tripling of university fees in England, a master's degree is no longer an option for her. 由于最近英国大学费用翻了三倍，硕士学位已经不再是她的选择。

14. The work of these writers has been largely a continuance or extension of Symbolism.

这些作家的作品主要是对象征主义的继承或发扬。

15. Total Physical Response is in a sense a revival and extension of Palmer and Palmer's English Through Actions, updated with references to more recent psychological theories.

"全身反应法"在某种程度上是重提并发展了帕尔默的教学法及其"通过动作学习语言"的理论，同时参照较近代的心理学理论做了改进。

16. This appears to be simply a continuation of the family-tree application of linguistics referred to earlier.

这似乎只是简单继承了早些时候提出的与之有渊源的应用语言学理论。

17. The bicycle was a recent acquisition, for his fourteenth birthday.

最近才有的这辆自行车，是他的十四岁生日礼物。

18. And I believe he is a better judge of the circumstances than I am.

我相信他比我对形势更清楚。

19. I am also a strong believer that love is a universal language spoken and understood by each person on earth. 我坚信，爱是世界上每个人都会说，每个人都能理解的通用语言。

20. And if papa was not there that day—an omission of rare occurrence—they would ride a few fields with the hounds.

而且要不是爸爸那天在那儿——这种疏忽是难得的（爸爸不在的情况是罕见的）——他们会在猎犬的跟随下再骑几块地远。

21. It would be a violation. 那是违法的。

22. As long as accountability of the teacher to the student, or of the educational institution to the student, or of the educational institution to the client, is a consideration.

考虑到教师对学生，或教育机构对学生，或教育机构对客户的责任。

23. Is China's agricultural sector a threat to the nation's rapid economic growth?
中国农业会威胁国家经济快速增长吗？

24. Science was instrumental in bringing about this theatrical revolution.
科学促进了这次剧场革命的到来。

25. So for example if you are in child care work and some of the children you are looking after annoy you, you make a conscious effort to remain positive and not snap at them because deep down you believe that this is a better emotional state to be in than showing how irritated you are.
比如，如果你负责儿童保育工作，你所照看的一些孩子惹恼了你，你会有意识地尽力保持良好的心态，避免严厉呵斥他们，因为你从心底里相信，保持这种积极的情感状态比对他们发火要好。

26. It is a steady down pour.　雨一直持续地下。

27. A must for all visitors to Detroit, "Motor City, USA", is a visit to an automobile factory.
凡是到底特律来的客人，一定会去参观"美国汽车城"的汽车工厂

28. The Blackberry is many things: mobile phone, web browser, still camera, video camera, personal organizer, calendar, note taker, email organizer and GPS navigational system.
"黑莓"集多功能于一身：既是 GPS（全球卫星定位系统）导航，又是移动电话、网络浏览器、相机、摄像机、个人电脑记事本、日历、注意事项记录本和电子邮件管理器。

29. He is in the full conviction that real knowledge is the end product of a thorough study of the history. 他深信，只有对历史加以透彻研究，才能真正学到知识。

30. For 20 years we were passive witness to the deterioration of prices of our raw materials and an excessive increase of the prices of manufactured goods.
过去 20 年，我们坐视原料价格下跌，而工业品价格暴涨。

31. The typical Westerner wishes to be the cause of as many change as possible in his environment, the typical Chinaman wishes to enjoy as much as possible in his environment, the typical Chinaman wishes to enjoy as much as delicately as possible. This difference is at the bottom of the contrast between China and the English-speaking world.
典型的西方人希望能够推动周围环境做尽量多的变革，典型的中国人则希望能够尽量多、尽量细腻地享受生活。中国和英语世界之间的多数分歧，追其根源都因为人生观的不同。

32 It is a natural result/consequence of this preference that avarice is a widespread failing of the Chinese. 作为喜爱享受的自然结果，中国人一个普遍的毛病就是贪财。

33. The company said stagnant demand for medium and heavy-duty trucks is the result of a slowing economy. 该公司表示经济放缓导致对中型及重型卡车需求停滞。

34. In fact, these silent scholars are simply the inevitable product of an education style that has changed little since Confucian scholars sat mutely at their masters' feet.
其实这些沉默的学生仅仅是一种教育方式的必然产物。自从孔氏门徒沉默地坐在老师的脚旁以来这种方式就没有多少改变。

35. The two years he served in the Army were the making of him.
两年的军中服役使他身心发展良好。（在部队得到了锻炼。）

36. One interesting event in Singapore was an exhibition of rare stamps depicting Sun and his contributions. 新加坡发生了一件有趣的事情，人们展出了一些罕见的邮票，那些邮票讲述了孙中山及其所做的贡献。

37. It is a great predicator of a second date. 很明显会有第二次约会。

38. John and I wrote the book jointly, so John is the coauthor of the book.
约翰跟我合写了这本书，因此约翰是这本书的合著者。

39. They are believers in Direct Method. 他们相信直接教学法。

40. Wilkins's contribution was an analysis of the communicative meanings that a language learner needs to understand and express.
威尔金斯的贡献是对语言学习者需要理解和表达的交际目的的分析。

41. The imperative is a powerful facilitator of learning, but it should be used in combination with many other techniques.
虽然强制可以有力地推动学习，但应与许多其他技巧结合使用。

42. Local colorist were consciously nostalgic historians of a vanishing way of life, recorders of a present that faded before their eyes.
乡土文学有意识地反映对正在消失的生活方式的怀旧情绪，记录他们眼前消失的当下生活。

43. I'm a teenager trapped in an aging body and, like a lot of my peers, there's an increasing desire to stop the clock.
我现在陷入了心未老而体渐衰的困境，就像我的很多同龄人一样，日益希望时间停止流逝。

44. I am a strong believer in brushing and scraping the tongue.
我是一个坚信刷舌和刮舌的人。

45. I've never been a fan of word games. 从不喜欢填字游戏。

46. This book is an introduction to contemporary views of second language course design, as well as a practical manual for the preparation of course materials.
本书介绍了一些当代二语课程设计观点，并指导如何准备课程材料。

47. They are all characterizations of the interaction of subjects of systems of rules in verbal behavior.它们都反映了言语行为规则体系主体相互作用的特征。（与"be characteristic of"结构对比）

48. The pupils are a credit to their teacher/school. 学生为他们的老师（学校）增光。

49. You must be a fan of World Cinema. 你一定喜欢世界电影院。

50. One of the most startling surprises for many Americans when they first arrive in Britain is the discovery that their mother tongue, which has been serving them faithfully all these years, is suddenly not up to dealing with the intricacies of the English language as practiced in the British Isles.
许多美国人在第一次去英国时，其中最让他们惊讶的是，他们这些年来忠实地为他们服务的母语突然不能适应不列颠群岛当地复杂的英语。

51. She was a revelation to Horace. 她的出现对霍拉斯来说是件意想不到的事。

52. I am a protector of things myself. 我本人就维护这些事物。

2.4 英语谓语译成汉语状语

1. The New Year's Day bombing of a Coptic church in Alexandria, Egypt was preceded a month earlier by an online warning of an attack if Catholics did not intervene in the Christian-Muslim dispute in Egypt. 新年这一天，亚历山大港科普特教堂发生了一起恐袭爆炸案，埃及政府在此前一个月收到一份网上警告，声称如果天主教不介入埃及国内的基督教与穆斯林教之间的冲突，将会发动袭击。
2. Switching from honeymoon mode back to training was tough, she said, especially after experiencing the greatest competition of her career, followed by the greatest moment of many people's lives, capped by a few weeks fishing and snorkeling on an island off Cairns.

她说从蜜月状态又回到训练是艰难的，特别是在经历了自己运动生涯中最大的赛事后，又经历了许多人一生中最美好的时光——蜜月是在凯恩斯港外的一个岛上过了几周时而钓鱼、时而潜泳的幸福日子。

3. And a deadly rampage at a U.S. Army base in Texas in November 2009 was followed by online praise for the alleged gunman by American-born Muslim cleric Anwar al-Awaki, presumably from Yemen.

2009 年 11 月在德克萨斯州美国陆军基地发生一起致命的骚乱，随后自称枪手者受到美国出生的牧师安瓦尔·阿瓦基在线表扬，据称此人来自也门。

4. It was followed by the entrance of a young man whom I at once saw to be a foreigner and who proved in fact an Italian acquainted with no English word but my name, which he uttered in a way that made it seem to include all others.

接着进来一位年轻人，我立刻看出他是一位外国人，事实证明他是一名意大利人，除了我的名字外，他并不知道其他英语单词。说我的名字时发音似乎也像是说其他的名字。换言之，发音极不准，张三李四的名字都有些像。

5. The hall was flanked by two towers. 大厅的两侧各有一座高楼。

第三节 宾 语

本节将分三部分介绍宾语在英汉互译时的转换。

3.1 宾语转译成定语

前面提到的形容词与它所修饰的名词具有逻辑动宾关系，使用这种结构基本上都可以把汉语宾语转换成英语定语。

1. historical description of football development 讲述足球发展的历史
2. rural description of Britain 描述英国的乡村
3. Palmer, Hornby and other British applied linguists had prepared pedagogical descriptions of the basic grammatical structures of English, and these were to be followed in developing methodology. 帕尔默、霍恩比等英国应用语言学家已经描述了英语基本语法结构的教学法，我们在制定教学方法时应遵循这些要求。

4. The group used studies of the needs of European language learners, and in particular a preliminary document prepared by a British linguist, D.A Wilkins (1972), which proposed a functional or communicative definition of language that could serve as a basis for developing communicative syllabuses for language teaching.

该小组对欧洲语言学习者的需求进行了研究，特别是英国语言学家 D.A・威尔金斯（D.Wilkins，1972）编写的初始文献，该文献提出了语言的功能或交际定义，可以作为交际法语言教学大纲的基本原则。

5. This is not the youngest record of laughing. 还有比他更小的婴儿会笑。

拓展学习：parental age of concern 父母关注的年龄

6. They even kept physical record of some of the people they dealt with.

他们甚至记录了被拘留者的体征。

7. Hong Kong arrival 到达香港

8. autobiographical writing 写自传

9. This poem presents his heroic portrait of Satan and his heroic portraits of the fallen angles

他在这首诗中描述了撒旦及众堕落天使的英勇形象。

10. a problematic moment of revelation 揭发问题的时刻

11. The other got himself a shilling bottle of Ammoniated Quinine which was tolerably cheap considering. 另一个花了 1 先令买了一瓶阿芒奎宁，还不算贵吧。

12. You see a gradual decline in the cultural idealization of virginity.

童贞文化的理想化呈现逐渐下降趋势。

13. We also do things to them in scientific research labs that would make a Josef Mengele blush.

我们还在科学研究实验室里对动物做一些让约瑟夫・门格勒感到脸红的动物实验。（Josef Mengele，人称“死亡天使”，德国纳粹党卫队军官和奥斯威辛集中营的“医师”。）

3.2 状语译成宾语

状语译成宾语这种译法在上册已经提到。

1. We may continue to advance in our understanding. 我们就可能继续提高认识。

2. think differently 思维差异，观点不同

3. As William Empson writes convincingly and brilliantly, although mischievously, in a wonderful book called *Milton's God*.

正如威廉・艾普森雄辩妙语横生，尽管有些戏谑的书中所写的那样（《弥尔顿的上帝》）。

4. extraordinary tendency to write autobiographically 特别想写自传

5. by helping them rebuild economically 通过帮助他们重振经济

6. They were painting here ethnically with a very blunt brush.

用一只粗糙的画笔描绘出各个民族。

7. dress identically 穿着相同

8. vote differently 不同选举结果

9. speaking culturally 谈文化

10. I have done professionally. 那是我的职业。

11. We had a training October that was really attended BU.

十月我们拥有专门针对 BU 的学习安排。

12. No one writes 19th-century novels about 20th—and now 21st—century America better than Allegra Goodman, whose omniscient narrators and impeccably polished storytelling seem borrowed from an era when authors were expected to issue cool moral judgements rather than exorcise inner demons.

用 19 世纪小说笔法来讲述 20 世纪（现在是 21 世纪了）美国故事，没有人能比阿莱格拉·古德曼更拿手。她那运用多位全知式叙述人的手法和细致得无懈可击的故事行文，仿佛移植自某个旧时代，那个时代只要求作家做出冷静的道德判断，而无须驱除作家笔下人物内心中的魔障。

13. He is sitting（for）an entrance exam at Leeds University as an insurance against failure at York. 他正参加利兹大学的入学考试以备约克大学考不取。

14. I worked a few clubs and so forth. 我曾在几家俱乐部以及诸如此类的地方工作。

15. Silence accompanies the mournful sheriff as he drives his Texas highways, and silence is what hangs in the air after Chigurh raises his grotesque, sound-muffling weapon to snuff out one life and then another, cold as hell.

寂静中忧郁的警长驱车行驶在德克萨斯的公路上；而每当奇古尔举起他那怪里怪气的无声武器干掉一个又一个人后，空气中弥漫着地狱般冷酷的寂静。

16. Lumber, corn, tobacco, wheat, and furs moved downstream to the delta country; sugar, molasses, cotton, and whiskey travelled north.

木材、玉米、烟草、小麦和皮货可以顺流而下，到达河口三角洲地区，而砂糖、糖浆、棉花和威士忌酒等货物则北上。

17. Whether words can travel that path, through truth, absurdity, simplicity, to silence I do not know, nor what that path can be like. 我不知道言语是否可以通过真理、荒谬、简单、沉默穿行那条道路，也不知道那条道路是什么样子。

18. The lion paced the floor of his cage restlessly. 狮子在笼子里不安地来回走动。

19. I will wander the face of the earth. 我会在四方流浪。

20. wander through the woods 徘徊于林中

21. When rain started to become scarce around 5,500 years ago, they migrated east to the Nile Valley. 大约 5500 年前，雨水开始变得稀少，人们向东迁徙到了尼罗河谷。

22 It doesn't make strategic sense for China to depend on foreigner to communicate internationally.

从战略上说，依赖外国人与国际交流对中国不利。

3.3 汉语宾语从句转换成英语宾语

1. 当然这意味着他会失去工作。Surely this would mean the loss of his job.

2. 说起来很奇怪，这位作家非但不生气，反而承认我的批评公正中肯，并和我继续讨论对这些不足之处进行改进的办法。

Strange to say, my interlocutor, instead of getting angry, admitted the justice of my criticism and proceeded to discuss possible remedies.

3. 我永远不会忘记我初次经历爱尔兰生活以及随后的那天晚上是如何度过的。

I shall never forget my first introduction to country life in Ireland, or the manner in which I passed the evening afterwards.

4. 周围一切物质的东西，都在可怕地反复申明它们不负责任。

All material objects around announced their irresponsibility with terrible iteration.

5. 你通知了他们你想离去么?

Have you informed them of your intended departure?

6. 一封写于政府宣布其购买方案三天之前的信件

a letter written three days before the Government announced its own purchase.

7. 熙凤认为这是可能的。Xi feng considered the probalities.

8. 通过调查，我们相信计划是合理的。

Investigation assured us of the soundness of the plan.

9. 我可以证实他的话是千真万确的。

I can attest to the absolute truth of his statement.

10. 长期以来，人们从科学和文化上都认为身体的衰老是不可避免的，这些研究结果对此提出了质疑。The findings cast doubt on long-held scientific and cultural beliefs regarding the inevitability of the body's decline.

11. 我完全相信这条消息是可靠的。

I have full assurance of the reliability of the information.

12. 阐明这种需要并开发语言教学的替代方法被认为是高度优先事项。

The need to articulate and develop alternative methods of language teaching was considered a high priority.

13. 这导致他被迫辞职。It leads to his forced resignation.

14. 一些微弱和不正确的努力导致他们完全失败。

Some feeble and ill-directed efforts resulted in complete failure on their part.

第四节 状 语

本节分为两部分：定语转换成状语，状语转换成补语或宾语。

4.1 定语转换成状语

1. No doubt that was how the idea was introduced to the man with the **uneasy** knowledge that he carried a diamond worth many thousands in his jacket pocket.

无疑那人知道了自己上衣兜里装着的是一块价值好几千块钱的钻石，心里会怎样忐忑不安。

2. From the unhealthy brew of emergency funding, multiple sets of books, and **chronic** underestimates of the resources required to prosecute the war, we have been spending—and how much we will, in the end, likely to have to spend. The figure we arrive at is more than $3 trillion.

从通过非正常途径筹集的应急资金、多套不同的账簿以及对维持战争所需资源的长期低估这几个方面，我们已经尝试着确定我们已经花费了多少——和最终可能要花多少。我们所得出的数字超过了 3 万亿美元。

3. With a grin he raised an **enquiring** eyebrow at the groom.
他莞尔一笑，对着新郎抬起眉毛作询问状。

4. My heart is overcome with sadness for the **devastating** loss of my true friend Michael.
痛失我真正的好朋友迈克尔让我的心充满悲伤。

5. The findings cast doubt on **long-held** scientific and cultural beliefs regarding the inevitability of the body's decline. 长期以来，人们从科学和文化上都认为身体的衰老是不可避免的，这些研究结果对此提出了质疑。

6. That's about thirty five very rich New Yorkers and two **token**（*adj.*）historians. They have us there for window dressing.
大约请了 35 名很富有的纽约人，并象征性地请了两位历史学家。他们请我们为了装饰门面。

7. *Madame X*, a strikingly sexual portrait that Sargent considered one of his finest works, developed tiny, almost **microscopic**, bumps under her right arm and along the back of her head, the deepest blacks of the painting.
《某夫人》是一幅引人注目的性感肖像画，萨金特认为该画是他最精美的画作之一，画中夫人右臂下面和沿着头部后面鼓起来许多微小的、几乎只有用显微镜才能看到的疙瘩（画中颜色最深的黑斑）。

8. The author wants to express a **humorous** evaluation of human intelligence.
作者想用一种幽默的方式评价人类智慧。

9. When Singapore became independent in 1965 it faced an **immediate** challenge of water resources because the city-state has no groundwater. 当新加坡于 1965 年独立时，由于这个城邦之国家没有地下水，因此立刻面临着水资源的挑战。

10. have a quick breakfast　迅速地吃早饭

11. Give either a written or oral description of a picture. 口头或用文字描述一幅图。

12. The teacher models an utterance while creating a visual realization of it with the colored rods. 老师每次示范读音时都用彩色棒指着它。

13. technical definition of ageing population　人口老龄化的科学定义

14. academic presentation of ageing population　人口老龄化的学术研讨

15 Not only do you get a wonderful beginning library of classic music but in effect you get a lifetime service contract with it.
你不仅开始拥有一个很棒的古典音乐图书馆而且享受终身服务。

16. Not plant trees big, but grow them big. 不栽大树，而是让它长大。

4.2 状语转换成补语

1. The attractive force between the molecules is negligibly small.
分子间的吸引力小得可以忽略不计。

2 The number of molecules in any object we can see is unimaginably large.

我们可以看到的任何物体中的分子数量是难以想象的大。（大得难以想象）

第五节　汉语“兼语式结构”译成英语动宾结构

汉语的“兼语式结构”可译成英语的“动宾结构”“动词加介词结构”或“双宾语结构”。

1. 他想强迫她注意。He wanted to compel her attention.

类似动词: declare，prove

2. 奥德先生立刻阻止她继续讲授。

Mr. Auld promptly forbade the continuance of her instruction.

3. 我介绍他加入协会。I recommended him for membership of the association.

4. 帮助她母亲送别客人。Laura helped her mother with the good-byes.

5. 有一次，他的车坏了，我开车载他回家。

Once I gave him a lift home when his car had broken down.

6. 她最终打破了沉默，为了使自己将来再婚的可能变得顺理成章，她向他保证很长一段时间内她不会再婚，直到他能够完全独立生活。

She ultimately broke silence, **qualifying her announcement of a probable second marriage** by assuring him that it would mot take place for a long time to come, when he would be living quite independently of her.

7. 仿佛她期待他们的注视，并不在意满足他们的好奇，甚至她还直接与几个注视她的人对视。 As if she expected their glances, and did not mind gratifying their curiosity, she met the eyes of several of her observers by lifting her own.

8. 富兰克林喜欢有聪明女性作伴，因而显然两人彼此留下了深刻印象。

Franklin enjoyed the company of intelligent women, and the two evidently left impressed with each other.

9. 比正常的健康体重减少五公斤**会让你**变得美丽。

Stay a beautiful five kilos below your natural healthy weight.

10. 正因为不是大河流才让人倍感亲切。They are perhaps more intimately known for that.

11. 发报员也在徘徊，他想等着稿纸堆到一定程度好工作，但又要确保能跟上写稿人的速度。The operator also wandered about, waiting for an accumulation of pages upon which he could work but making sure to keep up with the writer.

第六节　汉语“连动式结构”的翻译

汉语的“连动式结构”可以译成英语的“动宾结构”或“动词加介词结构”。

1. 一切爱好和平的人民都**要求**全面**禁止**核武器，彻底**销毁**核武器。

All peace-loving people **demand** the complete **prohibition** and thorough **destruction** of nuclear weapons.

2. 我没有等着继续谈判，而是直接走出了房间。

I waited no further parley but immediately walked out of the room.

3. 当诺拉再次回到家中时，钢琴也带来了，是她的儿子彼得**负责搬运**的。

When Nora came home again, the piano came with her. Her son, Peter, had **arranged its removal**

4. 沃伯顿先生**点头示意**他离开。Mr. Warburton gave him a little nod of dismissal.

5. 她浸入沉思。She fell into reverie.

6. 展馆在最后一天正常运行，所有的工作者都坚守岗位，确保圆满结束。

The pavilion ran steadily on its last exhibition day. All workers are sticking to their positions, to ensure a successful end.

7. 含泪关上展馆 tearful closing of the pavilion

8. 美国环保署建议容许使用吸尘器清除汞，但必须采取一些预防措施。

EPA's recommendations allow for vacuuming, with some precautions.

9. 它并不要求一定要获得成功。It does not demand guaranteed success.

10. 欢迎品尝啤酒 enjoy welcoming beer

11. 他出国留学去了。He has **gone abroad for** further studies.

12. 她与另外两个同学**代表**她们班 13 名同学**出席**了波士顿的会议——在会上，全国独立学校协会因她们工作出色，向她们颁了奖。

She and two other students **represented** their class of 13 **at** the conference in Boston, where the team was given an award from NAIS for their work.

13. 例如，Krashen（1981）**认为提供**可理解的输入和减少压力是语言学习成功的关键，它不仅使输入可理解并使压力最小化。

Krashen（1981）, for example, **regards provision** of comprehensible input and reduction of stress as keys to successful language as a means of making input comprehensible and minimizing stress.

14. 他们**上楼来到**客房，客房之美让索菲亚羡慕不已。

They **ascended to** the guest's room, which drew Sophia's admiration for its prettiness.

15. 预言说 speak prophetically

第七节　汉语的表语译成英语的状语或定语

这里用到了“形容词名词化”“形容词副词化”。

1. 首先我能够说的是，那种要把喝的东西带上飞机的需要是可以理解。

What is within my competence to dispute is the perceived need for carrying drinks into aeroplanes.（译成定语）

2. 把“时间不够”作为没有完成某事的理由是不可接受的。

I suggest “not enough time” is not an acceptable explanation of not getting something done.

3. 帕克尔泰夫人对这一发现感到恼怒，这是有情可原的。

Mrs. Packletide was pardonably annoyed at the discovery.（译成英语状语）

4. 再试一次是可行的/明智的。Hence the advisability of trying again.

5. 我认为我成为领导有点意外。I think I myself is a bit of accidental leader.

拓展学习：accidental elected official 意外当选的官员

6. Asher 认为需要注意的不仅是世界语言的意义，还有其结构的细微之处。

Asher sees a need for attention to both the global meaning of language as well as to the finer details of its organization.

7. 他又快乐起来。He felt a happy man again.

8. 你可以说那是偶然。You also say that occasionally.

9. 河流下游的情况是多种多样的。

The lower stretches of rivers show considerable variety.（宾语）

10. 例如，许多社会群体都认为在单位里工作职责与人际关系是重要的，但是不同的社会群体对两者的重要性排序是不一样的。

For example, many societies value the importance of the duty of work and human relationship in a workplace, but different society will put these two factors in a different order.

第九章 汉式英语例句修改

中国学生在写英语作文时，分不清汉式英语与地道英语，原因是汉式英语与地道英语之间既有差别，也有一些相同之处。加上老师在批改作文时，只是关注学生的语法错误，很少指出中国式英语并给出修改的建议，这就导致学生不会用英语思维模式组织英语单词。

第一节 汉式英语与地道英语对比

下面这些句型选自蔡基刚的《英汉写作对比研究》，句型 a 是中国学生写作中的句型，句型 b 是修改后的句型。通过这种对比，学习者可以揣摩汉式英语与地道英语的区别。

1. a）Most Chinese people had a strong anti-rural attitude, for in their minds, countryside is a place where people are poor.

b）A strong anti-rural attitude runs through the mainstream of Chinese mentality because of the association of the countryside with poverty.

句型 b）运用了非人称主语和动词名物化，把句型 a）中的两个句子合成一个简单句。

2. a）The mayor said that he was very grateful because the construction workers were very dedicated and competent.

b）The mayor expressed his appreciation of the dedication and competence of the construction workers.

句型 b）运用了动词名物化，并使用了形容词性物主代词“his”作逻辑主语，把复合句 a）变成简单句 b）。

3. a）This incident helps me to understand the nature of human beings deeply.

b）This incident deepens my understanding of the nature of human beings.

句型 b）通过动词的替换，把原先的宾补结构改为动宾结构，从而使句子变得简洁。

4. a）The first step is to make people all realize that smoking has a harmful effect on them.

b）The first step is the common realization of the harmful effects of smoking.

句型 b）通过动词的名物化，把句型 a）中的使役结构，转变为名词短语，并使用了形容词“common”作逻辑主语，从而压缩了句型。

5. a）I am very glad that he will accompany me to travel on the long journey.

b）I am very glad of his company on the long journey.

句型 b）通过动词的名物化，把句型 a）中的宾语从句变为名词短语，同时使用形容词性物主代词“his”作逻辑主语。

6. a）We all see that it is very necessary to revise our education system.

b）We all see the necessity of the revision of our education system.

句型 b）通过使用形容词和动词的名物化，把句型 a）中的宾语从句变为宾语。

7. a）When I become a college student, the whole family felt proud of me and even the whole village talked about me.

b）As a college student, I become the pride of the family and even the talk of the village.

把句型 a）中的从句变为一个短语，通过形容词“proud”的名物化，改变主句人称主语，从而把并列主句合为一个简单句。

8. a）In economic development, we must control our population, conserve our natural resources and protect our environment.

如知道“give an priority to”或“attach much importance to“这个搭配

b）Great importance must be attached to population control, the conservation of resources and environment protection in economic growth.

句型 b）使用了被动结构，去掉了人称主语；动词名物化的使用，改变了汉语中动词连用的现象。

9. a）We always believe that the social systems of two sides of the Straits shall not prevent the fact that we can contact and cooperate.

b）We always believe that the social systems of two sides of the Straits shall not be an obstacle to our contact and cooperation.

通过动词名物化的使用，去掉句型 a）中的动同位语从句。

第二节 汉语复合句与英语简单句转换

汉语中习惯使用复合句或一些短句子，受这种思维模式影响，学生在英语写作中习惯使用英语复合句或一些短句，使整篇文章看起来汉式英语味很浓。如果想把汉语复合句变成英语简单句，首先要学会把短句压缩成一个短语，可以通过以下几种方式：非谓语动词、副词、同位语、动词及形容词的名物化等。

2.1 分 词

分词包括现在分词和过去分词，关于它们的使用，在前面已经详细探讨过，这里只是介绍在写作中如何运用。

1. a）Yet all of history has taught us that if we deny these ulitmates and place man or state at the core of the universe, the result is that everyone will become selfish. That will paralyze everything. The first signs of it are already evident, and this is really frightening.

b）Yet all of history has taught us that the denial of these ultimates, the placement of man or state at the core of the universe, results in a paralyzing mass selfishness; and the first signs of it are already frighteningly evident.

a）的写法，汉语味较重，因为所用的句法单位级别基本和中文句法单位级别相同：

如果我们否认这些基本原理，把个人或国家置于宇宙的中心……

the denial of these ultimates, the placement of man or state at the core of the universe…（通过动词“名物化”的使用把汉语条件状语从句变成一个名词短语）

The result is that everyone will become selfish.

其结果是大家就会变得自私自利。这使一切都处于瘫痪。

results in a paralyzing mass selfishness（通过现在分词和形容词的“名物化”，把汉语的两句话压缩成一个动宾短语）

这方面表现出来的迹象已经十分明显，达到了十分怕人的地步。

and the first signs of it are already frighteningly evident.（通过使用“副词加形容词”结构，把汉语的两句话压缩成一句）

2. 他猛然倒在一把椅子上，椅子被压得吱吱响。

由于受汉语句法的影响，学生在英语写作中首先想到的是句子。因此上面的句子可翻译成：

a）He crashed down on a chair which produced a protesting sound.

而英语可能只用一个分词：

b）He crashed down on a protesting chair.

3.在我们学校里这一点表现为：教鞭消失了，心理老师出现了。

a）In our schools this is reflected by the fact the stick has vanished and the psychiatrist has emerged.

b）In our schools this is reflected by the vanishing stick and the emerging psychiatrist.

4.允许美国战俘接受红十字会的食品包裹，允许他们写信，但要经过审查。

a）American prisoners are permitted to receive Red Cross food parcels and write letters which must be censored.

b）American prisoners are permitted to receive Red Cross food parcels and write censored letters.

2.2 同 位 语

使用同位语化繁为简。

1. 打工能帮助我们接触社会。这是学习知识的另一个方法。

a）Doing part-time jobs can help us contact with society. This is another way of to get knowledge.

b）Doing part-time jobs can help us contact with society, an alternative way to get knowledge.

2. Soon I would be on my own, making my own decisions, doing what I wanted without someone looking over my shoulder and it meant going to school with boys—a welcome change coming from all-girl school.

2.3 副 词

运用形容词或名词副词化技巧，把短语或句子副词化，有时用到转移修饰法。

1. 他在讨论会上沉默不语，这不是他的个性。

He was uncharacteristically quiet at the discussion.

2. 理想的做法是，将浪漫编织在爱的关系中，而不时重温是一种表达爱意和承诺的最好方法。

Ideally, romance will be woven through a loving relationship. And reviving it now and then is an excellent way to express affection and commitment.

3. 从海岸线延伸入海数英里至数百英里不等，是坡度徐缓的大陆架斜坡。就地质上来说，它属于大陆的一部分。

From the shore-line out to a distance which may be anywhere from a few miles to few hundred miles runs the gentle slope of the continental shelf, geologically part of the continents.（L. G. Alexander *Fluency in English*）

4. 大概四川人好久没有看到过外国人了，所以我游泳时，旁边来了一大群好奇的观众。而单凭我的游泳技术，是不配引来这么多人来看的。

So I swam, presumably because of the long distance of foreigners from Sichuan, before an undeservedly large and enthusiastic audience.

5. 不吸烟者要求政府采取行动禁止公共场合吸烟，是完全有道理的。

Nonsmokers justifiably urge the government to take action to ban public smoking.

6. 当时，友谊商店只对外宾开放，中国人不能进。

At that time the friendship store was open to foreign visitors, not to Chinese customers.

At that time the friendship store was exclusively open to foreign visitors.

拓展学习：in an exclusive interview with *China Daily* 《中国日报》独家采访

7. 他对自己所取得的成绩充满了自豪，这不是没有道理的。

He is proud of his achievements, which is justifiable.

He is justifiably proud of his achievements.

8. 学纯正英语，做国际人才。

Learn Genuine English. Be an International Talent.

Change to: Speak Bilingually, Think Globally.

2.4 运用名词结构

一个名词或名词短语往往可以表示一个句子的意思。在英语中，句子包括从句一定要有主、谓、宾，其中主要成分一般不能省略。而用了名词结构，它的一些成分就可以省掉，使行文更紧凑。R.Quirk 在《英语句法大全》中举了一个例子：

a）Lanzarotti was disappointed by the fact the reviewers criticized his play in a hostile manner.

b）Lanzarotti was disappointed by the reviewers' hostile criticism of his play.

c）Lanzarotti was disappointed by the reviewers' hostile criticism.

这个例子说明名词词组是一种简练的语言形式，运用名词结构，可以省掉前文说到的"his play"，而句子结构不能省，结果名词短语起到了句子的作用。

2. 他每天花三小时看体育节目。他把心思都放在体育上，这对他的学习是有妨碍的。

a）He spent nearly 3 hours on watching sports events. The fact that he was completely absorbed in sport interfered with his studies.

b）He spent nearly 3 hours on watching sports events. His complete absorption interfered with his studies.

在上句已说到 sport 的情况下，要在这句中避免重复 sport, a）句的句法是不允许的。而 b）句可以，这样为句子压缩为词组创造了条件。

3. 我的观点是，一代人经常去抱怨他们下一代人，这是不可避免的。

a）My point is that one generation frequently complains about the one that immediately follows it, which is inevitable.

b）My point is that the frequent complaint of one generation about the one immediately following it is inevitable.

4. 孩子们看到这个菜就眉开眼笑，可知他们是难得吃这种菜的。

a）The children are delighted when they saw the dish. It showed that it was a rarity.

b）The delight of the children at the sight of the dish showed that it was a rarity.

5. 违反这些规则，将会被吊销执照。

Disregard for these rules will result in revoking of the licenses.

6. 我从未忘记第一次在我的花园里看到一只蜂鸟时的那种心跳的感觉——一只披着炫目的羽、小得令人难以置信的生灵正勇敢地在花丛中飞来飞去。

The thrill of seeing my first hummingbird in my garden has never left me—the sight of seeing this unbelievably tiny creature with dazzling plumage flitting boldly from flower to flower.

第三节 英语简单句拆成汉语复合句

对于英语中的简单句，翻译成汉语时，往往需要"解压缩"，把英语的简单句译成汉语复合句或几个短句；而汉语中的几个短句子或复合句翻译成英语时，一般需要压缩，译成简单句。

1. Footsteps announced his return. 听见脚步声，知道他回来了。

2. The sight of a tailor-shop gave me a sharp longing to shed my rags, and to clothe myself decently once more. 我一看到一家服装店，心里就起了一阵强烈的愿望，很想扔掉这身褴褛的衣服，重新穿得像个样子。

3. I am very sorry that the pressure of other occupations has prevented me from sending an earlier reply to your letter. 我因为近来忙于各种事务，未能早些复信，深感抱歉。

4. His presence would have added only another and needless agony to the last moment of the dying man.（Nathaniel Hawthorne）

他若在场，也只是给垂死的人在临终时刻多添一阵不必要的痛苦。

5. A lack of information and formal educational training had left many persons without any generalized standards of judgment applicable to this novel situation.

由于许多人消息不灵通，或者由于没有受过正规的教育训练，因此不能用一般的判断标准去判断这种新奇的现象。

6. My total ignorance of the connection must plead my apology.（J. Austen）

恕我孤陋寡闻，对此关系一无所知。

7. The combination of this Oriental city's geography and the absence of import taxes has long made Hong Kong the ideal storehouse for transit goods to and from Asia.

由于香港地理位置优越，加上免征各种进口税，这个东方城市长期以来成了各种进出亚洲货物的理想的中转储运基地。

8. The knowledge of this nuclear fission process has made it possible to use uranium as fuel to obtain nuclear energy.

由于人们知道了这种核裂变过程，（人们）就有可能用铀作为燃料来取得核能。

9 A little flattery will fetch him. 稍一奉承就会把他迷惑住了。

10. To accept this position would involve my living in London.

如果我接受这个职位，我就必须住在伦敦。

11. Our mastery of the behavior of objects requires a study of motions.
为了掌握物体的性能，我们需要研究物体的各种运动。

12. The development of an economical artificial heart is only a few transient failures away.
只需要再经过几次失败，就能造出价格低廉的人工心脏了。

13. The sight of the orphan always reminds me of her parents.
一看到那孤儿，我便想起她的母亲。

14. My mind goes reeling down dark corridors teeming with agonizing flashbacks, and a chill from within fills me with dread.（Nancy Rigging）
我思绪万千，恍恍惚惚进入了一条条幽暗的通道，回忆起许许多多的往事。心里一阵凄凉，不禁感到毛骨悚然。

15. Jane's kindly and gentle nature could not but revolt at her sister's callous behavior.
珍妮心地善良、性情温和，对她妹妹这种没心肝的行为实在看不顺眼。

16. The happiness—the superior advantages of the young women round about her, gave Rebecca inexpressible pangs of envy.（*Vanity Fair*）
丽贝卡看见她周围的小姐那么福气，享受种种权利，却有说不出的眼红。

17. The satisfaction of Miss Bennet's mind gave such a glow of sweet animation to her face.
贝内特小姐心满意足，不禁桃腮泛晕，流露出一丝激动的神情来。

18. Controlled rural urbanization gives farmers a taste of the good life.
控制农村城镇化让农民尝到生活的甜头。

19. Its gleaming sands and backdrop of pinewoods and distant hills lend it a pleasant and restful atmosphere. 这儿沙滩闪烁，松林掩映，远山连绵，自有一种心旷神怡的气氛。

20. The abuse of basic human rights in their own country in violation of the agreement reached at Helsinki has earned them the condemnation of freedom-loving people everywhere.
他们违反在赫尔辛基达成的协议，在国内侵犯基本人权，这已受到各地热爱自由的人们的谴责。

21. You can believe that I have worked that moment over and over again, in a sad attempt to send time back and resolve the event in a less tragic way.
真的，我一次又一次地回忆当时的情景，带着忧伤的心情，想把时间倒转回去，以求用一种不那么悲惨的方式来处理这个意外的情况。

22. My two great isolating experiences have given me an almost mystical sense of identity with all the suffering humanity. 我有过两次不同场合的重要经历，这使我产生了一种几乎带有神秘色彩的同情心而站在一切受苦的人一边。

23. The sound of the waves brought to her mind the sunny summers of her childhood.
听到这些波浪声，她想起了童年时阳光明媚的夏天。

24. The proximity of involuntary and enforced death was what weighed upon him now.
随着不情愿的、强制性的死亡的临近，他现在心情沉重。

25. I had unforgivably, in a stealthy manner, peeped at her correspondence.（*Rebecca*）
我偷偷摸摸地看她的信，这实在是难以宽恕的行为。

26. The sailors swarmed into a laughing, cheering ring around the two men.
水兵们欢欢笑笑，蜂拥而至，把这两个人围了起来。

27. All this time our poor bewildered families had been kept in secret at Brioni.
整整这段时间，我们可怜的家属，一直被秘密地留在布里俄尼，不知所措。

28. Over the years, the inability of patients and others to believe that I am a doctor has left me utterly demoralized.
多年来，（由于）病人和其他人都无法相信我是一名医生，这使我彻底心灰意冷了。

第四节 英语中的主语省略现象

省略是为了避免重复，突出新信息，并使上下文紧密连接的一种语法修辞手段。在对话中，交谈双方都知道谈论的对象，则可以省略句子的主语，这一点与汉语有相通之处。

1. Skin-like immaculateness had grown over Soames（整洁干净已逐渐成为 Soames 的癖性），as over many Londoners; impossible to conceive of him with a hair out of place.
他逐渐变得像许多伦敦人一样，一定要做到无疵可击；你决不可能想象他有一根头发弄乱。

2. Sounds like a good idea.

3. This way, please.

第十章 与汉语思维顺序不同的结构

按照英语语法，英语修饰语的词序是：限定词 评价 体积 形状 条件 年龄 颜色 本质 名词，如：“a/n ugly big round chipped old blue French vase”。而汉语的修饰语则不同。它习惯上把表明事物本质的修饰语放在前面，然后才是评价、体积、形状、条件、年龄等。

限定词主要包括：冠词、指示代词、不定代词、所有格、数量词。

评价分为：1. 主观判断（Epithet 性质特征），2. 客观描述（大小、形状、新旧、颜色）。

分类性：1. 来源（German /Chinese），2. 物质（gold, brick），3.（动）名词。

1. a very valuable old German gold watch
2. a famous German medical college
3. five previous nights 之前的五个晚上
4. north London house 伦敦北部的房子
5. southeast 东南
6. South China 中国南部
7. two remaining ones 剩下的两个
8. remaining few weeks 剩下的几周
9. one last question 最后一个问题
10. ten next days 再过十天
11. at dawn the next morning 次日早上拂晓时分
12. a list of his arguments 他的论点清单
13. central Thai province 泰国中部省份
14. Central China’s Hunan province 中国中部湖南省
15. on the top left 左上部
16. inner left thigh 左大腿内侧
17. upper right-hand corner 右上角
18. upper class Chinese girls 中国上流社会女孩
19. in the upper ranks of society 在上流社会里
20. upper middle class family 中上阶层家庭
21. upper middle income 中上收入
22. ancient Chinese poets 中国古代诗人
23. one November afternoon 十一月的一个下午
24. The Royal Swedish Academy of Sciences 瑞典皇家科学院
25. Air France 法航
26. Winners of the 2007 Nobel Prize in Physics 2007 年诺贝尔物理奖获得者
27. I live in the real world 24/7.
我生活在一周七天、一天 24 小时的现实世界里。
28. according to a preliminary Coast Guard investigation 据海岸警卫队初步调查

29. former Virginia governor 弗吉尼亚前州长
30. early one morning 一天早上
31. early in the morning 清早
32. miss their bus home 没赶上回家的班车
33. On his road home Simpson in his car would meet Hale in his.
在辛普森开车回家的路上碰到黑尔开着自己的车。
34. in high northern latitudes 在北部高纬度地区
35. for constant easy reference 为了方便经常查阅
36. in the entire previous history 以前的所有历史
37. a dozen other cities 其他 12 个城市
38. other American city 美国其他城市
39. stretch out both her arms 伸出她的双手
40. a neat new pocket-book 一本整洁的新口袋书
41. about half a mile south of the courthouse 在法院以南约半英里处
42. a mile and a half south of the village of Concord 在康科德村南部一英里半处
43. Ten years later, he won the first two golds in rapid-fire pistol—after teaching himself to shoot left-handed.
10 年后，他在自学用左手射击后，首次获得了奥运速射手枪射击比赛的两枚金牌。
44. Phrase I training 第一阶段培训
45. The night of 18 June 1815 was one to remember.
1815 年 6 月 18 日晚是个值得记住的日子。
46. in the early part of the 19th century 十九世纪初
47. in the latter half of 1863 在 1863 年下半年
48. a long classical poem 古典长诗
49. Nobel Prize of mathematics 数学界的诺贝尔奖
50. major western economies 西方主要经济体
51. collaberative regional initiative 区域协作计划
52. per capita global emission 世界人均排放量
53. sensuous human activity 人类感官活动
54. Novartis China 中国诺华
55. less than 25 percent of the average global level 不到全球平均水平的 25%
56. average monthly salary 平均月薪
57. in the mid and long term 中长期
58. I participated in joint U.S-China study of urban land reform.
我参与了中美城市土地改革联合研究。
59. She needed one last thing for her trip. 她的旅行还需要准备最后一样东西。
60. After a tempestuous two-month voyage they landed at what is now Plymouth, Massachusetts, in icy November.
在海上颠簸航行两个月后，他们在冰天雪地的十一月登陆于今天的马萨诸塞州的普利茅斯。
61. Our basic five senses are seeing, hearing, taste, touch and smell. The five basic verbs

referring to the senses are usually followed by an adjective rather than an adverb.

我们五种基本感觉是：看、听、尝、触和闻。指五种感觉的动词后面通常跟形容词，而不跟副词。

62. Shops with names such as Dancing Wolves, Wolf Zone and Temptation of Wolves could be found just meters away from each other on streets in central Jinjiang.

在晋江市中心的大街上，可以看到诸如与狼共舞（Dancing Wolves）、狼道（Wolf Zone）和狼的诱惑（Temptation of Wolves）等名称的商店，彼此相隔仅几米远。

63. Was central London really carpeted with flowers?

伦敦市中心是不是真的都让鲜花淹没了？

64. nestled in north-central Italy/west-central Italy 位于意大利中北部/中西部

65. central northern Germany　德国中北部

66. Poor Pluto is crowded by thousands of other icy bodies in the outer solar system, some bigger than Pluto itself, so it fails the test.

在太阳系的外围，可怜的冥王星和成千上万颗冰冷的天体挤在一起。

67. The best-known television advertisement in the land of the maple leaf is a 2000 Molson beer commercial that emphasizes the differences between Canada and its large southern neighbour.

这个枫叶之国最著名的一条电视广告是2000年莫尔森啤酒公司的一则商业广告，该广告强调了加拿大和它那个国土广阔的南部近邻的不同。

68. Time off is generous. 休息时间十分充裕。

69. Millions of the middle-class retired continue working at everything from lucrative consultancies to teaching literacy or finally finishing that PhD.

数以百万计的中产阶级退休人员继续工作，从利润丰厚的咨询服务到教学素养等方面，或者最终完成博士学习。

70. a syllabus for the teaching of English at the upper secondary level in Malaysia

马来西亚中高级英语教学大纲

71. I can still remember the day I opened up *USA Today*.

我还记得这一天，我翻开《今日美国》。

72. The old hands only take large and medium-size first class sedan cars such as Benz, Lincoln and BMW. 老手们只要大中型高级轿车，如奔驰、林肯、宝马。

73. the lives of middle-and lower-class Cairenes 开罗中产阶级和下层人民的生活

74. in elementary-to advanced-level classes　从初级班到高级班

75. This is already starting small business but medium and large enterprises will start to adopt Google within 10 years.

小公司已经开始采取行动，而大中型企业也将纷纷在10年内采用谷歌的新技术。

76. Focusing on the lower and middle end—with some famous designer names also in the rack—has meant Bangladesh has withstood changing global fashions.

集中在中低端——还有一些着名设计师的名字也在机架上——这意味着孟加拉国经受了不断变化的全球时尚。

77. The cost of direct US military operations—not even including long-term costs such as

taking care of wounded veterans—already exceeds the cost of the 12-year war in Vietnam and is more than double the cost of the Korean War.

美国直接军事行动的开销——甚至都不包括像料理伤退老兵抚恤事宜这样的长期费用——也已经超过了 12 年越南战争的开销，而且比朝鲜战争开销的两倍还多。

78. Insurers estimate that the costs of rebuilding would range between double and triple the amount of the annual California state budget.

保险公司估计，灾后重建所需的费用会是加州年预算的 2 倍至 3 倍。

79. Just ask Ford or Gap, which lost 19% and 15% of their brand value, respectively, in this year's *Business Week*/Interbrand annual ranking of the **100 Best Global Brands**.

在今年的《商业周刊》/Interbrand 年度全球百大品牌排行榜上，这两家公司的品牌价值分别降低了 19%和 15%。

80. Some 396 people died on Ireland's roads in 2005, a four-year high.

大约有 396 人死于道路交通事故，是 4 年以来新高。

81. She has wrapped the drama *Becoming Jane*, in which she plays a young and in-love Jane Austen. And, she had costarred in "*The Devil Wears Prada*", an adaptation of former *Vogue* employee Lauren Weisberger's 2003 novel.

她参演的电影《成为简》已经杀青，她在这部电影里扮演恋爱中年轻的简。她还是此前《穿普拉达的女王》（又译《时尚女魔头》）一片的主角之一，该片改编自《时尚》杂志的前雇员劳伦·维斯贝格尔 2003 年出版的小说。

82. The obscurity of Can Fables seems odd since the restaurant is one of only four in Spain to have earned three Michelin stars and routinely draws an international clientele.

"康·法贝斯"餐馆这么低调似乎有些奇怪，因为西班牙只有 4 家获得了米其林三星的餐馆，而它就是其中之一，经常有食客从世界各地慕名而来。

83. Andrew Young, a former US ambassador to the United Nations and a close friend of the King family, told reporters she died in California.

前美国驻联合国大使安德鲁·杨是金家族的一位亲密朋友，她告诉记者，金夫人在加利福尼亚去世。

84. MBA student, Svetlana Novoseltsev, a 30-year-old former investment banker who is studying at Judge Business School, in Cambridge.

今年 30 岁、之前做过投资银行家的斯维特兰娜·诺沃谢莉采娃目前在剑桥的佳奇商学院读 MBA。

85. The rise of domestic Chinese consumer brands to challenge their famous foreign counterparts has become a defining trend in China's industrial development.

中国本土消费品牌日益崛起，对外国名牌构成挑战，已经成为中国工业发展的一个标志性趋势。

86. a local Jinjiang company which raised HK$1.06bn（US$136m）in November through a Hong Kong stockmarket listing

一家晋江本土公司中国利郎（China Lilang），于今年 11 月在香港上市，融资 10.6 亿港元（合 1.37 亿美元）。

87. He looks like a macabre Tim Burton puppet and is voiced by Peter O'Toole, who lends

dramatic oomph to lines like "If I don't love it, I don't swallow!"

尹果看上去就像蒂姆·伯顿影片中令人毛骨悚然的木偶，由彼得·奥图尔配音，他在处理像"我要是不爱吃，就绝不下咽！"这样的台词时，赋予了极大的热情。

88. Judo is a traditional Japanese wrestling sport. 柔道是日本传统的摔跤运动。

89. a well-known contemporary Chinese writer and scholar 中国当代着名作家和学者

90. Shipping is also a significant British success story.

海运业也是英国的一部重要的成功史。

91. Savon also dominated the heavyweight class at three consecutive Olympics（1992—2000）then added six world championship titles to his Olympic hat trick.

萨文也是连续 3 届垄断了奥运会重量级拳击项目金牌（1992—2000），接着又给他的奥运三连冠的成绩增加了 6 项世界冠军的头衔。

92. This perhaps explains why a list of the 100 top British intellectuals, in *Prospect*, caused such a flutter among men and women of letters: those on the list are uncertain whether to be flattered or aggrieved; and those left off it, even more so.

这也许可以解释《展望》杂志推出的"百名顶尖英国知识分子"排行榜为什么会在文学界的男男女女中引起这么大的骚动：上榜的人拿不准这是奉承还是诋毁；落榜者呢，就更难说了。

93. The Audi brand has long suffered in comparison with its more prestigious German rivals.

奥迪品牌与其他更负盛誉的德国汽车品牌相比一直并不尽如人意。

94. Kaverts dropped under the table, and the stool struck the grass inner wall of the room.

凯尔茨倒在了桌下，凳子砸到了房屋的草墙内侧。

95. The biggest was magnitude 6.9 in 1989 in the mountains south of San Francisco.

最大级别的地震是 6.9 级，1989 年发生在在旧金山南部山脉。

96. Today's Cairene peddler is more likely to hawk **cheap imitation Rolexes and pirated DVDs**, but the same frantic spirit for entrepreneurship remains. They are adroit entrepreneurs and have perfected the skill of bargaining to an art form.

尽管今天开罗的小商贩更可能兜售**仿制的廉价劳力士手表和盗版 DVD 光盘**。他们是精明的实业家，讨价还价的本事已达到炉火纯青的地步。

97. The research report was published in the prestigious US journal *Science*.

该研究报告发表在颇负声望的美国杂志《科学》上。

98. China had proven its mettle four years earlier by becoming only the third member of the elite club of nations capable of flying humans in space.

中国在四年前成为了能够实施载人航天飞行的精英国家俱乐部仅有的第三个成员，以此证明了自己的奋斗精神。

99. On day seven we were safely past the Grand Banks and well ahead of schedule.

第七天，我们安全通过了大浅滩，比预计时间提前了许多。

100. The precious few tales of a painful past are what inspired Wilder to help found the United States National Slavery Museum, a $ 200 million project opening late this year in Fredricksburg, Va.

正是这仅有的一些关于痛苦的过去的宝贵故事启发了怀尔德协助创立了美国国立奴隶博

物馆，这个工程耗资 2 亿美元建成，今年晚些时候在弗吉尼亚弗雷德里克馆开馆。

101. Wrong. According to the 2003 World Robotics Survey produced by the United Nations.
根据 2003 年联合国的“世界机器人技术调查”而论，这个说法错了。

102. “I am hard pressed to think of any other technology that has been such a success so quickly,” says Barry Engle, president of Ford Brazil.
巴西福特公司总裁巴里·恩格尔说：“我真很难想象有另外哪种技术能这么快就取得了这么大的成功。”

103. But expensive gas, changing tastes, and trendy new offerings like the Yaris and Versa will probably drive that up. 但高昂的油价、消费品位的转变以及像威姿和骐达这样的流行新款车型很可能会使这一数字提高。

104. Coached by former Major League Baseball manager Jim Lefebvre, Team China is looking to make an impression on its Olympic debut.
由美国职业棒球大联盟前经理吉姆·拉斐尔执教的中国棒球队正期盼在北京奥运会上首次亮相时能给人们留下深刻的印象。

105. “Ultimately, an illusion only takes place in the minds of the audience,” says master illusion designer Jim Steinmeyer.
幻术设计大师吉姆·史泰因迈尔说：“说到底，幻觉只会发生在观众的意识里。”

106. In a recent German study, subjects taking three probiotics found that their colds were shorter and less severe.
在德国最近的一项研究中，服用了 3 种益生菌受试者们发现，他们患感冒的时间比以前短了。

107. We need more than pleasure to live the best possible life.
为了过上可能的最好生活，我们所需要的不仅仅是愉悦的感受。

108. Several such stories emerged in this year’s ranking, which is compiled in partnership with leading global brand consultant Interbrand Corp. and calculates brand value by using publicly available data, projected profits, and such variables as market leadership.
本年度排行榜中就出现了这样几家品牌复兴的企业，这个排行是全球领先的品牌咨询公司 Interbrand 合作编制的，用公开的可用数据、预期利润以及像市场领先度这样的变量值来计算品牌价值。

第十一章　与汉语思维模式一致的结构

由于人类同处一个地球上，各民族面对的自然环境既有差异也有相同的地方，因此各民族思维模式既有差异也有一致之处。当然也有现代汉语欧化的影响，或有些表达法本来就是外来语，久而久之成了汉语的一部分。下面是一些与汉语思维模式趋同的表达法。

1. There is no turning back.　没有回头路。

2. Overnight, the restaurant **turns hot**. But can Remy and Linguini triumph over the evil **head chef**, a sawed-off Napoleonic control freak（Ian Holm）?

一夜之间，餐馆火爆。但是雷米和林圭尼能击败那个可恶的主厨，一个专横跋扈的矮个怪人（由伊恩·霍尔姆配音）吗？

3. while his own country was racked by Japan and, finally, civil war, Qian became a **star pupil** of the director of Caltech's Guggenheim Aeronautical Laboratory, the Hungarian-American engineer and physicist Theodore von Karma. 当时他的祖国遭受日本人的蹂躏，后来又发生了内战，而这个时期，钱成为加利福尼亚理工学院古根海姆航空实验室主任、美籍匈牙利工程师和物理学家西奥多·冯·卡门的得意门生。

4. **Representative John Lewis**, a Democratic congressman from Georgia and civil rights leader, said her death was a "very sad hour". 来自佐治亚州的众议员约翰·刘易斯是民主党国会议员和民权运动的领导人，他说她的去世是"一个非常令人悲伤的时刻"。

5. the prevailing public opinion　主流民意

6. postdoctoral research associate　博士后研究伙伴

7. If there's the slightest suspicion about the death, he'll be the Number One suspect.

如果对死亡有丝毫怀疑，他将成为头号嫌犯。

8. the world number-two carmaker's head of research and development

世界第二大汽车制造商的研发首脑

9. That's the conclusion of a recent report in the online journal *Science Express*.

这是网上杂志《科学快报》中最近一篇报告的结论。

10. Cormac McCarthy's marvelous, throat-gripping, best-selling 2005 novel **of the same name** describes a contemporary American West（the action is set in 1980）where drug trafficking dirties the parched, wide-open landscape that was once home to cattle rustling.

科马克·麦卡锡2005年出版的这部精彩绝伦、引人入胜的**同名**畅销小说描写了当代美国（背景设定在1980年）西部的生活，这片曾是放牧盗牛发源地的广袤热土如今被毒品交易所玷污。

11. Too beautiful to be a character actress, she had no interest in traditional leading-lady roles（i.e., wives and girlfriends）. And her marriage to Kenneth Branagh had made her too famous to exist in the margin.

过于漂亮的容貌使她不适合做一个性格演员，她对传统的女主角角色（即妻子和女友）不感兴趣。而她与肯尼斯·布拉那格的婚姻使她名噪环宇，无法再处于配角地位。

12. MMUBS student Lynn Hughes agrees.
曼彻斯特城市大学商学院学生林恩·休斯表示赞同。

13. It was her company's annual picnic, and he **walked her home**.
那是她公司一年一度的野餐聚会，之后他步行送她回家。

14. *Geophysical Research Letters*（GRL）《地球物理研究通讯》

15. In a *China Daily* article in 2004, Keino bemoaned the attitude of the present day athletes, calling them too selfish. 在 2004 年《中国日报》的一篇文章中，凯诺对当今运动员的心态表示了遗憾，认为他们太自私了。

16. "People have become so selfish that even in daily life the phrase national development is slowly but surely being replaced by personal development," he said.　他说："人们变得这么自私，就连'国家发展'这个词儿在日常生活中都显然被'个人发展'逐渐取代了。"

17. with a history rich in heroes dating back to former world champion
历史上英雄辈出，可追溯到前世界冠军

18. break down the achievement 各个击破（目标分解）

19. Ralph Weyler, the management board member in charge of global sales and marketing, credits a plan put in place 20 years ago to make "bold technological and design statements".
负责全球销售和市场营销的董事会成员拉尔夫·魏勒把成绩归功于 20 年前实施的一项打造"大胆鲜明的技术和设计主张"计划。

20. Israel's hawkish Prime Minister-designate Benjamin Netanyahu met with his moderate rival.
以色列鹰派总理内塔尼亚胡当天会见了温和的对手。

21. Currently, China can only produce less than 30 percent of its annual domestic soybean consumption.

22. **News anchor Tom Brokaw** recently held a bottle up to the camera.
新闻节目主持人汤姆·布罗考就把一个瓶子举到镜头前说。

23. an imitation sub-machine gun 一把仿制的冲锋枪

24. These frigid, starkly beautiful mountains of floating ice turn out to be bubbling **hot spots** of biological activity.
这些寒气逼人、十分美丽的浮动冰山最终会成为生物活动的极为热门场所。

25. I suspect **this is because** their men like to be constantly listened to, and a whopping pair of diamond-drop earrings draws attention to one's good-listener equipment.
我猜想**这是因为**，她们的男人喜欢别人总是对自己洗耳恭听，而一副大得出奇的砖石吊坠耳环可将注意力引向自己那善于倾听的耳朵。

26. See a ghost. 见鬼了。

27. You meet Buddha. 送你上西天。

28. Coming up next is a man who... 接下来这位是……

29. An ethic of don't talk about family business outside the family. 家丑不可外扬。

30. First impression are firmly entrenched. 先入为主。

31. I have no illusion. 不抱幻想。

32. Don't need to fire a shot. 不需要放一枪一炮。

33. exaggeration wind　浮夸风

34. Fail and come back. 东山再起。

35. The marriage blows up. 婚姻吹了。

36. The report is partially ritualistic. 报告部分是形式化的。

37. Arising water raises all boats. 水涨船高

38. To pour new wine into old wine skins. 旧瓶装新酒。

39. Wagner does turn our emotions one hundred eighty degrees at this point.
在这一点上，瓦格纳确实让我们的感情发生了180度的转变。

40. to make this hundred-eighty turn 180度大转变

41. It's a sea change. 180度大转变。

42. From each according to his abilities, to each accroding to his needs.
各尽所能，按需分配。

43. This clock doesn't go. 这钟不走了。

44. Is your watch going? 你的表在走么?

45. I like to stay up until midnight or even later on my natural clock.
我很喜欢熬夜，一直到午夜或者更晚，这是我的生物钟。

46. Go to sleep. 去睡觉。

47. I am a night owl. 我是一个夜猫子。

48.This memento also had significance in my career.
这个纪念品也在我的职业生涯中有意义。

49. Everything goes black in front of my eyes. 我的眼前一黑。

50. If I hadn't seen it with my own two eyes and heard it with my own two ears, I would not have believed it. 如果我不是亲眼看到并亲耳听到，我不会相信的。

51. It's like trying to find a needle in a needle track. 大海捞针。

52. a needle in a haystack 大海捞针

53. She left town, no goodbye, no nothing. 不辞而别，什么都没留。

54. Virtue is always rewarded and evil punished. 善有善报，恶有恶报。

55. the captain of an empty ship 光杆司令

56. Fight fire with fire. 以毒攻毒。

57. New song, same dance. 换汤不换药。

58. I broke out all over in a cold perspiration as I looked at him.
看着他时，我出了一身冷汗。

59. "Kill one, warn a thousand", goes one Chinese proverb.
一句中国谚语："杀一儆百"。

60. But the sound may enter in one ear and go out through the other.
但可能是一个耳朵进，另一个耳朵出。

61. American educators had best look to China's example, return to the "3Rs", lest future generations be capable of building only castles in the air.
美国教育家最好看看中国的例子，回到"3Rs"去，免得后代子孙只会建造空中楼阁。

62. We got the wolf by the ears, with slavery. 有奴隶制在，我们就骑虎难下。

63. Some would say purple in its blood . 有些人认为这句诗鹤立鸡群。

64. Just throw three or four shells among those blue-bellied Yankees and they will scatter like sheep. 只需扔三四颗炸弹，他们就会鸟兽四散。

65. It's like throwing gas on the fire. 火上加油。

66. It was just like picking out fish in a bowl. 瓮中捉鳖。

67. Big fish eat small fish. 大鱼吃小鱼。

68. The equality genre was now out of the bottle, and for better or worse it could never be put back. 平等的观念现在已经出了瓶子，不管好坏，都是覆水难收。

69. It takes a thief to catch a thief. 解铃还需系铃人。

70. Don't cry over spilled milk. 覆水难收。

71.That's about thirty five very rich New Yorkers and two token historians. They have us there for window dressing.

共有 35 名非常富有的纽约人并象征性地请了两位历史学家，他们请我们装饰门面。

72. Which will open the door to us being able to talk. 打开天窗说亮话。

73. It's like taking the veil off my eyes. 豁然开朗。

74. It did not come out of a vacuum. 并非空穴来风。

75. become silosis（for a frog at the bottom of the well, the sky is very small）坐井观天

76. To my knowledge which is limited, at least twice before he accepted.

据我所知，三顾茅庐后他才接受。

77 Chinese politeness calls for three refusals before one accepts an offer.

78. There is no valor in foolishness. 勇者无谋

79. They are beating him with a scourge so that they cut through the skin on his back all the way to the bone.他们用鞭子把他打得皮开肉绽，直到骨头。

80. A grain of dust may be as wonderful as a whole mountain. 一叶知秋。

81 A single flower may reveal as much as a whole forest. 一叶知秋。

82. He runs off with another woman. 与另一个女人跑了。

83. He is going to have a bark that's much bigger than his bite. 雷声大雨点小。

84. We will be completely head over heels into internaitonalism.

我们开始彻底转向国际主义。

85. Wilson is between a rock and a hard place. 威尔森进退两难，前有狼后有虎。

86. He was caught on the horns of a dilemma. 他陷入进退两难的境地。

87. World War Ⅱ came on the heels of the great depression.

第二次世界大战紧随着大萧条。

88. like your snapping your fingers 仿佛只是弹指间（眨眼间）

89. Come back with a roar. 大张旗鼓回来。

90. Pendergast however will finally come enter the eye of grand jewelry.

然而彭德格斯特最终掉入钱眼。

91. So he doesn't have to go through congress. 因此他不必经过国会。

92. Play our last card. 杀手锏。

93. "Here, you must vote for me, have another," and the candidates themselves would have been present, helping to pour, and **mingling with** prospective voters.

“来来，你可得选我啊，再满上（喝酒），”参选人会亲自到场，给人倒酒，和可能投自己票的人打成一片。

94. Even brutes do not devour their young. 虎毒不食子。
95. I know people. 我有熟人。
96. green card 绿卡
97. Don’t put all the eggs in one basket. 不要把所有的鸡蛋放到一个篮子里。
98. That was like oil and water. 有点像水火不容。
99. I’ll beat my chest saying. 我敢拍胸脯说。
100. I want my children to be able to hold their heads high as Americans.
我想让我的孩子作为美国人能够昂首挺胸。
101. We decided to each sell five things. 决定每人卖 5 件东西
102. He is a little rusty in his math skills. 数学荒废了。
103. If you want, say a word. 如果你有需要，说一声就行了。
104. Fish or cut bait. 要么全力以赴要么放弃。
105. So come by, don’t be strangers. 来吧，别见外。
106. and also the ones that can cause you the most headache
也可能是让你最头疼的
107. fill the vaccum of…填补……空白
108. It’s not money thing. 不是钱的事。
109. It’s not been repeated in history since and not before it either. 前无古人，后无来者。
110. You can’t have your cake and eat it too. 鱼与熊掌不可兼得。
111. tunnel vision 一管之见
112. By the age of 24, she was over the hill. 当她到了 24 岁时，她开始日薄西山。
113. make overnight changes 立竿见影
114. give somebody an eye roll 翻白眼
115. It starts good and goes bad. 虎头蛇尾。
116. Let nature take its course. 顺其自然。
117. Let it be. 顺其自然。
118. In consequence, even the most attentive and experienced foreign listener will ofter find himself at least half a beat behind in almost any conversation. 结果，甚至那些注意力最专注的，经验最丰富的外国听众经常会发现他们在任何会话中都慢一拍。
119. the difference between heaven and hell 天壤之别
120. a frog in a pot of hot water 温水煮青蛙
121. a wide canyon 鸿沟
122. You are a minnow in a vast ocean. 沧海一粟。
123. That’s only a drop in the bucket. 沧海一粟，九牛一毛。
124. A law firm where from the outside everybody wanted to get in, and from the insile, everybody wanted to leave .
律师事务所是一个外面的人想进去，里面的人想出来的地方。
125. A small problem turns it into a foreset fire. 星星之火可以燎原。

126. A single spark can start a prairie fire. 星星之火可以燎原。
127. It had turned yellow because of age. 年久发黄了。
128. If you can change direction a little bit at the beginning, it's dramatic when it gets few miles on space. 开始时失之毫厘，结果会谬以千里。
129. A miss is as good as a mile. 差之毫厘缪之千里。
130. They almost become like a one-trick pony. 江郎才尽，黔驴技穷。
131. And I actually drag him with me this afternoon. 今天下午我把他拽来了。
132. I am drawn like a moth to the flame. 我就像飞蛾扑火一样。
133. First, the tortoise is given a slight head start. 起初，乌龟被允许先跑一段距离。
134. Run around like a chicken with its head cut off. 像个无头苍蝇般乱撞。
135. See your soft underbelly. 看到自己的软肋。
136. There were founding mothers whispering smarter things in the ears of founding fathers.
一些开国之母在开国之父耳旁轻声细语地指点一些高招。（吹枕边风）
137. So when the dust settles. 当一切搞定后。（尘埃落地）
138. I applauded with my two hands. 我双手赞成。
139. He is difficult to manage. 他难管理。
140. the overnight sensation a century in the making 台上十分钟，台下百年功。
141. If you help me do this, we're golden. 再帮我一次，我们就金盆洗手。
142. We fight income inequality. 劫富济贫。
143. his right-hand man 红人（左右手）
144. They are not even on the radar screen. 他们根本上不了台面。
145. I've burned my bridges. 我已经自断后路。
146. To make money doing nothing. 等着天上掉馅饼。
147. If you want, say a word. 说一声就行了。
148. What produces goose flesh? 什么让你产生鸡皮疙瘩？
149. Help his soul to reach western paradise. 超度他的灵魂到天堂。
150. Eggs have no business dancing with stones.
鸡蛋永远不要和石头一起跳舞。（以卵击石）
151. to plan for rainy days 未雨绸缪
152. You said Japan gets a cold and the New York Stock Exchanges sneezes.
日本感冒了，纽约证券交易所会打喷嚏。
153. When at last we checked, you could count the number of movies about Negro League Baseball on one hand.
当最后我们核对无误后，关于黑人棒球联盟的电影屈指可数。
154. **One thing led to another** after Liddy Fitz-Gerald visited the school where I'm principal with a box of miniature sculptures made by her husband, Clark.
丽迪·菲茨杰拉德带着一盒由她丈夫克拉克制作的微型雕塑访问了我当校长的这所学校之后，事情便**接踵而至**。
155. If you give a man a fish you can feed him for a day, but if you give him the means to fish he can feed himself forever.

授人以鱼（能让他吃一天）不如授人以渔（能让人吃一辈子）。

156. So that's about it—my most recent brush with death.

这就是事情的大概——我最近一次与死神擦肩而过的险情。

157. In Munich, Stevenson took the hope of a poor nation and years of Soviet-style training, knocked out American Duane Bobick and Peter Hussing of West Germany, then won gold without breaking a sweat when Ion Alex of Romania showed up with a broken thumb.

在慕尼黑，肩负着一个穷国的希望又接受了苏联式训练的斯蒂文森，将美国的杜安·鲍比克和西德的彼得·修星先后击倒出局，随后，当大拇指受伤的罗马尼亚选后伊翁·亚力克斯露面时，斯蒂文森不费吹灰之力便赢得了金牌。

158. For one sickly sheep infects the flock. 害群之马。

159. I am so very sad and confused with every emotion possible.

我太难过了，内心里五味杂陈。

160. I am not a tough guy, I just have a big mouth with little to back it up.

我不是一个粗人，我只是话多，嘴上没什么把门的。

161. Scarcity enhances value, and it was such a rare sight. 物以稀为贵。

162. I throw my knapsack over the wall. 破釜沉舟。

第十二章　一些常用短语的英文表达法

这一章的目的是让大家在学习时注意积累英语中一些同义的结构或词语。

第一节　覆　　盖

1. Green orchards of coffee and clove trees carpet some hillsides. Rice terraces like giant stairs cover others. 一些山坡上覆盖着绿色的咖啡园和丁香树，其他一些山坡上有稻米梯田，看起来像巨大的楼梯。

2. a lawn **carpeted** with fallen leaves　落叶覆盖的草坪

3. The whole valley floor, and the foothills too, would **be carpeted with** lupiness and poppies.
整个谷底和山麓都被覆上了一层厚厚的羽扇豆和罂粟花。

4. Any sharp corners, especially those facing you, should **be covered with** decorative photos or green, leaf plants.
任何尖角的地方，尤其是对着你的，应该用装饰性的照片或绿色的大叶子植物盖上。

5. They can **be topped with** poached eggs for a satisfying meal.
上面再加个水煮荷包蛋就是一顿令人心满意足的饭了。

6. She **cloaked** her sorrow with laughter. 她用笑来掩饰她的悲痛。

7. cloud-capped　乌云所笼罩的

第二节　比……活得长

1. He **outlived** his wife. 他比他的妻子活的时间长。

2. The old lady has **survived** all her children.
那位老妇人的子女都先她离世了。

3. Rome Columns **outlast** the civilization that built them.
古罗马文化业已衰亡，而象征罗马文明的圆柱依然存在。

第三节　超　　过

1. exceed　*vt.* 比……大；胜过

a. Their success exceeded all expectations. 他们的成功出乎一切预料。

b. exceed in size　规模突出

2. excel　*vi. /vt.* 优于他人；胜过他人

a. He excels in courage/ as an orator. 他在勇气（演说）方面胜过他人。

b. He excels all of us in/at tennis. 他的网球胜过我们所有的人。

3. overtake　*vt.* 赶上；压倒；突然来袭

a. The driver overtook a line of vehicles. 司机超过了一长列车辆。

b. He overtook in the face of oncoming traffic.
他不顾迎面而来的车流强行超车。

c. Germany rapidly overtook Britain in industrial output.
在工业产量方面德国迅速超过了英国。

4. surpass *vt.* 超越；胜过，优于

a. The beauty of the scenery surpassed my expectations.
该处的风景之秀丽超出我的预料。

b. Pre-war levels of production were surpassed in 1929.
战前的生产水平在 1929 年被超过。

c. Since China surpassed the US to become the largest automotive market in the world in 2009, industry players are in a fierce race to expand.
自 2009 年中国超越美国成为世界最大的汽车市场以来，业内车企都在快速扩张。

5. outstrip *vt.* 超过；胜过；比……跑得快

I think, to date, women have been in the shadow of men, but now two things are happening—women are getting better and the female retail sector is growing massively, outstripping the men's in many areas. 我认为，迄今为止，女性一直被男性的光彩所掩盖，可是现在，有两种情况正在发生——女性的表现越来越好，而且，女性用品零售业正在大幅度增长，在很多方面超过了男性用品零售业。

6. outclass *vt.* 远高于；远胜于

He was outclassed from the start of the race. 比赛一开始他就落后许多。

7. outdo *vt.* 超过；胜过

You will meet many people who will try to outdo you, in school, in college, at work.
你会遇到一些人他们总是试图超过你，在中学、大学，在工作中。

8. outmatch *vt.* 胜过；优于；凌驾于

He is outmatched in skill and endurance. 他技术与耐力不如人。

9. eclipse *vt.* 使黯然失色

eclipsing road accidents, cancer and coronary heart disease
甚至比交通事故、癌症和冠心病死亡率都高

10. outweigh *vt.* 比……重要；比……有价值

outweigh freedom 比自由更重要

11. dwarf *vt.* 使矮小

These new revenue flows dwarf aid. 这些新的收入使援助金额相形见绌。

12. In the season of joy I present my sincerest wishes and kindest thoughts. May this Christmas outshine all the rest.
在这欢乐的时节，我把最真的祝福和亲切的思念送给你，愿你今年的圣诞比往年更璀璨。

第四节 充满……

1. Dominating the square are a couple of silver-barked trees which in spring are **alive with**

nesting birds. 一对树皮呈银灰色的大树矗立在广场上，春天有很多鸟儿在树上筑巢。

2. I was jogging down the street, my mind **swimming with** petty worries.
我顺着街道慢跑，脑子里充斥着恼人的小事。

3. The soup was **swimming with** fat. 汤里满是脂肪。

4. The big streets and hidden alleys of my hometown were **swarming with** people at this time of the year. 到了年关这个时候，家乡的大街小巷到处是人。

5. Every garden is **teeming with** wildlife. 每座花园都满是野生生物。

6. The strip of sand is crowded with thousands of vendors.
长长的沙滩上挤满了成千上万的小贩。

7. This area **abounds with** caravan sites. 这个地区到处是大篷车队的营地。

8. The air **is thick with** dust/snow. 空气中充满了灰尘/雪花。

9. a musical gallery **complete with** 96-piece orchestra 一个拥有 96 支乐队的音乐走廊

10. And the place **was bathed in** delicious smells of breathing leaves and the warm sweetness of hawthorn **perfumed in** the air.
整个地方沐浴在树叶儿的新鲜气味中，空气中弥漫着山楂的香甜味儿。

11. Flowers perfumed the air. 空气中弥漫着花香。

12. a garden **perfumed with** flowers 弥漫着花香的花园

13 a sky **flecked with** clouds 布满点点云朵的天空

14. trees **laden with** apples 结满苹果的树

15. It was laden with food. 它满载食物。

16. Eyewitnesses reported that some ponds were so **stuffed with** corpses that they disappeared, the water（was）completely displaced.
目击者说有些池塘因堆满了尸首而消失了，水已不见踪影。

17. Admittedly it was not a prospect **fraught with** hope, but I decided to give it one more try.
不可否认这不是一个充满希望的前景，但我决定再试一试。

18. The air was **scented with** the sweet-smelling flowers of a tree that grew at the entrance to the arbour, and the fireflies, sparkling dimly, flew with their slow and silvery flight. The moon made a pathway on the broad river for the light feet of Siva's bride, and on the further bank a row of palm trees was delicately silhouetted against the sky. Peace stole into the soul of Mr. Warburton.
凉亭入口处有一棵树，空气中弥漫着这棵树散发的花香，还有萤火虫发出的微暗的光，在夜空中缓缓划出银白色的飞行轨迹。月光倾泻在宽阔的河面上，为步履轻盈的湿婆神的新娘照出一条路来。天空中映出了较远处河岸上棕榈树婀娜多姿的轮廓。此时沃伯顿先生的心情渐渐平静下来。

19. Mr. Warburton's chimney-piece during the season was **packed with** cards for one great function after another.
在社交季节，沃伯顿先生的壁炉架上摆满了请他参加盛大宴会的请帖。

20. The bus was **packed with** noisy children.
这辆公共汽车里挤满了吵吵嚷嚷的小学生。

21. The countries within the ring of "civilization"（that is, organized misery）were **glutted with**

the abortions of the market.

那些进入“文明社会”（换句话说，有组织的痛苦）的国家充斥着堕胎市场。

22. His round eyes **suffused with** tears. 他圆圆的眼睛噙满了泪水。

23. And the air was **charged with** their perfume. Then she drank a deep draught of the scent.

空气中弥漫着浓郁的花香，于是她深深地吸入一口花香。

24. It was towards evening that Ichabod arrived at the castle of the Heer Van Tassel, which he found **thronged with** the pride and flower of the adjacent country.

天快黑的时候，伊克波德来到了老凡富丽堂皇的农庄，那里有许多邻村的仪表堂堂的人物和如花似玉的姑娘。

25. The pavements are thronged with people. 人行道上挤满了人。

26. a home **replete with** every modern convenience 有各种现代设备的家庭

27. The apparently dismal monotony of a school was **replete with** more intense excitement than my riper youth has derived from luxury.

明明是沉闷、单调的学校生活，偏偏热闹非凡，后来在稍为成熟的青年时代，过的虽是奢侈生活，倒没有这么热闹呢。

28. We bought the house **complete with** furniture.

我们买了一套带有全部家具的房子。

29. The beach plums hung on the hillsides, their branches **heavy with** blossoms.

海梅立在山坡上，枝条上挂满沉甸甸的花朵。

30. The existing law **is riddled with** loopholes. 现行法律漏洞百出。

31. He is **brimming with** ideas. 他满脑子的主意。

32. Her accent is pure New Yorker and her speech is **littered with** the teenage verbal staples of “you know” and “basically”.

西格勒操一口纯正的纽约客口音，言谈中满是十来岁的青少年经常挂在嘴边的“你知道”“基本上”等口头禅。

33. When my youngest child was a baby, I took him to another neighbor, Janice, whose voice **overflowed with** softness. 我最小的孩子还是个婴儿时，我把他送到了另一位邻居——嗓音温柔甜美的贾妮丝——家托管。

34. politicians **imbued with** a sense of their own importance 自大的政客

35. words **pregnant with** meaning 富有意义之言词

36. store-houses **bursting with** grain 装满谷子的谷仓

第五节 出生、来自

1. Sigler **hails from** a tight-knit family in Long Island, New York State.

西格勒出生在美国纽约州长岛一个温馨和睦的家庭。

2. It is very well to say that you **came of** unhealthy parents.

可以这么说你的父母并不和睦。

3. The answer is ready enough at hand, and it amounts to this—that if you had been **born of** healthy and well-to-do parents, and been well taken care of when you were a child, you would never have offended against the laws of your country, nor found yourself in your

present position.

答案是显而易见的，也就是说——如果你出生在一个富有的家庭，父母感情和谐，在你小的时候得到细心呵护，你就不会触犯本国法律，更不会处于现在的境地。

4. He is a Philadelphian **by birth**. 他出生在费城。

5. the country **of his birth**　他出生的国家

6. Born to a British mother, Tanya Streeter was **brought up** in the Carribbean.

坦雅·斯特里特的母亲是英国人，在加勒比海长大。

7. This kid had been **born into** a decent, hard grafting family—he came along at the end of a string of seven. 这个孩子生活在一个体面的辛勤劳作的家庭——是 7 个孩子中的老幺。

8. John Nikolakis **came from** a privileged family.

约翰·尼科莱基斯出身于一个条件优越的家庭。

第六节　错　位

1. Let us reconsider the problem of derangements . 让我们重新考虑错位问题。

2. main body's misplacement of public opinion supervision 舆论监督主体角色错位

3. on procedure dislocation of criminal procedure in china 论中国刑事诉讼的程序错位

4. The cause of gender identity disorder is not known.

引起性别错位症的原因尚不清楚。

第七节　多嘴多舌的

1. talkative　多嘴多舌的

2. wordy　唠叨的，多话的

3. mouthy 话多的，嘴碎的

4. speak out of turn　多嘴

5. shoot off one's mouth　多嘴；信口开河

6. gossip and meddlesome　多嘴多舌的

7. long-tongued　多嘴多舌的

第八节　归　因　于

1. He **ascribed** Jane's short temper **to** her upset stomach.

他把简的暴躁脾气归因于她的胃部不适。

2. He **attributed** the firm's success **to** the efforts of the managing director.

他把公司的成就归功于总经理的努力。

3. Champagne houses **owe** their success **to** brand image.

香槟酒店的成功要归功于品牌形象。

4. And while many **credit** Gamblers Anonymous **with** rebuilding lives, one study found that only 8 percent of those who entered GA were still attending after a year.

尽管好多研究把重建生活的功劳都归于 GA 疗法，可是有一项研究也发现，在 GA 项目参加者中，能坚持到一年以上的人只有 8%。

5. A painting such as *The Boating Party*, with its broad areas of color, bold lines and collapsed space, suggests Cassatt's **debt to** Japanese prints.
例如《划船聚会》一画，它以宽阔的色域、大胆的线条和被压缩的空间提示了卡萨特受惠于日本版画之处。

6. Before you listen, make a guess of the possible reasons **attributable to** the phenomenon, and try to arrange them in order of importance.
听之前，不妨猜一下造成这种现象的可能原因，并试着按它们的重要性进行排序。

第九节 话到嘴边

1. Though her sympathy was deep, words stopped on her lips.
尽管她深表同情，但欲言又止。

2. She had just begun to say—the word died on her tongue before it was spoken.
她正要开口，话到嘴边又咽了回去。

3. It was on the tip of my tongue to ask his name when Jordan looked around and smiled.
我正要开口问他的姓名，乔丹转过脸来朝我笑了笑。

4. But something choked the words in my throat. 如鲠在喉，说不出话来。

第十节 怀有

1. He nursed feelings of revenge. 他蓄意复仇

2. bear a grudge against somebody 对某人怀恨在心

3. Each tag bore a code to indicate the exact place where the butterfly had been tagged.
每个标签上都有一个代码用来表明这只蝴蝶是在哪里被贴上标签的。

4. For years she cherished the hope that her husband might still be alive.
多年来，她一直心存希望她的丈夫可能仍活在人世。

5. Washington entertained little hope of an early improvement in relations.
华盛顿对早日改善关系不抱希望。

6. I had never for a moment entertained a hope that I should find anyone in that house whose boot I could wear. 我想都没想过在那座房子里会有一个人，我能穿上他的靴子。

7. They entertained a firm belief in final victory. 他们对最后胜利抱有坚定信心。

8. Singapore has enjoyed/boasted a very robust residential property cycle.
新加坡已经有过一个欣欣向荣的房地产业周期。

第十一节 回响、回荡

1. The room echoed with/to the sound of their happy laughter. 房间里回荡着他们的欢笑声。

2. The house echoed with shouts and thundering feet. 屋子里充满了叫喊与跺脚的回声。

3. Their experiences echoed the complaints voiced by many of my book reviewers who teach at some of the nation's best schools.
评论过我作品的不少书评家在国内几所最好的大学任教，也和这些教授们的抱怨有同感。
4. I used to answer with a resounding no, feeling that facts interfered with esthetics.
我过去会毫不犹豫地说“不”，认为这些事实影响了美学。
5.The house resounded with singing, laughter, whistling, trampling of heavy boots, and riotous scuffing.
房间旦回荡着歌声、笑声、口哨声、沉重的靴子的踩踏声，还有拖着脚走路的狂欢。
6. The office resounds with the metronomic clicking of keyboards.
办公室内回响着键盘机械呆板的噼啪声。
7. The hall reverberated with gaiety and laughter. 大厅里回荡着欢笑声。
8. There are tears and smiles, pure delight ringing in the laughter of seeing someone who has been gone. 泪水、笑容和由衷的快乐洋溢在久别重逢的欢声笑语中。
9. The room rang with laughter. 屋里笑声欢腾。

第十二节 聚集、集结

1. Troops are massing / are being massed on the frontier. 军队在边境集结。
2. The small bags are grouped together. 把小包放在一起。
3. Group the roses together. 把这些玫瑰花放在一起。
4. The police grouped（themselves）round the demonstrators. 警察围住示威者。
5. They were mustered every morning and told off to different tasks — grass-cutting, fence-building, tree-felling. 每天早晨，他们被召集在一起，按照白人的吩咐去干各种不同的活儿——割草、筑篱笆、砍树。
6. The station hands mustered every morning to the sound of the bell.
每天早上，站内工作人员听到铃声后便集合到一起。
7. The crowd is gathering. 人群正在聚集。
8. The teacher gathered all the pupils in the auditorium.
老师把全体同学集合在礼堂内。
9. assemble in the school hall　在学校礼堂集合
10. We drove them slowly like cattle till they were all assembled in one place.
我们缓缓地像赶牛一样驱赶他们，直到他们聚到一起。
11. The children clustered round her skirts. 孩子们围聚在她裙边。
12. Most of the foreign embassies are clustered in this area.
大多数外国使馆都聚集在这里。
13. The children flocked round their teacher. 孩子们聚集在他们老师的周围。

第十三节 捐款、捐助

1. The proceeds（收益）will be donated to an Aids awareness charity.
所得将捐赠给艾滋意识慈善会。

2. The donation will be the largest ever to the management school by one of its graduates.
这将是迄今为止耶鲁管理学院收到的最大一笔毕业生个人捐款。

3. He endowed the Church with lands. 他向教会捐赠地产。

4. He subscribed £400 to the campaign. 他向这项运动捐助了 400 英镑。

5. He subscribes liberally to charities. 他慷慨地捐助慈善事业。

6. The monument was erected by public subscription.
该纪念碑是由各届捐款建立的。

第十四节 对……的渴求

1. The fields are thirsty for rain. 这些田地急需要雨。

2. The orphan child was hungry for affection. 这个孤儿渴望得到爱。

3. She is desperate for money. 她急需要钱。

4. thirst to learn 渴望学习

5. He yearned to ask her to marry him. 他一心想着向她求婚。

6. long for the early unification of one's motherland 渴望祖国早日统一

第十五节 连 续 的

1. five consecutive /successive years 连续五年

2. two-hour straight live concert 连续两小时的直播音乐会

3. Continuous bombing spearheaded the way to occupying the city.
持续不停的轰炸为占领该城铺平了道路。

4. running water 自来水

5. It had three straight years of revenue and profit growth.
（公司）已经连续 3 年获得了收入和利润的增长。

第十六节 面向、朝向

1. a window that looks toward the jail 面朝监狱的窗户

2. My house confronts his. 我家与他家对门。

3. a house looking towards/ to the south 面朝南的窗户

4. The house looks south. 房子面朝南。

5. The cinema fronts toward the south. 电影院朝南。

6. The hotel fronts on the main road. 旅馆朝向大马路。

7. The hotel fronts the beautiful lake. 这家旅馆面对着那座美丽的湖。

8. I turned onto East 16th Street and pulled into a parking lot fronting a crumbling, two-story apartment complex. 我转上东 16 街，驶进一处摇摇欲坠的两层公寓综合楼前的停车场。

第十七节　描 述 高 度

1. To either side of us towered sheer, 700-foot red-brown canyon walls—the first hints of the Grand Canyon. 在我们的两边，高高耸立着陡峭的、700 英尺高的红棕色峡谷岩壁——这是大峡谷出现的最初标志。

2. The pressing of the linseed pulp to extract the oil is done by a vast ramshackle apparatus of beams and ropes and pulleys which towers to the vaulted ceiling and dwarfs the camels and their stone wheels.
从亚麻籽浆中榨油这项工作是用一套快要散架的庞大设备进行的。这套设备由横梁、绳索和滑轮组成。它高高耸立，接近拱顶，相形之下，骆驼和石磨则显得矮小。

3. Ancient trees towers to the skies. 古木参天。

4. The president towered over everybody, stiff on braced legs.
总统比所有的人都高很多，两腿僵直，靠钢架支撑着。

5. With a clamor of bells that set the swallows soaring, the Festival of Summer came to the city Omelas, bright-towered by the sea.
随着一阵响彻云霄的钟声的敲响，一群燕子惊得展翅高翔，白塔映日的海滨城市奥米勒斯迎来了她的夏庆节。

6. The whole valley is dominated by this mountain. 这座山谷俯临着整个山谷。

7. Jolmo lungma dominates all surrounding mountains. 珠穆朗马峰高耸于群山之上。

8. The great cathedral dominates the centre of the city.
大教堂高耸于市中心的主要位置。

9 Along the island's central mountain range, volcanoes rises into the clouds.
沿着岛上的中部山脉，火山高耸入云。

10. Mountains jut into the sky. 山直插云霄。

11. This is a magnificent stretch of pale yellow sand overlooked by bamboos and a few trees, which stretches away to the horizon.
在竹林和树木的下方，一望无际的，是一片苍黄的壮丽的沙滩。

12. Above the central park hovers a giant monument overlooking the whole city.
一座巨大的纪念碑耸立在中央公园，俯视整个城市。

13. Above it all hovers Victoria Peak, its 1785 feet of height covered with the odd mixture of junglelike vegetation and residential towers.
香港岛上直入云霄的是维多利亚山——海拔 1785 英尺，上面零星地覆盖着茂盛的植被和可居住的塔楼。

第十八节　目 光 闪 烁

1. His small, rather piggy eyes **glitter with** enthusiasm.
他那双很像猪眼的小眼睛闪烁着热情洋溢的光芒。

2. Her eyes **gleamed with** satisfaction. 她的眼睛闪烁着满意的光芒。

3. His cheeks **glistened with** tears. 他的脸颊因流泪而闪闪发亮。

4. As Alice rose from her knees, where she had sunk by the side of Cora, she threw herself on the bosom of the latter, and sobbed aloud the name of their aged father, while her soft, dove-like eyes **sparkled with** the rays of hope.

爱丽丝原本跪在科拉身旁，当她站起来时，扑向科拉的怀中，哽咽着说出他们年迈的父亲的名字，这时她那温顺的像鸽子一样的眼睛闪烁着一丝希望。

5. her sparkling blue eyes　她的蓝眼睛闪烁着光芒

6. His eyes were **sparkling with** happiness. 他眼里闪烁着幸福的光芒

7. And Uncas stood, fresh and blood-stained from the combat, a calm, and apparently and unmoved looker-on, it is true, but with eyes that had already lost their fierceness, and were **beaming with** a sympathy that elevate him far above the intelligence.

昂科斯站在那儿，精神饱满，由于刚才的战斗身上血渍斑斑，内心平静，似乎是一个无动于衷的旁观者，确实如此，但他的眼神已不再那么凶狠，取而代之的是同情，一种超越智慧的情感升华。

第十九节　拟　声　词

1. crack open a safe 啪的一声打开了保险箱

2. “Hi! Hi!” said the cab driver, whose door popped open at the very sight of a traveler.

出租车司机一看见旅客就砰地一声把车门推开说“Hi!Hi!”。

3. The door clicked shut. 门咔嗒一声关上了。

4. The door slams. 门砰地一声关上了。

5. slam the door　砰然关门

6. He slammed his book shut. 他把书啪的一声合上了。

7. Just as I was beginning to find the ride long, the taxi **screeched to a halt**, and the driver got out and went over to the policeman to ask the way. 正当我开始觉得坐车的路程很长时，出租车“吱”地一声停了下来，司机下车向警察走过去问路。

8. It isn’t long before the lake awakens at the **flap** of a blue heron’s wings and the melodic call of a loon.

不一会儿，随着一只蓝鹭拍打着翅膀的声音和一只潜鸟婉转的鸣叫声，整座湖开始苏醒。

9. The bird was **flapping** its wings. 鸟儿拍动翅膀。

10. The heron came **flapping** over the water. 苍鹭振翅从水面上飞来。

11. After a brief **buzz** from a computer version of the compact disc, a list of relevant entries appears on screen. 等计算机版的光盘内发出滋滋响后，屏幕上会出现相关的目录单。

12. But the volume was already on maximum, and the speaker were **buzzing** and fuzzing like they were about to explode.

可是音量已经到最大了，扩音喇叭发出的模糊不清的嗡嗡声，好像要爆炸似的。

13. Her high heels going clack clack clack. 她走动时高跟鞋哒哒地响。

14. There was a crash in the hall as the front door **bust open** and a smaller crash close by as Cocky dropped a teacup.

大厅里一声巨响，前门哐的一声开了，接着身旁的贝蒂的茶杯掉在了地上。

拓展学习：They bust the tunnel wide open. 他们把隧道炸开。

15. We heard boots storming up the stairs. 我们听到一阵上楼的靴子声。

16. The Venetian blinds snap up. 百叶窗啪的一声开了。

17. The door was slapped to, a voice exclaimed "All right," and on we drove.
车门关上了，“好啦”，一声大叫，我们便上路了。

18. A book lay spread on the sill before her, and the scarely perceptible wind **fluttered** its leaves at intervals.
一本翻开的书摆在她面前的窗台上，几乎让人感觉不到的微风间或掀动着书页。

第二十节　排　　序

1. finish ahead　排名靠前

2. We are one above Slovenia. 我们只在斯洛文尼亚前面一位。

3. Otherwise, he must stand against the second-placed candidate in a run-off election within three weeks.
不然，在三周内即将举行的第二轮选举中，他必须面对排名第二的候选人。

4. tie for second place　并列第二

5. The next nearest was Jim Anderson's exactly half a mile away by the shortcut through a field.
离我们家又远一点的是吉姆·安德森家，抄近路穿过一片田地正好是半英里远。

6. Yet the College Catalogue for the years 1854 to 1861 shows a list of names rather distinguished in their time. Alexander Agassiz **led it**; H. H. Richardson **helped to close it**.
亚历山大·阿加塞斯是名人录的头名，而H·H·理查森几乎是最后一名。

7. Entering the last eight would be a satisfactory result for both the men's and women's teams.
对于中国男子和女子手球队来说，进入前八名就将是令人满意的结果了。

8. Our university can be listed in the biggest 10 universities in China.
我们的学校能够进入中国十所最大的大学。
或 People list our university in the biggest 10 universities in China.

9. Right at the bottom are journalist, politicians and businessmen.
排在最下面的是记者、政客、商人。

10. He has never before featured in the top ten world rankings. 以前他从未进入世界前十。

11. They have bucked the nation's medal skid in the last decade, taking three gold from each of the last three Games to **rank inside** the top two at fencing.
他们顶住了过去10年里意大利奖牌数下滑的颓势，在最近的3届奥运会上每一届都获得了3块金牌，在击剑项目上的排名始终保持在头两名之内。

12. He finished third in the overall artistic gymnastics rankings last year and has **stayed inside** the top four since 2001.
去年他在竞技体操运动员排名中名列第三。从2001年起，他一直排在前4名之内。

13. the top seven ranked counties in the nation　全国排名前七位的县

14. As a result, the company surged seven places, to No.44, in this year's ranking and boosted

its brand value by 18%. 结果，该公司在本年度排行榜上一路窜升 7 个名次，排名第 44 位，并且品牌价值提升了 18%。

15. And Audi has moved up six spots in the rankings, to No. 68, and increased its brand value by 17%. 而奥迪也在排行榜上上升了 6 个位次，名列第 68 位，品牌价值提升了 17%。

16. And the company moved up three places in the rankings, to No. 95, and watched its brand value jump 16%.

而且公司在排行榜的排名前进了 3 位，排在第 95 位，品牌价值也跃升了 16%。

17. Hungary may suffer in future Olympics if it does not broaden its compass, but it still ranks just outside the top 10 in terms of overall medal count.

如果不拓宽参赛项目的范围，今后在奥运会上可能够匈牙利受的，不过从整个奖牌总数来看，它依旧会紧随十强之后。

18. A survey of 65,000 people worldwide conducted since 2001 shows that Audi now **trails** BMW and Mercedes by only a narrow margin in Europe and Asia.

自 2001 年起对全世界 6.5 万人所做的一项调查显示，在欧洲和亚洲，奥迪品牌现在仅以微小差距紧随宝马和奔驰之后。

19. But it is one, as evidenced by a 12% jump in brand value, which extends a rankings winning streak after faltering in 2004.

但这是事实，品牌价值跃升 12%就说明了这一点——诺基亚的品牌价值在 2004 年跌落一次之后就连续几年在排行榜上夺得优胜名次。

20. Hull ended their four-game losing streak. 赫尔结束了他们的四连败。

21. Because methane has been one of the fastest-growing green-house gases, and is third only to carbon dioxide and water vapor in total volume, changing the chemistry of the upper atmosphere. 因为甲烷是增长最快的温室气体之一，其总量仅次于二氧化碳和水蒸气而居第三位，从而改变了大气层上部的化学成分。

22. China's GDP is second only to the US. 中国的 GDP 仅次于美国排第二。

23. next to oxygen　仅次于氧

24. Even so, most Americans would probably rate New Oreleans, San Francisco higher.

即便如此，多数美国人可能会把新奥尔良、圣弗朗西斯科排名靠前些。

25. Where did you finish in the 100 metres? I finished first.

你在 100 米赛跑中获得第几名？　我得了第一名。

26. Would you rank him among the world's great statesmen?

你会把他列为世界上伟大的政客么？

27. a tennis player who ranked third / is ranked third in the world

一名排名世界第三的运动员

28. And behind Douglass came Elliot, Bruce, and Langston.

排在道格拉斯后面的是艾略特、布鲁斯和兰斯顿。

29. He placed eleventh/ was placed eleventh in the long individual race.

在这次个人长跑中他取得了第十一名。

30. My horse wasn't even placed. 我的马未获名次。

31. A survey placed the company 13th for achievement. 调查显示公司业绩排第 13 位。

32. The next-to-last fledgling is now mostly out of the nest box.
这倒数第二只幼鸟如今身子几乎已全部出了鸟巢。

33. But we've never finished worse than 13th, so we are expecting to tie somewhere around that place in Beijing. 但我们从未获得过比第 13 名更糟的名次，所以我们期望在北京奥运会的排名保持在 13 名左右。

34. Our boys won gold in Sydney and Athens, so we hope that in 2008 we can be in a good position there as well. 我们的小伙子们在悉尼和雅典摘得了金牌，所以我们希望 2008 年我们也能在奥运会上取得个好名次。

35. At the Athens Games in 2004, Hungary ranked 13th, its **joint-lowest finish** to date（the other being Sydney）, with 17 medals. Of those 17, six came in canoeing, three in fencing and two in swimming—all traditional strongholds.
在 2004 年雅典奥运会上，匈牙利排名第 13 位，是迄今为止的两次最低排名之一（另一次是在悉尼奥运会上排名第 13），获 17 枚奖牌。在这 17 枚奖牌中，6 枚来自划艇，3 枚来自击剑，2 枚来自游泳——全是传统强项。

36. While these may have been enough to see it rank third overall in 1952 at the Helsinki Games（where it bagged its best-ever haul of 16 golds）, nowadays it is a different story.
尽管这些奖牌数过去可能足以确保它在 1952 年赫尔辛基奥运会上总体排名第三(在那里，它收获了空前最多的 16 枚金牌），但如今已是时过境迁了。

37. Hungary's nine golds at the Melbourne Games in 1956 saw it finish fourth, whereas the same haul five decades later in Athens would have placed it somewhere between ninth and 12th. In fact it finished 13th with eight golds. 1956 年墨尔本奥运会上，匈牙利夺得 9 枚金牌，名列第 4，然而，50 年后在雅典奥运会上获得同样数目的金牌，却只能排在第 9 到 12 位之间。事实上，匈牙利在雅典是以 8 金排在第 13 位。

38. But unless it moves with the times and compensates for its shrinking returns at the Olympics, it risks sliding further down the table.
但除非他能与时俱进，并且能补足奥运会上缩水的奖牌数，否则它还会有在排名表上进一步下滑的风险。

39. She admitted that the nation got lucky in Athens, where it ranked 17th overall for its best finish since the 1952 Helsinki Games on the back of five golds.
她承认，挪威在雅典奥运会上运气很好，那届奥运会上最后排名第 17 位，不仅获得了 5 块金牌，还是自 1952 年赫尔辛基奥运会以来取得的最好成绩。
on the back of 在……之外，紧接着……

40. The beverage giant claimed the top spot for the seventh year in a row mostly because it is big and everywhere.
这家饮料巨头连续 7 年荣登榜首，主要是由于它的业务庞大，无所不在。

41. Volkswagen's premium brand has been ranking high in consumer surveys, with some of its models even **placing ahead of** BMW and Mercedes.
大众汽车的优质品牌在消费者调查中也一直受到很高的评价，大众的一些车型甚至排在宝马和奔驰前面。

42. Indeed, Citi posted a 9% gain and held on to its position as the No.11 global brand, thanks to a concerted effort to boost its retail presence.

确实，由于公司上下为加强在零售市场占有率所做的一致努力，花旗银行品牌价值实现了9%的增长率，稳稳保持住了在全球最佳品牌排行榜上第11名的位置。

43. Japan leads the way in high-tech gadgets that help prevent accidents.
日本在预防交通事故的高科技装置上领先。

44. The device leads the world. 这种装置领先于世界。

45. It goes to the top of the list if only for that hollowed-out volcano.
如果只看那个被挖空的火山，本片可以名列榜首。

46. The hedge fund manager/Russian industrialist who dominates today's rich list shirks this in favor of shiny shoes and cufflinks.
今日在富豪榜上占据支配地位的对冲基金经理或者俄罗斯实业家则对此不屑一顾，他们更喜欢发亮的皮鞋和佩戴领扣。

47. The same can't be said of many later designs. 后来的许多设计难望其项背。

48. The area under cultivation increased by 12% last year, to 114m hectares globally. American topped the list. 其耕作面积去年增加了12%，全球达到1.14亿公顷。

49. Chicago and Los Angles are the next top consumers of hot dogs.
芝加哥和洛杉矶的热狗销量仅次之。

50. But the other companies that make up our annual ranking have hatched plenty of their own brilliant ideas. The pay-off? It keeps them strong in good times and bad.
但是其他在我们年度排行榜上的公司也想出了很多它们自己的聪明创意。益处何在呢？无论顺境或逆境，这可以使它们始终保持强大。

51. Apple not only takes the No. 1 slot on this year's list of the World's Most Admired Companies, but also tops the U. S. survey—and wins the highest marks for innovation too.
苹果公司不仅在今年的"全球最受尊敬公司"排行榜上名列第一，而且在"美国最受尊敬公司"排行榜上名列榜首，在创新方面的得分也是最高。

52. He ranks among the best pupils of his grade. 他是他们年级最好的学生之一。

53. Canada has not ranked inside the top 20 countries at the Summer Olympics since the Barcelona Games in 1992, where it finished 11th.

54. Guy's 1961 recording of "*Stone Crazy*" made the list at Number 78.
盖伊1961年录制的唱片《疯狂的石头》排名第78位。

55. The 2011 Human Development Report shows China lies at 101 in a list of 187 countries.
2011年人类发展报告中，中国在187个国家中排名第101位。

56. the third-to-last of those emperor　倒数第三个

57. rank information　排名信息

58. the next youngest　第二年轻的

59. the second oldest　年龄第二大的

第二十一节　承担责任

1. I take/ bear /shoulder /accept/ claim responsibility for that and apologize.
我对此负有责任，并感到抱歉。

2. pin responsibility on　把责任推到某人身上

3. Russia does not want to assume responsibility for the problems of Tajikistan and other Central Asian countries during the current global economic downturn.

在全球经济下滑中，俄罗斯不愿意为塔吉克斯坦和其他一些中亚国家的问题负责。

4. You do feel a responsibility for her legacy, it's quite interesting.

我们确实感到对她所遗留下来的东西负有责任，这很有趣。

拓展学习: 1）In 2007, the three events were directly and indirectly responsible for injecting nearly $95 million into the local economy. 2007 年，这三件事直接或间接地为当地经济吸引投资 95 000 000 美元。2）the person in charge　负责人

5. To most drug companies, donating medicines may be the most convenient way to implement corporate social responsibility.

对于大多数医药公司来说，捐赠药品可能是公司履行社会义务最方便的方式。

第二十二节　前　进

1. Little donkeys with harmoniously tinkling bells **thread their way** among the throngs of people entering and leaving the bazaar.

小毛驴在集市上熙熙攘攘的人群中寻路穿行，身上系的铃铛叮当当，和谐悦耳。

2. The river had **channelled its way** through the soft rock.

河水已在松软的岩石中冲出一条小道。

3. Slowly the weary, dispirited creatures **wound their way** into the room.

那些疲倦的、沮丧的人们慢慢地进入了房间。

4. The din of the stall-holders crying their wares, of donkey-boys and porters **clearing a way** for themselves by shouting vigorously, and of would-be purchasers arguing and bargaining is continuous and makes you dizzy.

摊主的叫卖声，牵驴少年和搬运工为自己开出一条道路的高喊声，以及商贩和顾客的争辩声、讨价还价声——这些喧闹声混杂在一起，持续不断，让你头晕眼花。

5. For now I found myself clumsily **hobbling my way** through such newly difficult tasks as going up and down stairs.

因为我正在完成一项新的有难度的任务，就是一瘸一拐地上下楼梯。

6. They were **feeling their way** towards an agreement. 他们正谨慎地试着达成一项协议。

7. "Evening, Nan," I said, as I **felt my way** into the living room.

"晚上好，南"我一边摸到起居室，一边说道。

8. grope one's way（在黑暗中）摸索着走；谨慎

A blue heron rises from a distant shore and gently **fans its way** over the water.

一只蓝鹭从远处的岸边飞起，轻轻扇动着翅膀掠过水面。

9. Gingerly, we **pick our way** over slippery rocks and prickly pine needles, down 49 dew-covered log steps to the shore.

我们小心翼翼地踩在滑溜溜的岩石和扎人的松针上，走下布满露珠的 49 级原木台阶来到岸边。

10. This Italian sports car manufacturer has also **zoomed its way** into the top 10 most powerful brands this year after being knocked out last year.
这家意大利赛车制造商在去年被打败之后，今年已经跻身于10大品牌之列。

11. Through the windshield I could see the man's silhouette; like us, he was facing forward, toward the line of the highway beginning to **wind its way** through the hills.
透过挡风玻璃我能够看到那人的轮廓；他像我们一样面对着前方，朝向那条开始蜿蜒深入群山的高速公路线。

12. The stream **wound its way** across the field and then flowed right under their tent.
那条小溪弯弯曲曲穿过田野，然后正好从他们的帐篷底下流过去。

13. He is slowly **thumbing his way** through a thick report.
他正慢慢地翻读着一份厚厚的报告。

14. From the discouragement of his mining failures, Mark Twain began **digging his way** to regional fame as a newspaper reporter and humorist.
由于淘金失败而灰心丧气，马克·吐温从此开始艰苦努力，给自己开辟了一条道路，终于作为一名新闻记者和幽默大师在当地享有名声。

15. They **carved their way** into the international shipping trade by severely undercutting western shipping companies.
他们以低于西方船运公司的价格打入国际海运贸易。

16. The ship **nosed its way** slowly through the ice. 那艘船缓慢地破冰前进。

17. The water **inched its way** up the steps as first floor outside walls collapsed.
一楼的外墙倒塌之后，海水慢慢地浸上了楼梯。

18. Camille, meanwhile, had **raked its way** northward across Mississippi, dropping more than 28 inches of rain into West Virginia and southern Virginia, causing rampaging floods.
在此期间，卡米尔飓风横扫密西西比州后继续北进，给弗吉尼亚州北部和南部带来了28英寸以上的暴雨，致使洪水泛滥。

19. **bore one's way** through a crowd of people 从人群中挤过去

20. He **edged（his way）** towards the front of the crowd. 他侧着身子挤向人群前列。

21. The soldier wormed his way toward the enemy's lines. 战士向敌阵地爬去。

22. The train snaked（its way）through the mountains. 火车在山中蜿蜒而行。

23. This heavenly messenger **wings her way** outside of life altogether.
天使展翅飞翔于生活之外。

24. Slowly the silent company now **took its way** up the Sand River like whence it had come.
他们在沙河上缓慢地行走，都不做声，正如他们来时一样。

25. He left the stage, **elbowing his way** through the Big Man's retinue in the wings.
他下了台，从侧台"大人物"的跟班中挤了过去。

26. I made my way toward the sound of her creaking rocking chair.
我朝她那摇椅嘎吱作响的声音走去。

27. They try to make their way in the world. 他们试图走进这个世界。

第二十三节　容　　忍

下面几个动词后面都可以跟 *v.*-ing 或不定式。

1. Jasper could not forbear giving a special smile at Professor Clun, as though including him in a bond of peculiar pleasure at Rose's reminiscences.

贾斯珀忍不住专门对克伦教授微微一笑，仿佛他对罗斯的回忆录情有独钟。

2. I cannot stand seeing children smoking. 我无法忍受看见孩子们吸烟

3. I never could stand people telling me what to do. 我从不能忍受别人摆布。

4. I can't bear being kept waiting.我无法忍受人家让我长时间等待。

5. I couldn't bear to listen any longer, so I left the room.

我实在听不下去了，便离开了房间。

6. The teacher cannot tolerate eating on the class. 老师不容许在课堂上吃东西。

7. Thank you for tolerating my speech. 谢谢你们听我演讲。

8. I can't endure to see / seeing animals suffer like that.

看到动物那样受苦，我无法忍受。

第二十四节　受到……伤害的

1. flood-stricken areas　洪灾地区
2. frost-bitten　被冻伤的
3. a cold, frostbitten day　寒气袭人，并出现了霜冻
4. his weather-beaten face　他饱经风霜的脸
5. the storm-whipped British vessel　饱经风雨的英国军舰
6. "Stay away from the windows," he warned, concerned about glass flying from storm-shattered panes.

"离窗户远点!"他警告说，担心在飓风中震破的玻璃碎片会飞来伤人。

7. storm-tossed　暴风雨中飘摇的
8. a storm-devastated castle　暴风雨损毁的城堡
9. terror-stricken 受了惊吓的；恐怖的
10. some severely drought-stressed Grenache vines 饱受干旱之苦的格林那希葡萄藤
11 care-laden; care-worn　忧心忡忡的；劳碌的
12 nerve-racking 伤脑筋的；使人心烦的
13. conscious-smitten 良心受到谴责的
14. a weathered man 饱经风霜的人

第二十五节　用……装的

1. a boxed set of books by the same author 同一作者的盒装系列书
2 bottled water　瓶装水
3. canned fruit　罐装水果

4. bagged rice 袋装米

5. a caged lion 关在笼子里的狮子

第二十六节 时光流逝

1. The years slipped by. 岁月在不知不觉中逝去。

2. I grow very uncomfortable, meanwhile, for the afternoon wore fast away .
随着下午时光的逝去，我的心越来越焦急。

3. The day has simply flown by without any results .
稀里糊涂的一天就这么过去了。

4. Time presses, and I want to keep our question on the straightest line possible.
时间紧迫，我们最好不要偏离主题。

5. The autumn dragged on. 秋天慢慢过去。

6. A fortnight elapsed. 两个星期过去了。

7. Though many years have elapsed since I trod the drowsy shades of Sleepy Hollow
我离开睡谷宁静的居所已多年了

8. after a lapse of some months 过了一些月之后

9. And meanwhile the course of time were to take a turn backward instead of forward, and I were to wake up again in the nineteenth century.
与此同时时光会倒流，我会在十九世纪再次醒来。

10. with the passage of time 随着时间的流逝

11. Ten minutes rolled by, as did the wisdom of those greats.
十来分钟一晃而过，这些伟人的智慧也一样在我眼前一闪而过。

12. Time is moving so quickly. 时间过得真快。

第二十七节 描述眼泪

1. Her face was bedewed/ sprinkled with tears. 她脸上沾满泪珠。

2. Her eyes were bedimmed with tears. 泪水模糊了双眼。

3. Tears were beaded on her cheeks. 她双颊挂着成串的泪珠。

4. Her eyes were clouded（over）with tears. 泪水模糊了她的视线。

5. Her eyes were misted with tears. 她泪眼模糊。

6. Her face was streaked with dirt/ tears. 她的脸上点缀着泪珠。

7. Their grandmother, her red hair streaked with white, is already there.
他们的奶奶已经在那儿了，她的红发中夹杂着白发。

第二十八节 世俗的

1. worldly *adj.* 世俗的；世间的；尘世的
worldly possessions 身外之物

2. temporal *adj.* 世俗的，现世的，尘世的

the temporal power of the Pope 教宗的世俗权力

3. earthly *adj*. 地球的；尘世的

earthly joys/possesions 尘世的享乐（财产）

4. unearthly *adj*. 超凡脱俗的

5. secular *adj*. 世俗的

secular education 世俗教育

6. terrestrial *adj*. 世俗的

第二十九节 说、表达

1. He pronounced his opinion. 他发表了他的意见。
2. He voiced his opinion. 他表达了他的意见。
3. I would communicate my grief to him. 我将向他表露我的悲伤。
4. She was twittering about domestic trivialities.
他在喊喊喳喳地说着些家庭琐事。
5. He grumbled out his reasons from disliking the arrangement.
他嘟囔着说出了他不喜欢这个安排的理由。

第三十节 处于某个位置

1. The house is located by the river. 房子坐落在河边。
2. The firm finally located in Dallas. 公司最后落户于达拉斯。
3. Where is your company based? 你们的公司在哪里？
4. a London-based band 一只常驻伦敦的乐队
5. The council are trying to decide where to situate the new school.
委员会正讨论将新学校建在何处。
6. The supermarket lies opposite our college. 超市正对着我们学院。
7. a village sitting on the side of a hill 坐落在山边的一个村庄
8. The books sat unread on the shelf for years.
这些书在书架上搁了许多年无人读过。
9. The city sits on Israel's border with the Gaza Strip.
这座城市位于以色列边陲与加沙地带相邻。
10. The town stood on a hill. 那城镇位于小山上。
11. In one corner of the little room a couple of mops, with stiff, clotted, foul-smelling heads, stand near a rusty bucket. 小房间的一个墙角，靠近一个生锈的水桶立着几把拖把，拖把头发硬，结成一团，散发着臭气。
12. It was sited next to a nice little stream that froze in the winter and ran like a raging river in the summer.
它坐落在一条美丽的小溪旁，小溪冬天会结冰，夏天则像咆哮的河流一样水流湍急。
13. Tucked away in one corner of northwest England, the Lake District is unique.

湖区位于英格兰西北一个不为人知的地方，非常特别。

14. I recall seeing my daughter, the daughter I am going to visit, coming down that narrow corridor with her backpack slung on one shoulder, her overstuffed carry-on **cradled** in her arms, her headphones making her oblivious to the stream of people flowing along with her.

忆起我看见女儿，就是我现在要去见的女儿，正从那狭窄的通道走过来，肩上背着背包，怀里抱着塞得满满的行囊，带着的耳机让她无暇顾及身旁川流不息的人群。

15. villages nestling among the mountains　位于群山间的村庄

第三十一节　投入、专注于

1. The lady abandoned herself to the profound grief of losing her child in the accident.

这位太太沉浸在因为这次事故失去孩子的巨大痛苦中。

2. be completely lost in something　完全沉浸于……

3. My wife and daughters employed themselves in providing breakfast, which was always ready at a certain time. 我的妻子和女儿们忙于做早餐，早餐时间总是固定的。

4. He immersed himself in study during the vacation. 他在假期里埋头学习。

5. She was absorbed in study. 她专心学习。

第三十二节　笑

1. cackle.　*vi.* 咯咯笑

They have cackled on for hours. 他们高声谈笑了好几个小时。

2. giggle　*vt./ vi.* 咯咯地笑着说

They giggled at some private joke.

他们听到一些隐秘的笑话就咯咯地笑起来。

3. She smiled at me and then asked me if he could sit near me.

她冲我微笑了一下，问我她能不能坐在我的旁边。

4. grin　*vi.*　露齿而笑，咧着嘴笑

The boy grinned from ear to ear when his mother gave him the apple.

当小男孩的母亲给他苹果时，他咧嘴大笑。

5. The guests all laughed loudly. 客人们都大声笑了。

6. chuckle　*vi.* 咯咯笑；轻声地笑

She chuckled with delight. 她愉快地轻声笑了起来。

7. snigger（at/ over）吃吃窃笑

8. smirk　*vi.*　傻笑；得意地笑

He smirked his lewd delight at the scene. 看到这情景，他淫荡地一笑。

9. sneer　*vi.* 嘲笑；讥笑

sneer at religion　嘲笑宗教

10. titter　*vi.*　吃吃地笑，偷笑

He tittered at the joke. 他听了这个笑话吃吃地笑了起来。

第三十三节 新 兴 的

1. emergent countries of Africa（recently emerged） 非洲新兴国家
2. emerging industry 新兴产业
3. fledgling industry 新兴产业

第三十四节 蓄、留（发、须）

1. She grew her hair long. 她留了长发。
2. The students wore their hair long. 那些学生留着长发。
3. He's growing a beard. 他留胡须。

第三十五节 延 伸

1. A red scar extends from below my Adam's apple almost to my navel.
一块红色的伤疤从我的喉结下面几乎延伸到肚脐。
2. Another runs down my inner left thigh.
另一块伤疤从左大腿内侧向下延伸。
3. It stretches away to the horizon. 它一直延伸到远处地平线。

第三十六节 一群、一组

1. There were large crowds of people in the streets on New Year's Eve.
除夕的大街上有大批的人群。
2. a long string of tourists 一大批游客
3. a troop of musicians 一群音乐家
4. I remember feeling disdain for this collection of ogling humanity.
对这些色眯眯的人群，我感到不屑一顾。
5. There, at dusk, a group of local Balinese were chatting and bathing away the sweat and cares of their day's work.
傍晚时分，一群巴里当地人在那里一边聊天，一边洗去工作了一天的汗水和烦恼。
6. a host of reasons 多方面原因
7. a swarm of crawling locusts 一群爬行的蝗虫
8. I see also the dull, drilled, docile, brutish masses of the Hun soldiery plodding on like a swarm of crawling locusts. 我也看到大批头脑愚钝、受过训练、唯命是从而凶暴残忍的德国士兵，像一群爬行的蝗虫在蹒跚行进。
9. the mighty army of consumers 广大消费者
10. droves of sightseers 一群群的游客
11. clouds of airplanes 成群的飞机
12. a race of 一类的，一群

13. Outside the brush house in the tuna clump, a covey of little birds chattered and flurried with their wings.

在茅屋外面的霸王树丛中，一群小鸟一面喊喊喳喳地叫着，一面拍打着翅膀。

14. a knot of toads　一群蟾蜍

15. A vast mixed multitude of all ages, and of degrees, armed with all sorts of weapons.

一大群人佩戴着各种武器，他们来自不同的社会阶层，各种年龄段的人都有。

第三十七节　以……为动力

1. a horse-drawn dray　四轮马车
2. petrol-driven cars　汽油车
3. petrol-powered cars　汽油车
4. mechanically propelled passenger-carrying boats　机械动力客船
5. coin-operated telephone　投币电话
6. electricity-operated lift　电梯

第三十八节　赢得金牌

1. Some said Teofilo Stevenson got lucky at the 1972 Munich Games. They weren't saying that eight years later when he **picked up** his third straight heavyweight gold in Moscow.

有人说，在 1972 年慕尼黑奥运会上特奥菲洛·斯蒂文森是运气好；8 年之后，当他在莫斯科连续第三届夺得他的重量级拳击项目奥运金牌时，那些人不再说那样的话了。

2. Time would ultimately settle the debate as he went on to **claim his second** then third gold at the sport's greatest showcase.

时间最终平息了这场争论，因为他在最能展示该项运动竞技水平的赛场上，又继续赢得了他的第二块、第三块金牌。

3. Although Manus **earned** his maiden Olmpic medal in Athens at the age of 24…

虽然马努斯 24 岁在雅典获得了他破天荒的第一枚奥运奖牌……

4. Vezzali then went one better in Sydney, stamping her dominance to **capture** both gold.

维扎利后来在悉尼奥运会表现出胜人一筹的实力，获得了个人和团体两块金牌，标示出她的霸主地位。

5. After **walking away with five gold medals** at last year's Commonwealth Games, she **bagged another five golds** at the 2007 World Swimming Championships in late March in Melbourne.

在夺得 2006 年英联邦运动会 5 枚金牌以后，2007 年 3 月下旬，她在墨尔本举办的 2007 年世界游泳锦标赛上又将另外 5 枚金牌收入囊中。

6. If he **wins the gold** again, he will become only the fourth athlete in weighting history to capture three Olympic golds.

假如他再次获得金牌，他就将成为举重历史上屈指可数的获得三枚奥运会金牌的第四位运动员。

7. Four years later, in Munich, Keino **scored another gold** by winning the steeplechase.
四年之后，在慕尼黑奥运会上，凯诺获得了3000米障碍赛的冠军，又赢得了一块金牌。

8. The men's side is also hopeful of doing better than Athens where its powermen **lifted two golds**.
男子举重也同样有望取得比雅典奥运会更好的成绩，在雅典奥运会上，男子举重运动员们获得了2块金牌。

9. Now they hope to **add a fourth Olympic medal** after seizing silver at Seoul 1988 and bronze in Sydney in 2000.
他们希望在1988年汉城奥运会获得银牌和2000年奥运会获得铜牌之后，这次可以再增添第四块奥运奖牌。

10. He partnered with Fredrik Raaen Bekken four years earlier to **grab a silver medal** at the double sculls in Sydney.
在那之前4年的悉尼奥运会上，他和弗雷德里克·拉恩·贝肯合作获得了男子双人双桨的银牌。

11. Finn specialist Kusnierewicz **is responsible for** both of Poland's sailing medals to date and picked up his second, a bronze, in Athens.
专攻芬兰人级帆船比赛的运动员库什涅雷维奇是波兰迄今拥有的两块帆船奖牌的获得者，他在雅典获得了他的第二块奖牌——一块铜牌。

12. Margherita Granbassi, who beat Vezzai 7-6 to take gold at last year's World Fencing Championships and 24-year-old Elisa Di Francisca make Italy even more of a threat.
玛格丽塔·格兰巴锡在去年的世界击剑锦标赛上以7比6战胜维扎利获得了金牌，她和24岁的埃莉萨·迪弗朗西斯卡会使意大利更具威胁。

第三十九节 由……组成

1. The committee consistis of ten members. 委员会由十人组成。

2. The United Kingdom comprises England, Wales, Scotland, and Northern Ireland.
联合王国由英格兰、威尔斯、苏格兰和北爱尔兰所组成。

3. Fifteen separate republics comprise the Soviet Union.
苏联由十五个加盟共和国组成。

4. In 2006, to mark its 150th anniversary, Burberry mined its design archives and launched the Icons collection, comprising luxury hand bags, shoes, boots, trench coats, and small leather goods.
2006年，巴宝莉公司为了纪念品牌创立150周年，从它的众多设计档案中掘取精华，推出了“时尚风标”系列产品，包括奢华的手袋、鞋子、靴子、男士双排扣风雨衣和小皮件。

5. There course will be comprised of readings, discussions, guest speakers and group design sessions.
整个课程将涵盖阅读、讨论、客座讲授以及分组设计等几部分。

6 . the parts that compose the whole 组成整体的各部分

7. Our party was composed of teachers, pupils and their parents.

我们这一伙由教员、学生及学生的父母组成。

8. England, Scotland and Wales compose the island of Great Britain.
英格兰、苏格兰和威尔士组成大不列颠岛国。

9. These constitute the next three components of design in method analysis.
这些成为后面方法分析设计的三个组成部分。

10. It appears to be made of cotton. 看起来好像是棉花做的。

11. Wine is made from grapes. 葡萄酒是由葡萄酿成的。

12. A document is considered to be made up of a number of topics, each with its own information type.
文档被看作是由一些主题组成，每个主题都有自己的信息类型。

第四十节 发 型

1. long-flowing hair 飘逸的头发
2. wavy 波浪式的
3. parted 分头的
4. cropped 平头
5. braided 编头发的
6. pony tail 马尾辫

第四十一节 超过、有余

1. She is over 40 inches round the waist. 她的腰围四十几英寸长。
2. 12 pounds odd（plus） 十二英镑多
3. All the children here are twelve plus. 这里所有的孩子都超过 12 周岁。
4. More than two students have been concerned in this affair.
这件事情牵涉两个以上的学生。

第四十二节 与……匹敌、对等

1. Her hat-trick also equaled the country's previous total number of medals at swimming.
她在这一届奥运会上上演帽子戏法所取得的奖牌数也相当于波兰在游泳项目上以前所获得奖牌的总数。

2. No one can touch him as an actor of tragic roles.
作为一个悲剧角色的演员没人能及得上他。

3. There seems to be no other competitive techniques which can measure range as well or as rapidly as a laser can.
就测距的精度和速度而论，似乎还没有其他技术可与激光相比。

4. Even their technological development seems to parallel our advances.
甚至它们的技术发展也与我们的进展相对应。

5. He is following a brilliant career without (a) parallel in modern times.
他正从事着举世无双的辉煌事业。

6. Her album sales rival those of Madonna and Michael Jackson.
她的专辑销量赶上了麦当娜和迈克尔·杰克逊的专辑销量。

7. Thompson today equaled the world record for the 400 metres.
汤普森今天平了 400 米世界纪录。

8. His latest film doesn't match his previous ones.
他最新的一部影片比不上他以前的一些影片。

9. Few places on earth can match Madagascar as an ecotourism destination.
地球上没有几个地方能与马达加斯加作为生态旅游景点相媲美。

10. Yet no one matched Pavarotti at his best for sheer, prodigal outpouring of vocal beauty.
然而当帕瓦罗蒂处于最佳状态时，他那纯净的、纵情倾泄的美丽歌声，无人能媲美。

11. Having encroached on traditionally male territory, such women are proving the equal of men—and are reaping lucrative rewards.
已经进入传统男性领域的这些女性证明她们完全可以与男性相匹敌——而且正在获得经济利益的回报。

12. Peach Blossom Land is the Chinese equivalent of Eden.
世外桃源是中国版的伊甸园。

13. Shanghai is the equivalent of New York. 上海可以媲美纽约。

14. the equivalent of a shilling 相当于一先令

15. The 46-year-old Obama is among the youngest serious contenders for the American presidency since JFK, who was just 43 when he took the oath of office. And Obama's campaign has been eager to invite parallels to the youthful president.
46 岁的奥巴马是继肯尼迪（入主白宫时年仅 43 岁）之后美国总统宝座的有力争夺者中最年轻的候选人之一。而奥巴马的竞选班子也一直热衷于激发人们对他与那位年轻总统相似点的比较。

16. One must go back to Coleridge to find in English a figure comparable to the Symbolist leader, Stephane Mllarme.
能够与象征主义领导人匹敌的。

17. At home something comparable would have cost well over $100.
在国内同样的东西花费将会超过 100 美元。

18. If it did occur to the Greeks to distinguish between a person's "inside" and "outside", they still expected that inner beauty would be matched by beauty of the other kind.
如果希腊人确曾想对一个人的"内在"与"外在"做出区分的话，他们仍然希望内在美能够有外在美与之匹配。

19. No one can stand very near the crashing sweeps of a windmill in half a gale without a tightening of the heart—a feeling **comparable to** that which comes from watching the waves break over a wall in a storm.
任何人在四五级风里站在发出巨响的风车翼板附近都会心情紧张——可以与之相比的是在暴风雨里眼看巨浪冲过壁垒时的感觉。

20. They will not influence the rate at which the body rids itself of toxins, and any beneficial effects would be matched at much lower cost by drinking plenty of tap water, eating fruit and vegetables and getting a few early nights.

这些东西不会影响人体自身排毒的速度，而多喝自来水、多吃水果和少熬点儿夜这些方法比吃排毒食品花的钱要少得多，但所起的养生作用却一点也不比后者差。

21. I don't think we can rule out the other main **competing** theory—that the temple was a meeting point between the land of the living and the dead.

我认为我们不能够排除另一种与之相抗衡的理论——这个寺庙曾经使生者与亡灵见面之地。

22. **Parallel to** the interest in developing rational principles for vocabulary selection was a focus on the grammatical content of a language course.

23. In a developmental sense, Asher sees successful adult second language learning as **a parallel process** to child first language acquisition.

在某种程度上，亚瑟认为成功的成人第二语言学习与孩子的母语习得过程是相同的。

24. Parallel to the processes of first language learning, the foreign language learner should first internalize a "cognitive map" of the target language through listening exercise.

外语学习者与与第一语言学习相同之处是首先通过听力练习内化目标语的“认知地图”。

25. These two types of interactions may be said to be microcosmically **equivalent to** the two major classes of human interaction-interaction between equals（symmetrical）and interaction between unequals（asymmetrical）.

这两类互动可以说在微观上相当于两种主要的人类互动——对等的互动（对称的）和不对等的互动（不对称的）。

第四十三节　越来越多的

1. There is **accumulating** evidence that much of medical work comes from interactions with people rather than things.

越来越多的证据表明，医务工作的很多压力来自于与人的交往而不是工作。

2. This basically means that we **increasingly** have jobs where we deal with people rather than things（such as components on an assembly line）.

这主要意味着，现在越来越多的工作要与人而不是与物（如装配线上的零件）打交道了。

3. Psychologists are now **increasingly** recognizing that this "emotional labour" may be more mentally taxing than the "physical labour" we did in the past.

心理学家们现在日渐认识到，这种“情感劳动”和我们以往的“体力劳动”相比，可能更费心费力。

4. In 1980, the American Psychiatric Association officially categorized pathological gambling as a diagnosable medical disorder, and since then there has been **increasing** understanding of the brain chemistry, the biology, even the genetics that plays a role.

1980 年，美国精神病协会将病态赌博界定为一种可以确诊的疾病。自那时起，人们对在赌博中起作用的脑化学、生物学甚至遗传学方面的了解越来越多了。

5. Record fuel costs pushed hrbrid cars to center stage at the world's biggest car show in 2006

but automakers argued over whether the **rising** popularity of petro-electric vehicles was just the result of marketing hype.

创纪录的燃油价格把混合（动力）型汽车推到2006年世界最大的汽车展的中心展台，而汽车制造商们却为汽油-电力车辆的日益流行是否只由于促销宣传所造成展开了争论。

6. Hurd also has focused on HP's **sprawling** global operations, using the same marketing strategy it is employing in the U.S. to ramp up consumer sales in emerging markets.

赫德还把重心放在了惠普公司范围日益扩大的全球业务上，使用了公司在美国的营销战略，增加在新兴市场上消费产品的销售额。

7. And during the last 20 years, despite **increasingly** clear scientific evidence regarding the dangers of climate change, the country's output of carbon dioxide had increased by a fifth.

在过去的20年里，尽管气候变化产生危害的明显科学证据不断增多，美国的二氧化碳排放量增加了1/5。

8. A **growing** number of low-power electrical goods are now available.

这正是人们自己现在开始利用人体自身发电产生浓厚兴趣的原因。

9. a rapidly **expanding** middle class 人数迅速增长的中产阶级

10. War or no war, as the generation passed, it became increasingly difficult for our young people to accept standards of behavior that bore no relationship to the bustling business medium in which they were expected to battle for success.

不论是否发生战争，随着时代的变化，要我们的年轻一代接受与他们必须在其中拼搏求胜的这个喧嚣的商业化社会格格不入的行为准则已经变得越来越难了。

11. Agriculture faces a growing problem. 农业面临的问题越来越多。

12. **Increasingly** over the past ten years, people have become aware of the need to change their eating habits.

在过去的十多年内，越来越多的人意识到需要改变他们的饮食习惯。

13 Consequently, there has been a growing interest in natural foods.

结果，越来越多的人对天然食物感兴趣。

14.With **expanding** interest in the process of as well as the product of language acquisition

随着人们对语言习得过程及其结果给予越来越多的关注

15. It continues to **grow in popularity** and strength in Canada and elsewhere, and it is being adapted for adult learners.

这种方法在加拿大及别处越来越受到欢迎，影响力也在不断增强，并被成人学习者接受。

16. The most persuasive signal is that Asia has decoupled, with a **decreasing** dependence on the US.

最有说服力的一个信号就是，亚洲经济已经相对独立，对美国的依赖越来越少。

17. Petroleum's **falling** energy return on investment will encourage many economies to burn more coal.

不断下降的石油能源投资回报率将鼓励更多的经济体转而燃烧更多的煤。

第四十四节　怎么样地说

1. I am just saying. 我只是随口说说。

2. hard to say　难说

3. It is easy for us to say… 我们可以轻易地说……

4. **On paper** these kids should not be succeeding, but they are.
从理论上说，这些孩子本不会成功，但他们成功了。

5. theoretically　从理论上说

6. logically speaking 从逻辑上说

7. objectively speaking 客观地说

8. On the demand side, one of the key issues is biofuels.
从需求方面来说，一个关键因素是生物燃料。

9. Maybe I missed that class, but I **honestly** had no idea that John Wilkes Booth spent 12 days evading a massive manhunt after shooting Abraham Lincoln.
可能那堂历史课我缺席了吧；老实说，我压根儿不知道约翰·威尔克斯·布斯枪杀亚伯拉罕·林肯之后，为躲避大规模追捕还逃亡了十二天。

10. Honestly, I struggled with God after going through this over and over and over again.
说句实话，经历一次又一次的挫折，我开始与上帝抗争。

11. **To be honest**, small cars like yours are not their target at all.
说老实话，像你这部小车，他们还看不上。

12. **To be precise** it was at Dick's Sporting Goods Park, Commerce City, Colorado that the Galaxy soccer（football）team went down 3-0 to the Rapids.
确切地说，这是在科罗拉多康默斯市的迪克体育用品公园球场，银河足球队 0-3 不敌科罗拉多急流队，以落败告终。

13. **To be accurate**, Yum first tested the market in 1992 but withdrew two years later.
准确地说，1992 年白胜首次尝试在墨西哥开设餐馆，但两年后黯然收场。

14. **Professionally speaking**, that's meant a career of virtuous heroines.
从职业角度来讲，那是指演艺生涯中炉火纯青的诸般表演，像道德上正直的文学作品女主角。

15. **Admittedly**, Japan, China, India and Southeast Asian countries have striking dissimilarities in business practices, much like the differences in US and European practices.
不可否认，日本、中国、印度和东南亚国家的商业惯例相互之间存在着显著的差异　就像美国和欧洲商业惯例之间的差异一样。

16. **Intuitively**, the globalization of manufacturing and labour markets had a significant impact in reducing headline rates of inflation and sustaining consumer confidence.
直观地讲，制造业及劳工市场的全球化在减少总体通货膨胀率和维持消费者信心方面产生了重要的作用。

17. **Technically**, *Manhunt* belongs in the history section（its author is a respected Lincoln scholar）, but it's as gripping a page-turner as anything you'll find on the mystery shelf.
严格地说，《追捕》一书应该跻身于历史著作之林（作者是颇受尊敬的林肯研究学者），但它读来像悬疑小说架上的作品一样扣人心弦，令人不忍释卷。

18. Suffice it to say that they were not considered suitable for this project.
简单地说，他们被认为不适合做这项工程。

19. In response to Sartre's obscure and self-righteous pronouncements, he could not resist the very British response, in his own words, to "give him a good boot".
对萨特晦涩和自以为是的陈述，他忍不住给出典型的英国式回应，用他自己的话说，"狠狠踹上这家伙一脚。"

20. It's closer to say that pigs were the mixing bowl for this virus.
几乎可以说猪是这种病毒的搅拌钵。

21. **On scans**, the climbers showed a reduction in both white matter and gray matter.
从扫描结果来看，登山队员们大脑中所含的白质和灰质都降低了。

22. East Asian societies tend to be more socially complex than Western societies.
从社会学的角度看，东亚社会往往比西方社会更加复杂。

23. ecologically speaking 从生态学的角度来说

24. Its women weightlifters were **in contrast** later starters.
泰国的女子举重选手相对来说是后起步的。

25. Truth be told. 说实话。

26. This can be said. 可以这么说。

27. It's safe to say that this is no easy feat. 这当然不是能简单达成的壮举。

28. I should say. 应该说…。

29. We could say…我们可以说……

30. What do you mean by saying this? 你说这话是什么意思?

31. metaphorically speaking 打个比方说

32. outwardly speaking 从表面上看

33. **In fairness**, the assault on high culture and tradition that has transpired since the 1960s has paid great dividends, bringing long overdue attention to marginalized voices.
公平地说，自20世纪60年代起出现的对高雅文化和传统的攻击，在这方面也起了重要作用，至少它让人们注意到长久以来一直被忽视的社会边缘人群的声音。

34. say something back 说回来

35. in essence 实质上

36. in effect 实质上，实际上

37. The minister's powers allow him, in effect, to ban programmes.
实际上，部长的权力使他能够取缔一些项目。

38. to be fair 公平地说

39. **To some degree**, dollar stores have weathered their tough times.
从某种程度上说，一美元店已经走出了它们的艰难时期。

第四十五节　重 要 人 物

1. a person of no account 一个无足轻重的人

2. a man of no importance 一个无足轻重的人
3. no ordinary man of business 了不起的生意人

第四十六节 驻 扎

1. Police officers had **stationed** themselves at all the entrances to the building.
这座建筑物的所有出口都有警察把守。
2. Guards **were stationed** round the prison. 警卫被派驻在监狱四周。
3. Two soldiers were **posted** at the factory gate. 工厂门口有两名士兵把守。
4. Children **were posted** night and day on the outskirts of the local jungle to head the tiger back in the unlikely events of his attempting to roam away to fresh hunting-grounds, and the cheaper kinds of goats were left about with elaborate carelessness to keep him satisfied with his present quarters.
为了把老虎吸引回来，让儿童日夜驻守当地丛林的周围，以免它企图走开去寻找新的游乐场所。同时经过精心设计，有意无意地把一些便宜的山羊放养在附近，让老虎对它现在的领地感到满意。
5. The army **encamped** there for the night. 部队安营度夜。
6. The soldiers **were encamped** on the edge of the forest. 士兵在树林边上安营。
7. Many **were quartered** in tents. 许多人住在帐篷里。
8. He **quartered** his men on the inhabitants in the town.
他把他的部队安置在镇上的居民家中。

第四十七节 抓住机会、提供可能

1. The idea for producing an Olympic-themed computer came in the middle of the torch design process. Lenovo marketers suggested it, and Yao and his team **jumped at the chance**.
生产奥运主题电脑的想法是在设计奥运火炬的过程中产生的。联想的销售人员提出了这个建议，姚和他的工作组立即抓住了这个机会。
2. seize an excellent opportunity 抓住一个绝佳机会
3. Who Would Not Seize the Chance to Live to Be 150? 谁不想活到 150 岁呢？
4. take chance to do something 抓住机会做某事
5. grasp the opportunity 抓住机会
6. grab the opportunity 抓住机会
7. I wanted to give you an opportunity to make any explanations.
我想给你一个解释的机会。
8.The kaleidoscope of shifting interests of the nations during the negotiation **made it impossible** to sort out the “winners” and “losers”.
9. This really **gives people a platform and an opportunity** to get feed back and to enjoy themselves.
这真的给我们提供了一个平台和机会让作品得到大家的回应——也让他们从中得到快乐。

10. These **permit** the generalization and incorporation into the course design of learners' needs, wants, and desires.
这些使得我们可以总结学习者的需要、所求及意愿并把它们融入课程设计。
11. It **allowed** the civil war to emerge. 引发了后来的南北战争。
12. It **induces** miscarriage. 导致流产。
13. A neighborhood which is a mostly vacant lots is an **invitation** to criminal activity.
大多数地方空置的区域简直是犯罪行为的天堂。
14. An unrealistic goal **invites** failure. 不现实的目标只会导致失败。
15. This passage **opens a possibility for** students' imagination of an English village and understand of English rural life.
这篇文章不仅可以引发学生想象英国的乡村是什么样子，而且让学生对英国的乡村生活有一个了解。

第四十八节 装备、配备

1. to provision a ship/ an army 为船或军队供应必需品
2. The ship was manned. 为船只配备了人员。
3. staff a new school 给新学校配备教职工
4. a well-staffed hospital 人员充足的医院
5. an under-staffed office 人员不足的机关
6. All bedrooms are equipped with a colour TV. 所有卧室都配有彩色电视机。
7. They equipped themselves for the campaign. 他们为战役做好了准备。
8 She armed them with brushes and mops. 她给他们刷子和拖把。

第四十九节 报 案

1. They took the crew member's cash and cell phones and warned them not to **report the robbery** or face punishment.
他们拿走了船员的现金和手机，并警告他们不要报案，否则会受到惩罚。
2. Taobao Mall said on Wednesday that it had **referred the matter to the police**.
淘宝商城周三说这件事已经交由警方处理。
3. I won't **go to the police**. 我不会报案。
4. I will **call the police**. 我会报案。
5. So when **the police are called** and the whole process is initiated.
因此报警以后，司法流程启动。
6. **report a case to** the security authorities 报案

第五十节 多才多艺的

1. A case in point: Domingo, the dominant tenor of the era, a more consistent tenor, versatile

and rounded singer than Pavarotti and a far more affecting actor.

相关的一个例子：与帕瓦罗蒂相比，同时代的另一位主要男高音歌唱家多明戈是一位更加稳健、多才多艺和全面的歌唱家，也是一位更令人动情的演员。

拓展学习：a versatile tool 有多种功能的工具

2. a man of many talents 多才多艺的人

3. a true mulitfaceted and interdisciplinary intellect

多才多艺又跨多个学科的天才

4. gifted in many ways 多才多艺的

5. all-round 多才多艺的

参 考 文 献

[1] Sapir E. The Status of Linguistics as a Science, Language Vol.5（1929）.Readings in Linguistics: Seventy-five Years since Saussure,Vol.1,北京：测绘出版社，1988.

[2] 列维.布留尔. 原始思维[M].丁由，译. 北京：商务印书馆，1985.

[3] 霍尔. 荣格心理学入门[M]. 冯川，译. 上海：三联书店出版社，1987.

[4] 钱冠连. 语言：人类最后的家园[M]. 北京：商务印书馆，2005.

[5] 王德华. 英汉思维方式对其语言、文字的影响[J]. 外语与外语教学，2003（3）：70

[6] 毛荣贵. 翻译美学[M]. 上海：上海交通大学出版社，2005.

[7] 蔡基刚. 英汉写作对比研究[M]. 上海：复旦大学出版社，2000.

[8] 林语堂. My Country and My People[M]. New York: John Day Company，1935.

[9] 陈保亚. 语言文化论[M]. 昆明：云南大学出版社，1993.

[10] 费尔迪南·德·索绪尔. 普通语言学教程[M]. 高明凯，译. 北京：商务印书馆，2001.

[11] 张忠勇. 整体性思维方式与中国古代文学审美特质[J]. 甘肃教育学院学报（社会科学版），2001（3）：25.

[12] 潘文国. 汉英语对比纲要[M]. 北京：北京语言文化大学出版社，1997.

[13] 伍铁平. “语言决定人的思想吗？”语言与思维关系新探[M]. 上海：上海教育出版社，1990.

[14] 刘宓庆. 当代翻译理论[M]. 北京：中国对外翻译出版公司，1999.

[15] 申小龙. 汉语人文精神论[M]. 大连：辽宁教育出版社，1990.

[16] 梁实秋. 略谈英文文法[J]. 英语世界，2008（6）：106.